STUDIES IN THE
LEGAL HISTORY OF THE SOUTH

Edited by Paul Finkelman and Kermit L. Hall

This series explores the ways in which law has affected the
development of the southern United States and in turn
the ways the history of the South has affected the development
of American law. Volumes in the series focus on a specific
aspect of the law, such as slave law or civil rights
legislation, or on a broader topic of historical significance
to the development of the legal system in the region,
such as issues of constitutional history and of law and society,
comparative analyses with other legal systems, and
biographical studies of influential southern
jurists and lawyers.

A PECULIAR HUMANISM

WILLIAM E. WIETHOFF

A Peculiar

HUMANISM

The Judicial Advocacy of Slavery
in High Courts of the Old South,
1820–1850

THE UNIVERSITY OF GEORGIA PRESS
Athens and London

© 1996 by the University of Georgia Press

Athens, Georgia 30602

All rights reserved

Designed by Sandra Strother Hudson

Set in 10.5 on 15 Bodoni by Books International

Printed and bound by Thomson-Shore, Inc.

The paper in this book meets the guidelines
for permanence and durability of the Committee on
Production Guidelines for Book Longevity of the
Council on Library Resources.

Printed in the United States of America

00 99 98 97 96 c 5 4 3 2 1

Library of Congress Cataloging in Publication Data

Wiethoff, William E., 1945–

A peculiar humanism : the judicial advocacy of slavery in high
courts of the Old South, 1820–1850 / William E. Wiethoff.

p.   cm. — (Studies in the legal history of the South)

Includes bibliographical references and index.

ISBN 0-8203-1797-7 (alk. paper)

1. Slavery—Law and legislation—United States—History.

I. Title.   II. Series.

KF4545.S5W55   1996

342.73'087—dc20

[347.30287]   95-20993

British Library Cataloging in Publication Data available

For Edward and Mary

CONTENTS

ACKNOWLEDGMENTS

Paul Finkelman and Kermit Hall have provided me with insightful, constructive criticism. The professional librarians and archivists, who made my research more productive than it could have otherwise been, remain anonymous here. My typical but nonetheless regrettable slight to these gracious people obscures my deep gratitude for their advice and assistance.

A PECULIAR HUMANISM

INTRODUCTION

In early nineteenth-century America and especially in the Old South, oratorical form appealed to legal professionals—judges as well as advocates. Consistent with the humanism proclaimed in classical and neoclassical works, appellate judges perceived their civic duties to demand oratorical skill as well as legal expertise. In the following chapters I assess the judicial use of oratorical form to advocate slavery, despite the customary and professional restraints on judicial advocacy.

My purpose is threefold. Most generally, I draw attention to a neglected intersection of law and letters: the proslavery discourse embedded in antebellum judicial opinions. Although these opinions have been analyzed extensively for other reasons, they have not been examined for their proslavery oratory. More specifically, I trace the humanist authority by which selected judges adopted the roles of advocates as well as reviewers of fact and law. The early nineteenth-century influence of classical lore is generally accepted but its judicial endorsement has not been specifically documented. Most pointedly, I analyze the judicial struggle to obey humanist ideals by enhancing the factual settings of cases, by equating humanity and interest, and by issuing apologetics for the frequently unsuccessful struggle itself.

These judges played an important role during the period in which a national identity was shaped. My roster includes those judges who occupied appellate benches in jurisdictions that eventually formed a southern Confederacy, and who overcame the professional decorum that typically suppressed oratorical form in writing opinions about slavery. Omitted by design are otherwise noteworthy judges in the Upper South and Deep South. Although they earned conspicuous places in legal history, these judges did not apply oratorical form to their opinions on slavery between 1820 and 1850. Moreover, the varying tenures of high courts and the idiosyncrasies of individual judges are reflected in disproportionate amounts of discourse, state by state. Due to a lack of relevant data, I make no claims about the high court of Texas—the sole adherent to the Confederacy missing from my roster.

The following parenthetical dates identify lifespans of judges whose advocacy of humanist ideals attracted my critical attention. Bracketed dates refer to the tenures of these judges' appellate duties in courts of law and equity.

ALABAMA
William P. Chilton (1810–71) [1847–56]
Henry W. Collier (1801–55) [1828–32, 1836–49]
Anderson Crenshaw (1783–1847) [1821–32, 1838–47]
Edmund S. Dargan (1805–79) [1847–52]
Henry B. Goldthwaite (1802–47) [1837–43, 1844–47]
Abner S. Lipscomb (1789–1857) [1820–35; Texas 1846–57]
John J. Ormond (1795–1866) [1837–48]
Silas Parsons (c. 1800–60) [1849–51]
Reuben Saffold (1788–1847) [1819–36]
John M. Taylor (c. 1788–1859) [1826–34]
Harry I. Thornton (1792–1862) [1834–36]

ARKANSAS
Edward Cross (1798–1887) [1845–56]
Townshend Dickinson (1797–c. 1860) [1837–43]
Thomas Johnson (1808–78) [1844–52]

FLORIDA
Thomas Baltzell (1804–66) [1846–59]
George S. Hawkins (1808–78) [1846–50]

GEORGIA
Joseph H. Lumpkin (1799–1867) [1845–67]
Eugenius A. Nisbet (1803–71) [1845–53]
Hiram Warner (1802–81) [1845–53, 1867–80]

LOUISIANA

Pierre A. C. B. Derbigny (1769–1829) [1813–20]

Rice Garland (1795–1861) [1840–46]

George Rogers King (1803 or 1804–71) [1846–50]

Francis-Xavier Martin (1764–1846) [1815–46]

George Mathews (1774–1836) [1813–36]

Alonzo Morphy (1798–1869) [1839–46]

Alexander Porter (1785–1844) [1821–33]

Pierre A. Rost (1797–1868) [1839, 1846–53]

Thomas Slidell (1805–64) [1846–55]

MISSISSIPPI

Joshua G. Clarke (d. 1828) [1818–27]

Alexander M. Clayton (1801–89) [1842–51]

William L. Sharkey (1797–1873) [1832–50]

James F. Trotter (1802–66) [1838–42]

NORTH CAROLINA

William Gaston (1778–1844) [1834–44]

John Hall (1767–1833) [1801–32]

Leonard Henderson (1772–1833) [1808–16, 1818–30]

Frederic Nash (1781–1858) [1844–1858]

Richmond M. Pearson (1805–78) [1849–65, 1866–78]

Thomas Ruffin (1787–1870) [1829–52, 1858–59]

John Louis Taylor (1769–1829) [1799–1829]

SOUTH CAROLINA

Elihu H. Bay (c. 1754–1838) [1791–1828]

Andrew P. Butler (1776–1857) [1836–46]

Charles J. Colcock (1771–1839) [1811–30]

Henry W. DeSaussure (1763–1839) [1808–37]

Baylis J. Earle (1795–1844) [1836–43]

Josiah J. Evans (1786–1858) [1836–52]

Edward Frost (1801–65) [1843–53]

William Harper (1790–1847) [1830–47]

David Johnson (1782–1855) [1817–46]

Abraham Nott (1768–1830) [1810–30]

John B. O'Neall (1793–1863) [1830–63]

John S. Richardson (1777–1850) [1819–24, 1836–50]

David L. Wardlaw (1799–1873) [1841–68]

Thomas J. Withers (1804–65) [1846–59]

TENNESSEE

John Catron (1779–1865) [1824–36]

Nathan Green (1792–1866) [1827–52]

Robert J. McKinney (1803–75) [1847–61]

Jacob Peck (1779–1869) [1822–34]

William B. Reese (1793–1875) [1831–47]

Archibald W. O. Totten (d. 1867) [1850–55]

William B. Turley (1800–51) [1835–51]

VIRGINIA

John J. Allen (1797–1871) [1840–65]

Briscoe G. Baldwin (1789–1852) [1842–52]

William Brockenbrough (1778–1838) [1809–30, 1834–38]

Francis T. Brooke (1763–1851) [1804–51]

William H. Cabell (1772–1853) [1808–51]

Dabney Carr (1773–1837) [1811–37]

William A. G. Dade (d. 1829) [1827–29]

Joseph L. Fry (fl. 1820s through 1840s) [1830–51]

John W. Green (1781–1834) [1822–34]

John T. Lomax (1781–1862) [1848–57]

Richard E. Parker (1783–1840) [1817–40]

Henry St. George Tucker (1780–1848) [1824–1841]

I address each of these persons as "Judge" as a matter of convenience. Many of them were addressed properly in their own day as "Chancellor" (in courts of equity) or "Justice" (in supreme courts). As appellate judges in the several jurisdictions that would ultimately form a southern Confederacy, these persons reviewed problems with slavery that resisted the easy solution of plantation justice. However, despite their uniquely influential positions, these judges have not been examined individually or as a group for their contribution to a "configuration of law of letters that dominated American literary aspirations."[1]

Apart from the advocacy of famous trial lawyers, professional uses of forensic eloquence in the early nineteenth century remain obscure.[2] This scholarly gap contrasts sharply with an allied recognition of the oratorical culture in nineteenth-century America, especially in the South.[3] Although a recent and authoritative definition of "the characteristics of the nineteenth-century rhetorical tradition in North America" accurately depicts the bias in educational curricula, this analysis does not account for the oratorical form adopted by antebellum southern judges.[4]

By scholarly convention and critical practice, the antebellum period has been located within the years from 1828 or 1832 to 1860 or 1861. However, my examination begins in 1820 because it essentially involves an analysis of rhetorical as well as legal compromises in composing judicial opinions on slavery. National debate over the Missouri Compromise is a relevant prompting event.[5] In addition, rather than founding my analysis on opinions that were peppered with transitory reactions to Denmark Vesey's conspiracy in 1822 or Nat Turner's revolt in 1831, and punctuated with high feelings about various tariffs—the 1828 version being "intolerable"—I widen my scope to transcend these events. In all instances, I look for pro-slavery advocacy that addresses related problems of an enduring nature.

Beyond mere symmetry my survey ends with the national debate over another great Compromise Act, including the Fugitive Slave Law: 1850 is a defining moment in my project both generally and specifically. Discernible changes occurred generally in law and politics. At the state level, penal statutes were fashioned to regulate spoken or written discourse against a master's right to slave property. At the regional level, the idea of secession was pursued in an organized though fruitless manner at a Southern Convention in Nashville. More effectually, southern courts increasingly resisted comity with northern courts in the matter of slaves' manumission.[6] At the national level, "[c]onstitutional development" relied on "extrajudicial factors," and an ill-fated Compromise Act was passed to replace its 1820 predecessor.[7]

More specifically, after 1850 judicial opinions cannot reasonably be examined without accounting for the influence of sectional fervor and "increasing politicization of the courts' environment," as distinct from the feelings attached to slavery.[8] "In 1850," remarked Judge O'Neall of South Carolina, "the war of words about secession was filling many a stout heart with alarm."[9] Related influences on the tenor of judicial discourse about slavery cannot be discounted. After 1850, this tenor became more "polemical," "more stridently pro-slavery."[10] Scarcely absent in judicial discourse before 1850, the heightened sectional fervor after 1850 requires a specialized analysis of jurisprudential style that lies outside my critical scope.

Within this thirty-year period, selected judges undertook the duties of advocates when reviewing slavery cases. Under the auspices of civic humanism, the "state's needs for a certain kind of public servant" were fundamentally linked to "training the orator."[11] My project illustrates how the formative influence exerted by classical literature may be traced beyond the eighteenth century and in the professional field of jurisprudence.[12] In the humanist tradition, the judges accepted an identity of civic and moral aspirations that in earlier ages had been acclaimed as the hallmark of *areté* (Greek for "human excellence"), *humanitas* (Latin for "good breeding"), or *virtù* (Italian for "valor"). The oratorical portions of appellate opinions were instruments for protecting social structures and routines, that is, for affirming the beliefs and values of a ruling class. Indeed, "much of the rhetoric of the law of slavery was derived, not from the English or Continental legal heritages, but from the discursive systems of other sectors of white antebellum Southern society."[13] As Georgia's Eugenius A. Nisbet explained, judges were among those who shouldered "the responsibilities of the ruling minds of a State."[14] Remarks to law students in an 1849 speech by Tennessee's Nathan Green illuminate the judicial sense of civic humanism:

You have, gentlemen, commenced a course of study which is to fit and introduce you to a profession which exercises, in all free governments a controlling influence; and which is more intimately connected with, and acts more powerfully in reference to the interests of society, than any other profession or pursuit known among men, save that of the holy ministry. Yes, gentlemen, establish it in your minds as a settled principle, that "*a lawyer must be a gentleman.*" By the word *gentleman,* I do not mean polish of manner, and courtesy of demeanor toward others, important as these are, and assiduously as they should be cultivated, but I mean to use the word in that higher sense which it has acquired in this republican country, and which implies that he is *honest, true,* and *just.*[15]

Conscious thought about exerting "a controlling influence" and heeding the demands of a "profession" is prominent in Judge Green's speechmaking. Dutifully protecting the interests of society, the judges saw themselves as trustworthy guardians because of their moral tendencies.

Analyzing judicial discourse illuminates the beliefs and values of the upper class. Arranged hierarchically, highest to lowest according to the scope of slaveholding in each class, were large-scale planters, small-scale planters and merchants/professionals, yeoman farmers, free blacks, and slaves.[16] The social hierarchy varied somewhat from region to region. These regions—distinguished by geography and readiness to secede from the Union—include the Upper South (Virginia, North Carolina, Tennessee, and Arkansas seceded after the surrender of Fort Sumter) and the Deep South (South Carolina, Georgia, Alabama, Mississippi, Florida, and Louisiana seceded before the surrender of Fort Sumter). Texas also is properly located among jurisdictions of the Deep South but, given the lack of oratorical addresses to slavery in Texas reports after statehood, this judiciary lacks treatment in the present study. Professional judges, whose holdings typically included at least a few slaves if not hundreds, ranked in the upper classes of both the Upper and Deep South.

The Upper South of Virginia, North Carolina, and Tennessee enjoyed a legal heritage that was relatively long-lived and, for this reason alone, the judiciaries in these states were widely respected. On the individual level, formal educational credentials and professional skill brought fame to several judges from this region. The Arkansas judiciary, as well as other benches across the Old South, were often staffed by emigrants from the prestigious bars and benches of the Upper South. As a result, judges from this region exerted considerable influence when they expressed themselves on points of law. Judge Lumpkin of Georgia, for one, declared that he would sooner consult the jurisprudence in Arkansas law reports than "the ponderous tomes" of traditionally influential British jurists.[17]

The Deep South benches of South Carolina, Georgia, Alabama, Mississippi, and Florida were distinctive in the tenor of their address to the slavery issue. These benches presented a relatively solid front in articulating the relationships among state, master, and slave. Just as significant, the judges were not shy about speaking out on related issues. Due to legal and cultural uniqueness, judicial artifacts from Louisiana tell a somewhat different story.

The judges did not advocate a distinction between morality and civics in reviewing slavery cases. Instead, exploiting the oratorical form, a diverse roster of high court judges explicitly and implicitly struggled to equate humanity with interest. In this equation, they endorsed humanist ideals by endorsing related standards in reviewing slavery cases: the conservation of property as well as the conservation of life. These equations disclosed personal priorities—the perceptions, beliefs, and attitudes chosen as "starting points" of argument—as briefly illustrated in the 1840 cases of *Green v. Robinson* and *Ross v. Vertner*.[18] During successive terms of Mississippi's High Court of Errors and Appeals, Judge James F. Trotter issued opinions whose arguments reflected an equation of humanity and interest but whose holdings reflected considerable differences.

In the first instance, an 1833 statute and a long-standing jurisdictional arrangement provided the judge with sufficient grounds to rule against the flow of money out of the state through interstate slave trading.[19] However, he also speculated on the public policy behind the statute, citing the "barbarities, the frauds, the scenes so shocking in many instances to our feelings of humanity and the sensibilities of our nature."[20] In so doing, Judge Trotter explicitly issued a blended appeal to humanity and interest.

Secondly, a statute on wills and trusts gave the judge clear enough direction that he explicitly scolded counsel for seeking a wider review on appeal.[21] Nonetheless, he did not resist elaborating on "the policy of the statute, which is opposed to an augmentation of free negroes in the state; a result hazardous to the safety of the owners of slaves, and the security of the public peace."[22] On this occasion, implying that the public policy of Mississippi was innately humane, the judge explicitly appealed only to interest.[23]

Collateral discourse at least partially explains Judge Trotter's style. Three years earlier, the judge had agreed to support a petition for pardon of Little Leader—an Indian convicted of murder in Trotter's court. Claiming to be "most cheerfully unite[d] in recommending the defendant to Executive Clemency," the judge explained: "I hope for it likewise in consideration of the hardship of his case in being compelled to submit his trial to a tribunal with whose rules he was totally unacquainted and to the language of which he was a stranger. To him the whole trial was of necessity a pantomime."[24] The fate of American Indians was typically not at issue in slavery cases between 1820 and 1850, although the distinction between Indian and African-American ancestry was crucial to the adjudication of several legal issues.[25] Freed from policy concerns, the judge appealed exclusively to humanity in supporting Little Leader's pardon.[26]

With numbing regularity other judges opined that relevant portions of a constitution or statute obviated the need for their own analysis or commentary—but then analyzed and commented on thorny questions of morality and policy. They accurately rejected a flawed analogy between black bondage in America and the British system of villenage—but then rendered decisions consistent with the analogy. They occasionally crafted opinions from their intuitions of race and slavery, measured legal rights against inchoate social norms, or simply threw up their hands and appealed to an undefined moral code. Thus, a strictly legal analysis of judicial discourse obscures the character, intellect, and passion behind words of judgment. As an early biographer of South Carolina's Andrew P. Butler stated: "Judge Butler's opinions . . . give you no correct idea of the man; they are tame, lifeless things compared with his speeches or his charges."[27] In contrast, the oratorical portions of judicial opinions were instrumental "in avoiding harsh moral-formal conflicts" in the appellate review of slavery cases.[28]

These oratorical passages deserve to be taken seriously as an index of the beliefs and attitudes that coexisted with legal decision making. The crafting of judicial opinions cannot be fully appreciated without "some notice of judicial self-fashioning, more concern for the projected assumptions in decision-making, and a deeper awareness of both the hidden perspectives and projected certitudes in the judicial voice."[29] Escaping the "law box" in judicial opinions, falling somewhere between the utterly logical and the sheerly arbitrary, oratorical discourse contains various forms of argument about matters of probability that rely on political, economic, social, and religious premises.[30] These warrants existed at both conscious and unreflected levels of the judicial mind, and merit scrutiny for their influence on legal decision making in the sense that "all parts of a judge's opinion are meant to inform, explain, and guide parties in future cases, whether or not the observations enjoy the technical weight of *stare decisis*."[31] The rewards of attending to these premises are analogous to the benefits offered to historians of law by adopting legal hermeneutics and by scrutinizing both textual and contextual evidence.

In essence, the discourse of the judges illustrates practical reasoning. Traceable to a system rooted deeply in ancient theories of forensic speech, practical reasoning is now studied as legal argumentation that combines the form and clarity of dialectic with the flexibility of rhetoric. Judges who approach argument this way may well have "a concern for history and context; a desire to avoid abstracting away the human component in judicial decision making; an appreciation of the complexity of life; some faith in dialogue and deliberation; a tolerance for ambiguity, accommodation, and tentativeness, but a skepticism of rigid dichotomies."[32] Judges who feel complimented by the characteristics attributed to practical reasoners nonetheless remain open to the criticism that their discourse implies rather than expresses the real reasons behind their opinions. Given the absence in many slavery cases of legal guidance, through precedent or statute, selected appellate judges in the Old South warmly embraced this allowance.

Between 1820 and 1850 these judges deferred to tradition and avoided oratorical form in their opinions, even though this form has always been closely allied with the language of the law.[33] In fact, surviving references to the "birth of rhetoric" place it amid fifth-century B.C.E. lawsuits.[34] Nonetheless, and specifically when reporting their opinions in cases of slavery, the judges avoided rhetorical expression despite allowances for "freer" argument in southern courts than in the North.[35] The general scarcity of oratory in judicial opinions adds to the value of this discourse as a source for uncommonly personal expressions of judicial sentiment. The judges who violated commonly accepted bounds of professional demeanor, and who expressed their minds on slavery for the record, deserve special attention. They endorsed classical models like Cicero and they knew what they were doing when they supplemented or supplanted their legal logic with oratory.

In one sense, given the high level of feelings about slavery in their milieu, holding their tongues was remarkable for the judges. The advantages and disadvantages of slaveholding evoked strong sentiment. For example, North Carolina's John Louis Taylor publicly recounted fear over slave revolts as a lively dread.[36] South Carolina's Henry W. DeSaussure privately expressed concern about the state of the economy in Charleston's slave market.[37] As Mississippi's Alexander M. Clayton confessed retrospectively, slavery was "the greatest material interest of the world."[38] For Judges Taylor, DeSaussure, and Clayton, avoiding the expression of personal sentiment on slavery taxed their professional abilities. And when the words did burst out, they took on exceptional significance.

In another sense, staid custody of oratorical form was understandable because of the professional restraint associated with appointment to the bench of a high court. "Polite learning," one observer noted, "should never be displayed too much or unnecessarily upon the bench . . . . The point ruled in a legal decision should never be covered under figures of speech or flourishes of rhetoric."[39] Judicial status had to be conserved. Even on the legal frontier, for example, Edward Cross was credited with being "one of the most honest and impartial judges that ever presided on the bench in Arkansas—a man who succeeded in almost any enterprise in which he was engaged. He ranked as one of the leading men of the state.

In every position he has commanded respect."[40] Conscious if not jealous
of their status, judges risked falling into disrepute through a careless use
of words.

In chapter 1, "Humanists and Advocates," I sketch the judges' familiarity
with the humanist tradition and their related endorsement of oratory.
The humanist program of professional formation cut against the advocacy of change in existing institutions. Rather, prevailing beliefs and
values were the topics of conservative eloquence. In turn, the judges explicitly endorsed classical and belletristic forms of oratory for advocating
a conservative agenda. Whether specifying curricula and reading lists for
the education of young gentry, or criticizing the forensic speechmaking
of contemporaries, the judges made clear their personal commitment to a
humanist art of advocacy.

Chapter 2, "Intuition in Judicial Advocacy of the Upper South," and
chapter 3, "Intuition in Judicial Advocacy of the Deep South," contain assessments of the narratives within judicial opinions on slavery. The judges
recounted life in the Old South and these narratives were richly endowed
with evidence of judicial perceptions and recollections of their personal
experience as planters, merchants, and slave owners. Judicial narratives,
by affirming the southern system and the planter class as viable and desirable, confirm that the judges shared upper-class perceptions. The more
provocative function of these narratives was the provision of both premises and evidence in judicial advocacy. Susceptible to attack as circular and
fallacious reasoning, the judges' discourse reveals the authority they assumed to interpret the facts of southern life and to fashion arguments that,
at least in appearance, deserved canonization in the law reports.

In chapter 4, "Equations of Humanity and Interest in the Upper
South," and in chapter 5, "Equations of Humanity and Interest in the
Deep South," I assess the humanist urge behind judicial appeals to morality and policy. By advocating the conservation of property as well as
the conservation of life, the judges articulated a humanism that was peculiarly adapted to their needs as agents of the planter class. Addresses to
humanity and interest—the moral imperative to treat slaves humanely

and the South's interest in maintaining slavery—are examined prominently in legal histories and jurisprudential analyses, but my analysis shows that the judges did not intend to prompt a choice between the two standards. When used in isolation, each type of advocacy remained sketchy. When combined, however, these appeals became useful. In theory, pairing these appeals was effective in addressing partisans as well as citizens who were becoming disaffected with slavery. In the Upper South, a blended appeal to humanity and interest ultimately took root in the professional culture of the judges. In the Deep South, physically and psychologically distant from the forces of abolition, judges struggled less successfully to articulate a fully humanist defense of slavery—often relying exclusively on appeals to interest. When merged with its moral partner, however, this appeal remained useful in advocating that state laws were moral as well as expedient.

In chapter 6, "Judicial Apologetics," I illustrate how the judges defended their struggle to be humanists. In their opinions and private correspondence, they addressed the maintenance of professional status and the everyday discomforts of their jobs. If their apologetical discourse is genuine, then it substantively reflects a devotion to humanism: the judges expressed regrets over their frequently unsuccessful struggle to accommodate humanity and interest. If the apologetics are sheerly rhetorical, they at least confirm judicial commitment to conservative advocacy.

In my conclusion, I weigh the evidence that the judges fulfilled oratorical norms as well as legal duties when addressing the issue of slavery. I argue that, although they may have spoken artfully about the rightful places in their world of judges and slaves (confirming later indictments of their paternalism and chauvinism), they either ignored the classical ideal of epistemic rhetoric or failed to satisfy its demands. Although they crafted a rhetoric of slave laws, they also became creatures of that rhetoric.

My notes and list of works consulted identify routes by which interested readers may gain access to texts of judicial discourse and relevant scholarship. The list of abbreviations is a convenient index to the locations of these sources.

Chapter One

HUMANISTS AND ADVOCATES

D espite ambiguity on other issues, historical and legal accounts indicate that judges of high courts in the Old South knew the roles they were expected to play. If Nathan Green's 1849 speech on the powers and duties of lawyers is a reliable indication of self-consciousness, the judges knew that they should act nobly as public servants. For selected judges, this recognition reflected a deference to the civic humanism proclaimed by classical and neoclassical authorities. Public action, not private meditation, was the ideal. In professional practice, this ideal prompted the judges to advocate traditional beliefs and values as readily as reviewing issues of facts and law.

Judicial endorsement of classical standards and oratorical models is meaningful beyond the anecdotal level. This endorsement, as an emblem of their allegiance to a professional culture, made even more likely their advocacy of tradition. The antique philosophers and orators who earned judicial admiration innovated a brand of morality wedded to politics; the "good" man was identified with the civil servant who valorously defended useful institutions. Classical models of eloquence were unabashedly conservative in their political philosophies. As models, these Greek and Roman authorities provided the judges with commonplaces about social order in a world where slavery itself was commonplace.

Judicial regard for neoclassical authorities is similarly meaningful. Leading authorities of "taste" and other belletristic norms favored elegant variations on a theme rather than substantive revisions. Not surprisingly, then, judicial opinions favored arguments for the preservation of existing institutions, including the peculiar institution of slavery.

JUDICIAL HUMANISM

When they urged their successors to be "honest, true, and just," the judges were sanctioning a classically humanist program of social and professional formation for their sons and other upper-class southrons. Consciously or unconsciously, the judges were also extending an eighteenth-century phenomenon in the American educational system.[1] From the humanist perspective, virtue should be defined in relation to tradition and should be demonstrated publicly.[2] In view of its traditional roots, the humanist program endorsed by the judges has been denigrated as "moral and intellectual training for the elite."[3] Honesty, truth, and justice would never be defined differently from what the ruling class preferred. Indeed, the American legal institution itself has been analyzed persuasively as an economic instrument of the privileged class between 1780 and 1860.[4] Setting aside for now its effect on nineteenth-century social engineering, judicial endorsement of the humanist program reflects the authority of selected classical authors.[5] Whether the judges enjoyed a formal education in the classics or merely endorsed its benefits, they explicitly deferred to the same authorities.

Based on prehistoric and sophistic customs in ancient Greek culture, Protagoras declared in the fifth century B.C. that "[o]f all things the measure is man."[6] In the following century, Isocrates defined human excellence as the fulfillment of one's civic duty, as practical politics; he articulated this ideal in the form of a forensic oration that was designed to rebut charges of tax evasion ("impiety").[7] Isocrates insisted that, in order to be moral, a person should disdain the contemplative life in favor of participating in public affairs or "liturgy," a blend of civil and religious activities. This participation would demonstrate virtue in the conservation of traditional beliefs and values.

In the pragmatic tradition of ancient authorities such as Protagoras and Isocrates, humanism has consistently been analyzed in terms of civic or community duty. From one perspective, humanism has been linked to civic leadership reflecting not only "effectiveness" but also "the cruelty, the unfairness, and perhaps also the vulgarity of a proposed public policy." This dream envisions an exercise of power "grounded in explorations of the realm of humanistic values."[8] Consistent with American beliefs in democracy and progress, as idealized in the Declaration of Independence and Constitution, humanism can be construed as an urge to serve the community at the expense of individual rewards.[9] This urge is tied to present states of affairs, ignoring future consequences.

In an oral culture such as ancient Hellenism, political activity was oratorical. Conservative eloquence was accomplished through reasoning from pre-existing and approved commonplaces or "topics," a system authoritatively outlined by Aristotle in his *Art of Rhetoric*.[10] The system made sense. A virtuous orator could defend traditional norms no more clearly than by relying on argumentative premises derived from those norms. Proslavery argument in America, by stressing pragmatic issues and relying on experience, has been characterized as following Aristotelian precepts.[11]

Because of his own reputation for civic virtue, Isocrates influenced the form and content of later pronouncements on human excellence—notably that of the Roman advocate and orator Cicero. According to a standard reference, Cicero theorized "that the orator is the source from which flow all the forces that produce civilization and government; that the orator is the best statesman, and also teacher of morals."[12] Drawing on related sentiments expressed by Isocrates in his oration *Panegyricus*, Cicero pursued virtue through conservative eloquence. He represented the interests of Roman *optimates*—conservatives of senatorial rank.[13] He wrote *On the Orator* not so much as a work on eloquence but as a political act.[14] And by Roman definition, Cicero acted morally when he defended state interest.

Summarized in the first century A.D. by Quintilian,[15] the concept of *humanitas* prompted aspiring leaders to be politically eloquent—except for the mavericks who continued to indulge in meditative philosophies such as Platonism.[16] Though falling on hard times with the end of classical civilization, the notion of conservative eloquence—especially as expressed in the Ciceronian tradition—was eventually rekindled in western Europe.[17] The Venetians, for example, "carved time from busy lives to study the 'divine eloquence' of ancient masters."[18] Renaissance humanism has been characterized generally as the pursuit of eloquence.[19] Yet eloquence was not an end in itself for civic leaders. They pursued through their eloquence an elusive *virtù*, a blend of "moral energy" and "political expediency."[20] In fact, the study of eloquence (rhetoric) became allied with the study of moral philosophy during the Renaissance.[21] While struggling to accommodate morality and politics, humanists hoped that success would bring heroic or at least chivalrous status.[22] In the Old South, jurists pursued this chivalry by arguing for an accommodation of humanity and interest—the moral right to life and the civil right to property.

Never situated far from the tension between morality and expediency, legal practitioners were always found at the European centers of humanist development. Combing through the wisdom of the ancients, humanists sought "useful skills."[23] Whether it was Lorenzo Valla's instruction on dialectic in Italy, or Gabriel Harvey's lectures on rhetoric at Cambridge, the Ciceronian doctrines embraced in Quintilian's *Institutio Oratoria* were examined to satisfy the practical needs "of the lawyer and politician."[24] The "first beneficiaries of the humanist instauration," lawyers became the "continuators of humanism" across Europe through practical need and a general appetite for knowledge.[25] Professional needs related to the composition of persuasive discourse prompted lawyers and judges to master the oratorical form endorsed in humanist lore.[26]

Especially pertinent here is the *doctrina exemplorum* or "rule of examples" taught by Guarino Veronese and other humanists. According to this doctrine, the evidentiary weight of a single case takes on enhanced value: an example or testimonial based on personal experience does not merely illustrate a general or abstract principle; it authoritatively replaces generality and abstraction.[27] Moreover, the morally normative value of citing "custom" in ancient Roman oratory was translated into common law jurisprudence.[28] For antebellum judges, arguing from intuition and narrating what they perceived to be the facts of life were not only permissible but desirable. In advocating the laws of slavery, they cited examples from their own experiences as members of the planter class and assumed that these specific instances would be persuasive—so long as they matched the customary experiences and perceptions of their fellow planters.

During the Enlightenment, English teachers and critics of the common law and of jurisprudence sustained the moral focus of civic humanism.[29] In Scotland, the ideals of civic humanism prompted related assessments of jurisprudential theory.[30] Carrying these ideals as intellectual baggage, British subjects who were trained in this enlightened climate emigrated to America's leading institutions of higher education. In a pioneering effort, John Witherspoon reasserted the alliance of rhetoric and moral philosophy while lecturing at Princeton from 1768 to 1794. As a result, "[w]ell into the eighteenth century, both fields of study were still being influenced by the same two classical authorities, Aristotle and Cicero, whose civic humanist assumptions defined rhetoric as the art of political discourse, with moral philosophy defined by a complementary attention to civic ethics and practical politics."[31] Later authorities, such as John Quincy Adams and Edward T. Channing at Harvard and Timothy Dwight at Yale, affirmed the humanist doctrine by which orators held a civic duty "to articulate an established wisdom."[32]

But how specifically did the ancient regime of conservative eloquence flourish among professional judges in the Old South? After all, American lawyers learned their trade through apprenticeship more often than through academic study.[33] The answer to the question again lies in a lengthy historical tradition. Though an argument can be made that the nature of liberal education shapes the character of legal education in any given period,[34] it is sufficiently noteworthy that a heightened need for public discussion and debate spurred the growth of the ancient legal establishment.[35] Growing up in a golden age of oratory during the ascendancy of Rome, the legal profession maintained close ties with the art of oratory. Indeed, a rivalry developed between fully trained orators (advocates) and mere lawyers based on their disparate earnings as well as their relative skills.[36] Eventually, perhaps as early as the time of Cicero, a working balance was achieved that defused professional tensions. As centuries passed in those nations indebted to Roman law, various rules and protocols mirrored the Roman fusion of lawyering, advocacy, and oratory.

Not all modern Western nations were indebted to Roman law. Nonetheless, even in nations wedded to the common law, the notion of civic humanism pervaded developments in the arts and sciences.[37] And here a deference to the neoclassical expression of Ciceronian doctrines made conservative eloquence desirable in judicial discourse. As a modern authority for "half the educated English-speaking world," Hugh Blair's analysis of tasteful eloquence required the conservation of tradition. In the humanist tradition,[38] he issued a call to defend existing institutions as a matter of morality. For authority, Blair could look to Cicero and Quintilian. These classical authorities had borrowed Cato the Elder's definition of a truly eloquent orator as "a good man speaking well"—precisely as an admirer once said of Georgia's Joseph H. Lumpkin in the original Latin.[39] Thus James Kent asserted in his inaugural lecture at Columbia College, November 17, 1794, that a "lawyer in a free country, should have all the requisites of Quintilian's orator."[40]

The study of belles lettres was designed by Blair to "support a proper rank in social life." Moreover, he considered rhetorical taste to be a key for unlocking "the operations of the imagination, and the movements of the heart."[41] These operations and movements led to the execution of one's civic duty. "The elevated sentiments and high examples which poetry, eloquence and history are often bringing under our view," Blair insisted, "naturally tend to nourish in our minds public spirit, the love of glory, contempt of external fortune, and the admiration of what is truly illustrious and great."[42] This conception of eloquence was consonant with antebellum Southern judges' stated and unstated ambitions. Serving the public through their labors on the bench, the judges also pursued personal advantage, if not glory.

Adopting the roles of advocates in regard to the laws of slavery, the judges accepted Blair's assertion that orators invariably strive to convince their audiences "of something being either true, right, or good."[43] By extension, aspiring humanists argued for the truth of slave codes based on premises of righteous humanity and good interest. After all, commonplaces such as these—staples in "the writings of Aristotle, Cicero, and Quinctilian"—were the general ideas applicable to a great many different subjects.[44]

Despite criticism of their opinions from peers, much less from abolitionists, the judges could claim, perhaps unwittingly on Blair's authority, that they possessed a public and private devotion to the "truly illustrious and great" operation of the law. A dominant force in the education of English-speaking students, Blair's lectures were also popular on the Continent. Thus, even for émigrés to the unique jurisdiction of Louisiana, judicial recognition of forensic eloquence—and its humanist commonplaces about morality and expediency—may be traced to common sources of reference. Whether for the Louisiana judges who required "a good classical education" for admission to the Bar, or for Tennessee's William B. Turley who possessed "a fine classical and literary taste,"[45] training in the art of being lawyerly was related to training in humanism. It was this training and related values that the judges endorsed.

JUDICIAL ADVOCACY

The judges saw oratory as an end in itself, an art form that should be cultivated publicly for its intellectual, moral, and aesthetic values. The practice of oratory was essential to effective advocacy, but oratory was worthwhile regardless of its practical effects. No other explanation is nearly as persuasive when encountering sententious remarks in the opinions of otherwise little-noted judges. Henry Crabb of Tennessee, for example, inserted a model speech on "freedom" in reviewing *Vaughn v. Phebe.*[46] A black woman had successfully sued a white man for freedom and damages after he had seized her as a slave. Judge Crabb oratorically approved the trial court's reception of hearsay evidence but, as often happened, the court did not preserve the woman's freedom. Her case was remanded for a new trial because portions of the hearsay admitted into evidence had supplanted more probative records.

Notwithstanding the legal outcome, Judge Crabb's use of oratorical form illustrates judicial advocacy. He metaphorically distinguished the substance of freedom from the forms of chicanery: "Freedom in this country is not a mere name,—a cheat with which the few gull the many." He personified freedom, attributing to it the powers of mobility and social influence: "It walks abroad in its operations,—transfers its possessor, even if he be black, or mulatto, or copper-colored, from the kitchen and the cotton-field to the court-house and the election ground." In some jurisdictions, the judge declared, freedom renders its possessor a "politician, brings him acquainted with the leading citizens, busies him in the political canvass for office, takes him to the ballot-box; and, above all, secures to him the enviable and inestimable privilege of trial by jury." He indulged in rhetorical questions laced with anaphora and polysyndeton:

> Can it be said that there is nothing of a public nature in a right that thus, from its necessary operation, places a man in many respects on an equality with the richest and greatest and the best in the land, and brings him into contact with the whole community? Can it be said that common reputation is no evidence of a right, producing so many effects relative in their character, to that very society where the common understanding, report, or reputation is required to exist? Can it be said that the community or neighborhood, as the case may be, the "public" around a man, will too readily give credence to a claim by which the individual who makes it obtains among themselves so high a comparative elevation?

In sum, he applied panegyric to the execution of his judicial duty. "Freedom," Judge Crabb exclaimed, "embraces with its comprehensive grasp all the useful rights of man; and it makes itself manifest by many privileges, immunities, external public acts. It is not confined in its operations to privacy, or to the domestic circle." This judicial encomium of freedom's embrace glorifies the same equation of private and public acts idealized in civic humanism. Just as clearly, the judge's discourse is not a review of facts or law. It is advocacy.

Pragmatic as well as artistically inclined, the judges appreciated oratory as a means to advancement in the public eye. Mississippi's William L. Sharkey and Alexander M. Clayton contributed substantially to their state's legal history, but they also found time to address commencements of their university's law school in 1859 and 1860. After commending the legal profession, Judge Sharkey identified "arms, eloquence, and the study of civil law" as three roads to fame.[47] Evidence of widespread admiration for military credentials—a medal or wound was especially valuable—abounds in histories of the Old South. Regard for training in the martial

arts was unquestionably high but Judge Sharkey made a point of attributing equal power to training in eloquence. One year later, Judge Clayton
listed "moral philosophy"—identified with rhetorical training in curricula
of the period—among the several courses of study desirable for aspiring
lawyers.[48] For these two judges, speechmaking was central among civic
duties.

Not all of the judges were sufficiently educated in a formal sense to recognize the myriad techniques of rhetoric, but they all were clever enough
to recognize the fundamental place of oratory in their culture. Little evidence remains from the career of Arkansas Chief Justice Townshend Dickinson, but the Batesville *Gazette* faithfully reported his stirring oration on
July 4, 1822.[49] Louisiana's Pierre Derbigny also delivered a Fourth of July
oration at the first celebration of that occasion in New Orleans.[50] Not surprisingly, Judge Derbigny's court approved the 1819 rule requiring "a
good classical education" for admission to the Louisiana Bar.

When they had received a humanist education themselves, the judges
enthusiastically endorsed it as a preparation for entry into their oratorical
culture. For South Carolina's Henry W. DeSaussure, who had studied
under "a classical teacher of high reputation," rumors of "gambling & de-
bauchery" at his state's university were especially troubling.[51] The judge
no doubt wished to keep riffraff out of an upper-class enclave. He also and
explicitly applauded a young protégé's study of "the Latin and Greek classics" at Yale, insisting that "right knowledge of the Classics is often useful
& always ornamental."[52] In addition Judge DeSaussure self-consciously
praised the merits of selected classical orators in a Fourth of July speech.[53]
A colleague, Baylis J. Earle, had earlier declaimed on the character of Cicero in a graduation speech.[54] Humanist ideals aside, a mastery of oratorical form was "useful."

Based on classical models, South Carolina's William Harper declared
that "[t]here can be no true eloquence without good sense and just & vigorous thought. To this more must be added—the earnestness of thorough
conviction and the force of strong feeling."[55] Andrew P. Butler agreed,
but he specifically denounced a mindless imitation of the classical orators. "I never borrow from Demosthenes," he insisted, "and palm it off as

my own." Furthermore, Judge Butler argued, "liberty of speech . . . is the great conservative element of a Republic; it is to the political, what fire is to the material world, a subservient and affluent minister, when under the control of prudence and intelligence."[56] As both judges recognized, eloquence was a powerful tool that demanded prudent handling. Judge Butler more specifically voiced the "conservative" function of oratory.

For another South Carolina jurist, John S. Richardson, classical education always included a healthy dose of training in eloquence. In a notebook signed by the future judge and dated 1809, the entry on "Education" abounds with classical references to rhetoricians such as Aristotle and orators such as Cicero. In another entry on "Private v. Publick Education," the thirty-two-year-old state legislator contrasted Attic and florid eloquence.[57] For this judge, public life demanded discipline as well as flair—two qualities commonly attributed to successful advocates and orators since antiquity. South Carolina's John B. O'Neall held similar beliefs. In fact, he once praised Richard Henry Lee as "the Cicero of the old Congress" for advocating the Declaration of Independence.[58] Having initially developed skill in extemporaneous speaking at the Newberry Academy, Judge O'Neall attributed much of his fame for polished advocacy to his participation in a Saturday debating society during the year before his admission to the bar in 1814.[59]

The judge who dominated Georgia's early Supreme Court earned a sterling reputation for classical education and oratorical training. Joseph H. Lumpkin delivered the salutatorian address on the occasion of his graduation from Princeton, and his command of Latin was regarded highly enough that he was offered the professorship of rhetoric and oratory at his state's university while it was still known as Franklin College. Indeed, as noted above, an admirer gushed enthusiastically during the judge's lifetime: "We know few men who better answers to the Latin description of an orator—*Vir bonus dicineri peritus*."[60] By reputation, at least, the judge's formation had prepared him to be the "good man skilled in speaking" who was applauded by classical authorities.

Fellow Georgians Robert M. Charlton and Eugenius A. Nisbet expressed sentiments affirming Judge Lumpkin's formation. Asserting that "education" is a lifelong duty, Judge Charlton identified both "the rules of logic, and the principles of rhetoric" among basic tools in mental training.[61] In more passionate tones, Judge Nisbet advocated a belletristic program and exhorted his audience of female collegians to develop their sensitivity to beauty—lambasting insensitive people such as those "who sit beneath the voice of Tully [Cicero] and hear no eloquence."[62] Aptly bearing the middle name of Aristides, a leading sophist in the Roman empire, Judge Nisbet twice declined appointments as a professor of belles lettres.[63] Eulogizing him, Chief Justice O. A. Lochrane observed that Nisbet the advocate "was no orator, 'as Brutus is.'" Rather, "he was an orator whose purity of diction, ornate expression, and statesmanship of sentiment bore him onward and forward and upward to the highest regions."[64] Making allowances for eulogistic hyperbole, it remains ironic that Judge Nisbet once declared: "One might certainly say with truth, 'let me write the books, and make the speeches, and educate the youth of a country, and I care not who makes the laws.'"[65] For Judges Charlton and Nisbet, the "principles of rhetoric" and an appreciation of "eloquence" merited serious attention.

Thomas Ruffin, perhaps the most noteworthy of North Carolina's antebellum judges, revealed a passionate attachment to the art of eloquence. Early in the nineteenth century, he asked rhetorically:

> [W]hat inspires a man with more confidence in time of danger than a consciousness of his talents as an orator? Who is more effectual in laying prostrate and chastising the injurious and arrogant? Who is more capable of repressing intemperate desires? Whose admonitions do we receive with more submissive patience than those of the monitor by whose eloquence we are enraptured? Can you then bestow too much attention to this exercise?

Answering his query about the value of exercises in eloquence, he asserted: "No—you will never regret, assure yourselves from me, an almost incessant devotion in the study of oratory."[66] The equation of self-confidence with one's self-consciousness of oratorical skill is striking in Judge Ruffin's speech. Just as noteworthy by implication is his belief that judges may control litigants and their passions, ganing adherence to opinions, by judicious use of oratorical form. The judge paid special tribute to Demosthenes and Cicero as classical models for applying oratory to both public and private affairs. For modern guidance, the judge favored "standard authors in *Belles Letters*."[67] Thus were the precepts of Hugh Blair recommended to another generation. Other artifacts from North Carolina further illuminate the judicial endorsement of oratorical training: coursework in the "Catholic Seminary" experiences reported in 1822 by Richmond M. Pearson and in the 1867 brochure of his son's academy, the Oxford Classical and Mathematical School.[68]

As Judge Ruffin would do for his daughter, Catherine, North Carolina's William Gaston extended advice to his eldest daughter about dictaminal rhetoric: "Do nothing carelessly. Whatever you have to do let it be done as well as possible. . . . If you write dismiss not your letter till it is as perfect in all respects as you can make it."[69] Judge Gaston's advice was authoritative. By 1816 he had established his speechmaking credentials in Congress.[70] Two years later his courtroom oratory drew high praise from an educated observer:

> When he spoke of the helpless condition of the prisoner at the bar, many moist eyes were to be seen in every part of the house. As celebrated as he must know himself to be, & accustomed to public speaking as he is both on the floor of congress and in addressing the box or bench, he yet commences with hesitation—faulters and sometimes even appears at a loss, till warmed and fired by his subject he forgets himself and is totally lost in defending the interests of his clients. His influence on the verdict of the jury is almost proverbial.[71]

An accomplished if sometimes reluctant orator, Judge Gaston was also a speech critic whose technical assessments were prized for their accuracy.[72] No doubt, his critical insights were equally prized for their realism. While assessing the oratorical formation of civic leaders, for example, the judge asserted that "all the rules of Quinctilian, [Charles] Rollin or [Hugh] Blair, will never make a powerful reasoner or an eloquent orator."[73] The true humanist eventually must abandon the role of student and take action.

The education of Virginia's judges was consistent with the upper-class training endorsed in other jurisdictions. Classical studies and the development of oratorical skill were prominent.[74] Francis T. Brooke, for instance, recalled how his father had engaged a private tutor, "a Scotch gentleman, under the name of Alexander Dunham," to drill the future judge and his twin brother in "Latin and Greek" so that they could read the "higher classics."[75] Spencer Roane was another and more politically famous Virginian who attended "the best schools in the neighbourhood" and learned "the dead languages."[76] Always outspoken, Judge Roane once exclaimed (under the pseudonym "Amphictyon") that "Truth and liberty are dearer to me than Plato or Socrates."[77] This exclamation and others have been cited to illustrate that, in his speaking and writing, Judge Roane "had a taste for belles lettres."[78]

Henry St. George Tucker saw specialization as the key to improving forensic eloquence. Speaking at the 1841 opening of the law school in Charlottesville, the judge cautioned aspiring advocates that they should not hope to excel in all things. His choice of illustrations and authorities is notable. He observed, for example, that "the conquerors in the race and the champions in martial exercises were not the followers of Aristotle; nor did Cicero and Demosthenes aspire to excel their contemporaries in . . . the triumphs of the chase, or their skill in throwing the javelin."[79] Judge Tucker revealed how deeply he endorsed classical and neoclassical authorities on eloquence when seeking to influence his son's educational experiences. In a petition to the president of Yale, the judge recounted his son's prior exposure to the Greek and Latin classics and asked that his training include, above all, the study of "Belles Lettres."[80]

Virginia's judges were well versed in both classical and neoclassical eloquence. Dabney Carr, writing to his uncle, Thomas Jefferson, remarked about Carr's liberal education—including his readings in Cicero.[81] Later, when contributing a series of essays to the *Richmond Enquirer* under the pseudonym "The Old Bachelor," Judge Carr pointed out the need for improvements in elocutionary training so that nineteenth-century advocates might more closely approach the skill of Demosthenes, "prince of orators." Judge Carr specifically contrasted antebellum training in public speaking with the ancient education of Roman orators described by Cicero and Quintilian:

> Let us pause, here, to compare these advantages, thus gained by the Roman, in childhood, with the faults exhibited by the best of our public speakers, in the particulars just mentioned. In point of time, they are either so rapid and precipitate, as to disconcert their own understandings and make those of their hearers swim *in vacuo*, or so very slow, drawling and tedious, or so full of unnecessary and affected pauses, that it were just as interesting to attempt to watch the motion of the shadow on a sun-dial as to follow the equally imperceptible creeping of their minds. . . . Beside the management of the voice, in the articles of time, cadence and articulation, the Roman orator was attentively formed in his early years to all that easy and graceful flexibility of frame on which attitude and gesture depend, and all that management of the features, which insinuates, with such resistless energy, the convictions and feelings of the speaker into the minds of his audience.[82]

Judge Carr thus endorsed "the resistless energy" of oratory and its transfer of "the convictions and feelings of the speaker into the minds of his audience." Although he restricted his attention to presentational style ("action"), he revealed himself to be a competent historian of rhetoric:

> Now altho' more than two centuries elapsed between the age of Demosthenes and that of Cicero, yet during that period Athens had continued to be the school of eloquence, to Rome as well as to the rest of the world; and there is little reason to doubt that by the great orators of the latter city, as well as the philosophers and rhetoricians of the former, all the modes of action which distinguished Demosthenes had been transmitted, during this interval, both at Athens and Rome. Cicero studied eloquence under Grecian masters in both cities, and there can be no reason to doubt that the action of Demosthenes was intimately known to him and of course to Quinctilian, who lived so shortly after him.[83]

The authority of classical Greek and Roman masters of eloquence is prominent in Judge Carr's chronicle. More significant, he demonstrated an acquaintance with historical details that would escape anyone less taken with the inherent value of rhetoric, oratory, and their civic applications. This portion of Judge Carr's chronicle remains antique in its focus, but he elsewhere reported his recognition of more recent models of eloquence such as Bossuet.[84]

Just as revealing, Judge Carr's call for educational reform contains an endorsement of civic humanism. He criticized the founding fathers for not having insisted more vehemently on introducing "their children to virtuous hardihood, . . . as well as to policy and literature."[85] Understanding and appreciation of literature were the ordinary goals of education; his mention of virtue and policy within the same assertion reveals the judge's endorsement of humanist ideals. Later he asserted that "the *political* condition of the people must ever depend upon their *moral* and *intellectual*."[86] The intellectual condition of Virginians was his theme, and so the pairing of the other two conditions, political and moral, must be understood as an endorsement of the humanist program.

Some judges not only endorsed training in the art of oratory, they harped on it. William H. Cabell, for instance, pestered his son repeatedly during the summer and fall of 1837 with letters specifying which works on rhetoric and oratory were essential to higher education. Beginning in late July and continuing through early November, Judge Cabell wrote frequently to his son, Coalter, who was attending the University of Virginia. Usually in a scolding tenor, Cabell pointed out his choice of sources for rhetorical doctrine. Hugh Blair's *Lectures* and sermons were suitable; in fact, the judge recalled incorporating a passage from one of Blair's sermons into his own valedictory address at Hampden-Sydney College.[87] George Campbell's *Philosophy of Rhetoric* was also cited.[88] In addition, Coalter was reminded that his father possessed "translations of all the classics."[89]

Since merely obtaining a classical education was not the humanist ideal, Judge Cabell also exhorted his son to enter civic affairs: "A man who can speak & write well, may do what he pleases, in a government constituted like ours." More expansively, after announcing the civic value of rhetorical training, the judge outlined several methods based on his personal experience:

> I can confidently affirm that there never lived a more bashful man than I was, when I commenced the practice of the law. I felt, deeply felt, that in any effort I should make at public speaking, I should fall infinitely short of the just expectations of my friends. And such was the fact. But it did not prevent me from making the effort. I went on, floundering away, but doing my best, and I would have done so, at the risk of my immortal soul. Every successive effort was less painful; until, at last, I spoke without embarrassment. Let my example encourage you. When you begin to speak, do not aim at display. Try only to speak plainly & sensibly without any effort to procure admiration. To this end study the subject well before you attempt to speak on it. Get all the information on it that you can; arrange & methodize your ideas, without regard to the precise words or arrangement, and then speak as you would do, in arguing the same subject, with a friend in private. At first disregard tone or jesture. They will come to you naturally, after a while. But be cautious to acquire no bad habit of unseemly gesticulation, no screwing, squinting or shutting the eyes, no twisting or contortion of the features, no unnecessary clearing of the throat etc. etc.

The judge summarized his advice with a negative example, "a young lawyer at Lewisburg, a very sensible young man, & good lawyer, who spoils all that he has to say by what appears to be affectation." This unfortunate advocate illustrated everything to be avoided in humanist oratory: "He throws his head back, sometimes turning it to one side, and shutting his eyes, almost close, as if he were going into a swoon."[90] The overbearing Judge Cabell's opinions illustrate his belief in the instrumental power of the spoken word as well as his personal applications of oratorical form. He toiled on the bench of Virginia's highest court for

several years. However, consistent with the reluctance of all his colleagues
to use oratorical form in their opinions, he succumbed only twice when
reviewing slavery cases.

In March 1828, Judge Cabell joined four colleagues in reviewing *Randolph v. Randolph*, in which two daughters attempted to have several
slaves exempted from the assets of their deceased father's estate.[91] The
judge argued that the slaves should not be treated as property of the estate because the daughters had brought forward sufficient evidence of
having gained separate ownership of the slaves before the father's death.
Judge Cabell began his opinion with a sweeping generalization unsup-
ported by the facts of record in the case:

> Slaves are rational beings, and, as such, have moral qualities, which
> are calculated to render them of peculiar value in the estimation of
> their masters. It may be laid down as a position almost universal,
> that the master, unless obliged to sell, would think himself poorly
> compensated for the loss of a slave, by the price which a Jury might
> fix upon him. Moreover, slaves are human beings; and therefore, I
> do not think that even their attachments and feelings are to be dis-
> regarded. The inhumanity of wantonly invading these attachments
> and feelings, forms with me an additional argument.

This exordium is enthymematic in the Aristotelian tradition: it begins
with a premise that was predictably acceptable to the class of persons
constituting the audience, and reaches a conclusion that flows clearly if
not inevitably from the generalization.[92] The exordium also reflects
Cicero's theory of *insinuatio*.[93] Following the classical principle of insinu-
ating or subtle introductions, later confirmed by moderns like Hugh
Blair, the judge recognized that the case under review had a discreditable
character.[94]

Common law judges avoid tampering with clearly expressed directions
in a last will and testament, yet Judge Cabell's opinion teeters on the edge
of tampering with testamentary wishes. In such circumstances, using the
technique of insinuation, he tried to avoid unsavory appearances by fo-
cusing on moral agency instead of a discreditable act. The judge ampli-

fied his discourse in an epideictic mode rather than with strictly forensic technique. In the classical tradition, epideictic rhetoric is recognized as commonly applicable to judicial causes.[95] Judge Cabell's praise of slaves' personal attributes and qualities matched hellenistic models.[96]

The judge reviewed a second relevant case, *Paup's Administrator v. Mingo,* in January 1833.[97] In this case, former slaves sued for excess profits accruing to the administrators of an estate who continued to hold the slaves in bondage beyond the point at which they should have been freed. The slaves' master, William Walker, had executed a will that provided for their freedom as soon after his death as his affairs were settled and his debts were paid. Walker died in 1789. The slaves were not formally granted freedom until 1809, and even then they received no payment for labor that had produced income for the estate in excess of William Walker's debts. Finally, in 1827, the business affairs of the Walker estate were complete. At that time, survivors among the former slaves sued for the excess profits owed to them eighteen years earlier. Judge Cabell argued curtly that the former slaves were owed nothing: "I consider it the settled law of this country, that a person held in slavery, no matter how long or unjustly, cannot recover damages in the form of profits, or otherwise, for his illegal detention in slavery." The judge then revealed his personal stance toward such cases: "This being the settled law, I deem it unnecessary to inquire into its policy or abstract justice. I am not disposed to disturb it." Far from insinuation, the judge's blunt discourse reflects his righteous feelings about the cause of action. Indeed, he used one of the rhetorical tricks (feigned indignation) that Aristotle listed for emphasizing a high degree of wrongdoing.[98] In effect, the judge decreed indignantly, slaves were attempting to violate an unwritten law of right.

As William Gaston illustrated in North Carolina, abiding concerns about the study and practice of eloquence lured judges into speech criticism. Judge Carr, for one, evaluated the political eloquence of Benjamin Franklin.[99] In another of his "Old Bachelor" essays, the judge assessed forensic technique. Recalling a courtroom speech in defense of a woman accused of murdering her bastard child, Judge Carr lampooned the advocate's method:

The evidence was circumstantial; he was arguing against the probability of the fact, from the atrocious nature of the crime and its inconsistency with the feelings of a mother's heart. . . . He suggested
[relevant issues], but did not urge them; in other words, he threw
them out in a manner so cold and disengaged, that they produced
no effect, or if any, they produced an unfavorable one.

After quoting from the advocate's flawed speech (which included the affected waving of a handkerchief), the judge recalled that "in the men of
taste who stood around, the only emotions which he excited were those
of contempt and disgust." In conclusion, Judge Carr recommended that
advocates study Patrick Henry's technique—a mode of legal eloquence
that made "people's blood run cold and their hair stand on end."[100] The
prominence of delivery in Judge Carr's remarks reflects his deference to
the standards of all but a few classical critics. His reference to "men of
taste" suggests belletristic standards. More generally, his fascination with
the art of advocacy was not to be denied in his endeavors on the bench.

Little-noted judges like North Carolina's Henry Seawell also delighted
in speech criticism—perhaps as a salve to their egos. After visiting the nation's capitol, Judge Seawell poked fun at the art of advocacy as practiced
by the "great men in the Supreme Court." He lampooned these advocates
who "begin so low, as scarcely to be heard, and gradually swell until they
fairly rave; then they gently subside into a soft whisper, their gesticulation
is *menacing*, both to the Court and the bystanders."[101] In other discourse,
the judge complained of his professional status.[102] He may have engaged in
speech criticism to achieve the same end, a venting of his professional
frustration.

Oratorical form was important to the judges because they were expected
not only to reach just decisions but also to promote the justice they were
dispensing. Advocating what is just represents the practical limit of judicial duty, and requires a special skill. Furthermore, the judicial administration of justice may create a "rhetorical community" over time.[103]
In fact, when analyzing the goodness and badness of judicial opinions,
critics should attend to the criterion of effectiveness in constructing a po-

litical or ethical community with auditors: "The law indeed works by argument, and does so under circumstances where agreement cannot be compelled by resort to logic or data. It is thus a branch of rhetoric."[104] Judicial discourse does not always proceed relentlessly from statutory or common law premises, and conclusions are sometimes logically invalid though rhetorically appealing.

Judicial opinions are also models of justification—treated elsewhere as "rationalization."[105] From this perspective, the judge composes a formal opinion after having reached a decision that is not necessarily or completely derived from the arguments expressed in the opinion. These formal statements, however, do not lack rhetorical value simply because they may not match the judge's "inner deliberation."[106] As discourse that is addressed to contesting parties, other tribunals, and the public, the justifications of a judgment are proper when "socially and culturally conditioned" to suit the convictions and the aspirations of the audience.[107]

The judges wrote legal opinions as addresses to audiences.[108] The addressed nature of these opinions makes my critical approach fruitful. At the most basic level, each of the audiences agreed with the judges that life was hard. The frontier had not yet become an American myth. Alabama's Anderson Crenshaw, for one, could easily relate to the frontier audience because he was no stranger to hard times. He could easily recall deprivation during the Indian raids of his youth: "The hostile Indians are murdering the families on the limits of the territory every day."[109] Both audiences and judges also recognized that violence was systemic in their shared culture. For example, from the point of view expressed in his petition to arm the militia, Mississippi's Joseph S. B. Thacher seemed well aware of the commonly violent antidote to native Americans' presence in the Old South.[110] In more settled times and places, however, agriculture claimed the lion's share of everyone's attention—including, of course, judicial members of the planter class. Not surprisingly, then, did Pierre A. Rost of Louisiana grandly address "Sugar: Its Culture and Manufacture" at an 1845 exposition.[111]

Advocating their opinions on slavery to a community of professional colleagues, appellants, and the general public, the judges imitated classical models and obeyed antique rules. These models and rules lay at the heart of a liberal education that, as endorsed by the judges, sustained the tradition of conservative eloquence. The study of oratorical form was central to this education, which, once mastered, enabled a person to fulfill civic duties—primarily the advocacy of traditional beliefs and values.

Ironically, a leading proslavery propagandist denigrated the consequences of judicial preferences in personal and professional formation. "After the Romans had conquered Greece," George Fitzhugh wrote in 1857, "Athens became the school and center of thought for the civilized world. Men had but one set of ideas, but one set of models to imitate." For Fitzhugh, this lack of diversity was ruinous: "Improvement and progress ceased, and imitation, chaining the present to the past, soon induced rapid retrogression."[112] Fitzhugh's complaint about stagnation should not be dismissed out of hand. The oratory admired by the judges featured compelling arguments for preserving existing institutions as well as belletristic support for these arguments on behalf of tradition. To some extent, at least, the judges' reverence for classical thought and culture disabled them from addressing slaves and slavery any differently than prior generations had done. In any event, the judges were disposed to advocate a position on slavery rather than merely review trial records.

Chapter Two

INTUITION IN JUDICIAL ADVOCACY
OF THE UPPER SOUTH

Favoring advocacy as a humanist ideal, judges in Virginia, North Carolina, Tennessee, and Arkansas recognized that advocates stress those facts that help their causes. In theory, as they struggled to articulate a humanist defense of slavery, the judges would have favored details sustaining the aspirations of the planter class. In practice, added to the scope of judicial discretion already granted to them on the rough-and-ready appellate circuit, their authority to review the factual setting of each case gave judges a distinctly oratorical advantage. Late twentieth-century observers contend that courts seldom reach a unified interpretation of the facts and then decide how the law addresses these facts. Rather, judges develop a set of facts within the process of justifying a legal opinion.[1] Whether or not a similar dynamic prevailed in high courts of the Upper South, narrative portions of their opinions on slavery illustrate that the judges used oratorical form to assert their intuitions about the antebellum facts of life.

The judges reviewed slavery cases through a perceptual filter. For judges who perceived a lack of legal precedent on how to assess slaves, experience was the best teacher. For judges who perceived a lack of settled law on slavery, intuitions about the nature of slaves were compelling. No disembodied or distant narrator, each judge lived in the narrative he composed. As the foundation of humanist advocacy, judicial narratives expressed perceptions of slaves' physical and spiritual characteristics. These narratives identified slaves as economic assets that were troublesome to administer because they were inherently degraded creatures.

Judicial narratives were distinct from the citation of precedent or the recitation of legislative history.[2] John W. Green, for example, disclosed no personal intuitions when he composed a well-documented "review of the history of slavery and servitude in Virginia, and the laws relating thereto."[3] Thomas Ruffin did not adopt a narrative mode when rejecting arguments about the legislative intent behind an element in his state's penal code.[4] In addition, the judges did not simply adopt the published record of facts—the narrative pleaded by the winning advocate. Rather, judicial narratives illustrate that the judges invented authority for their opinions—occasionally the very facts upon which cases turned. Neither saintly nor devilish, this artful invention was a tool of advocacy endorsed in the humanist tradition.

In Virginia, Henry St. George Tucker relied on personal experience in reviewing *Paup's Adm. v. Mingo*. Concluding that former slaves should not be entitled to recover damages for labor they were illegally forced to provide, he argued that "the slave, in his birth and in infancy, has been a burden, and that if the master could have foreseen his emancipation and his demand for profits, he might have been altogether averse from incurring such a charge."[5] Judge Tucker cited precedential authority for his intuition about the "burden" placed on society by slaves.[6] Yet the story he told was also consistent with a culture in which former slaves did not escape several conditions of bondage, even though they had obtained their freedom. The judicial image of masters' regretting in hindsight the birth of a troublesome slave is especially powerful, calling to mind absolute power over life and death. This intuition or speculation on the godlike power of slaveowners, in addition to its plausibility for an audience of planters, echoed doctrinaire pronouncements by the judge's father.[7]

Other suitably experienced judges included William H. Cabell, John T. Lomax, and William Brockenbrough. Judge Cabell was well practiced in issuing orders to an overseer and making deals for slaves.[8] Judge Lomax received slave property from his father-in-law.[9] Judge Brockenbrough acknowledged paying the considerable sum of five dollars to a physician for "adjusting a Truss to an inguinal hernia" in a young slave.[10] However, in *Davenport v. Commonwealth*, the judge perceived a link between physical ills and mental weakness—asserting on his own authority that the "colour" of freed slaves "renders them an easy prey to the arts and violence of desperate and abandoned villians."[11] In contrast to Judge Tucker's attribution of exceptional powers to slaveowners, Judge Brockenbrough attributed abysmally poor abilities to slaves. As a result, the judge agreed with Judge Tucker—though on different intuitive grounds—that slaves had no place in free society.

Addressing lofty issues such as freedom and more down-to-earth concerns such as rights of inheritance, Dabney Carr and John W. Green expanded the judicial technique of extracting premises and evidence from personal intuitions about slavery. Judge Carr observed matter-of-factly in *Jones v. Mason:* "With us, nothing is so usual as to advance children by gifts of slaves. They stand with us, instead of money." Judge Green concurred: "With us, the advancement of children is most frequently in negroes; and a bequest or gift of negroes is generally made as an advancement for the better establishing the child in life."[12] Identifying with the audience ("us") and distinguishing themselves and their audience from slaves ("they"), the judges assumed for purposes of argument that their perceptions were authoritative. Unlike taking judicial notice of the weather on a certain day or the address of a residence, the judges' observations attributed a social norm and economic advantage to the transfer of slaves. These observations functioned as enthymemes, devices by which an advocate need not mention an argumentative premise because both orator and audience share a related experience or belief.

Judges Carr and Green also reviewed a case that turned on the question whether the sale of an estate could be enjoined when the property to be sold included slaves. Judge Carr argued in *Randolph v. Randolph* that a sale could proceed when the slave property had no peculiar value. In these instances, the aggrieved party could easily be compensated in a traditional suit for damages: "We must all agree, that there are many cases, in which a slave has no peculiar value with his owner; some, among the large slaveholders, where he is not even personally known; or he may be vicious or worthless." In effect, the judge intuited that slaves were unlike human beings of another race who retained at least some worth because of their very existence. The best assessor of peculiar value would be a member of the audience being addressed by the judge: "Whether the slave has a peculiar value with his master, none can so well know as the master himself. He can speak from his own feelings, his own knowledge." Again Judge Green concurred: "[Slaves] have moral qualities, which make them, in some instances, peculiarly valuable to their owners; but which could not be the subject of enquiry in each particular case, without great inconvenience and uncertainty."[13] By stressing the reliability of a master's "feelings, his own knowledge," Judge Carr simply transferred his own experience into the case at hand. He expressed the transference enthymematically by asserting that, in order to resolve the question, his audience "must all agree" with his experiential premise. In accord with what an audience of fellow planters might be expected to agree, the judge reasoned to his conclusions about the proper assessment of slaves. Judge Green added further commentary on the "inconvenience" of dealing with slaves despite their value as assets.

Conversely, a few judges bemoaned their experience. Francis T. Brooke, for one, implied a desire for wider and richer experiences when he noted obtaining "less than 20 negroes from family & patrons."[14] Wary of being distracted by the financial details of slaveowning, the newly appointed Briscoe G. Baldwin was probably delighted by the advice he received to sell off his stock and hire out his negroes upon assuming his duties on the judicial circuit.[15] The economics of slavery were troubling enough for Judge Baldwin in 1848 that he used his intuitions as collateral evidence in reviewing *Peter v. Hargrave*. Arguing that former slaves should not be entitled to recover damages for labor they were illegally forced to provide, the judge reflected:

> The owner of slaves . . . is usually condemned to a constant, permanent and anxious burthen of care and expenditure. It seldom happens that more than a small proportion of them are capable of productive labour; while provision must be made for the food, clothing and shelter of all; for the helplessness of infancy, the decrepitude of age, the infirmities of disease, to say nothing of the heedlessness, slothfulness and waste natural to persons in their con-

dition. Hence it is that the scantiness of net profit from slave labour has become proverbial, and that nothing is more common than an actual loss, or a benefit merely in the slow increase of capital from propagation.[16]

Though relying on well-established precedent, Judge Baldwin embellished his opinion with intuitions about the economics of slavery. His pecuniary meditation was based on "proverbial" truth. His observations were "usually" accurate and based on "common" experience.

Impressed with the probative force of his own testimony, Judge Baldwin expanded his argument to oppose emancipation itself:

Slavery is with us an institution founded upon a distinction of races, one of which is subject to the control and domination of the other. The servile race, from colour, and other physical traits, carry with them indefinitely the marks of inferiority and degradation; and even when relieved from bondage can never aspire to association and citizenship with the white population. Freedom to them is a benefit rather in name than in fact; and in truth, upon the whole, their condition is not thereby improved in respectability, comfort, or happiness. While they remain in what is here their original status, provided for as they are in infancy, old age, and infirmity, they are exempt from the cares and anxieties of a precarious subsistence, and the wretchedness of actual want; and those who are most familiar with the usual mild despotism to which they are subject, can best appreciate their sources of enjoyment from the common humane indulgence, and kind regards of their masters.[17]

Enlarging the scope of his argument, Judge Baldwin introduced as evidence his perception of slaves as a flawed race that did not benefit from freedom. In fact, he perceived that slaves enjoyed the "mild despotism" under which their lives were governed. Oratorical form is prominent in his opinion: the antithetical claim, "Freedom to them is a benefit rather in name than in fact," reflects axiomatic reasoning. No routine citation of precedential authority, the judge's statement was a claim of personal authority to interpret the facts of life in antebellum Virginia. Well beyond the customary scope of judicial notice, his opinion illustrates appellate advocacy in addition to judicial review.

For Judge Baldwin and his Virginia colleagues, slavery was an economically sound institution if not profitable. These judges also perceived that slaves, by their nature, were unsuited to any higher station in life. Deriving both principles and proof from their intuitions, the judges composed narratives of slavery that resisted counterarguments. If advocates of opposing intuitions were to appear in court—an unlikely event—they would need to change the judges' entire world view in order to be persuasive.

A similar situation existed in North Carolina where Thomas Ruffin either expressed or implied most of the intuitions to be found in his colleagues' opinions. Judge Ruffin profitably managed several tracts of land, attending carefully to details.[18] When advised of his overseer's plan for harvesting crops, the judge queried: "Will that be the case with the young corn at the gate and that in the old field at the river? How many times has that in the old field been ploughed? Say to Mr. Glass, that I think it ought to be ploughed *four* times, before it has been laid by: that is, all of it except the hill side at the bridge."[19] Although a successful planter, the judge experienced inevitable reverses. "Our agricultural prospects up the country," he once disclosed, "are gloomy enough to make us all despondent"; and revealing a lasting concern about disciplining his slaves, he confessed: "I want to make a crop, it is true; but I am more anxious to have my family well served and the domestics kept in due order."[20] Apparently, though, he saw his duty to keep good order among his "domestics" as a parental obligation. He described slaves as members of his family.[21]

Although his successful career as an advocate has been attributed to his command of logic and not rhetoric, Judge Ruffin's narrative technique illuminates his jurisprudence.[22] His speech to North Carolina's Agricultural Society summarizes his paternalistic view of slaves as childlike or thoughtless brutes who required the same type of cultivation as the land they worked. "Slavery, indeed, is not a pure and unmixed good," he observed. Acknowledging "instances of cruel and devilish masters, and of turbulent and refractory slaves," he distinguished these as exceptions "to the usages of our people." In fact, the typical master recognized a need "to be observant of the health and morals of his slaves; to care for them, and provide for them; to restrain them from baneful excesses, and employ them in moderate, though steady labor." As proof of his claim, the judge cited a self-evident "increase in the numbers of our slave population" based on "the abundant supply of the necessaries and comforts of life, and a contented state of mind."[23]

Narratives in the judge's opinions elaborate his perceptions of race and slavery. In *Heathcock v. Pennington* he perceived that a slave, "being a moral and intelligent being," was capable of self-preservation unlike "a lifeless thing, or . . . an irrational animal."[24] In fact, as the judge asserted in *State v. Watters*, their instinct for self-preservation disqualified black mothers as competent witnesses. "It is well known," he declared on personal authority, that women of color give biased testimony in order to create "the impression on others, that their illegitimate child is the issue of a white man."[25] Helping children to escape from degraded conditions was an understandable but unacceptable tendency on the part of slaves. This tendency, as noted in *Waddill v. Martin*, and other natural characteristics explained why a master might be reluctant to grant small favors to slaves such as permitting them to cultivate and sell for profit "little crops of cotton, corn, potatoes, ground peas and the like." Although "experience has proved so fully the advantages of these minor benefactions," a master rightfully might never trust his naturally cunning slaves with even a small taste of independence.[26] The "experience" mentioned by Judge Ruffin was personal, but he confidently assumed that fellow planters shared his perceptions.

Judge Ruffin's intuitions supply part of the evidentiary base for decisions of "an exceptionally able judge," perhaps "one of ten foremost American judges."[27] In *State v. Caesar*, he dissented vigorously from opinions by Frederic Nash and Richmond Pearson supporting the retrial of a slave convicted of murdering a white man, who was not his master, while defending a fellow slave. Refusing to accept the decedent's violent behavior as sufficient provocation for reducing the indictment to manslaughter, Judge Ruffin reflected on personal experiences that gave rise to the impressions disclosed in his speechmaking. "[I]t is an uncontestable fact," he declared, "that the great mass of slaves—nearly all of them—are the least turbulent of all men; that, when sober, they never attack a white man; and seldom, very seldom, exhibit any temper or sense of provocation at even gross and violent injuries from white men."[28] In his advocacy, the judge relied on an "uncontestable" premise—at least from an experienced planter's perspective. Whether his opinion cast him into the role of parent or master, two roles he preferred to blend, the judge fashioned an argument that was consistent with the intuitions of slavery and race he expressed away from the bench. In judicial review, he used the same narrative technique he used in ceremonial oratory.

Despite reaching a conclusion in *State v. Caesar* that contradicted Thomas Ruffin, Judge Nash drew on similar experiences of slaves and race. He casually mentioned his everyday mastery over slaves named Sue, Isaac, Ismael, George, and Henry in letters to his wife.[29] He also more pointedly issued directions for tending his crops of corn and oats: "[H]e who plays when ought to work, will have to work when he ought to play."[30] Yet, in the case of the slave named Caesar, Judge Nash queried: "Does the fact that the prisoner and his associate Dick are slaves alter the law? *This* point has not heretofore been decided by this Court. By the common law the prisoner's offense would clearly be mitigated to manslaughter [due to the degree of provocation by the white decedent]."[31] Emphasizing "mercy to human frailty" and the blindness of common law to "difference of caste," Judge Nash implied a factual premise about race that he had explicitly stated one year earlier in *State v. Lane.* Holding that a free man of color had a qualified right to bear arms, the judge interjected oratorically: "Degraded as are these individuals, as a class, by their social position, it is certain that among them are many worthy of all confidence."[32] Equally "certain" of his intuition, this judge expressed far less suspicion about a race of people than had Judge Ruffin, and the common law of North Carolina changed as a result.

Richmond Pearson also disagreed with Thomas Ruffin about the degree of provocation needed to mitigate a slave's homicidal act. Like his colleague, Judge Pearson eventually amassed a considerable fortune. He admitted to a taxable estate worth more than $20,000 in his petition for clemency after the Civil War, and, a decade earlier, he had been affluent enough to pay cash for three young slaves.[33] Yet he contradicted his colleague and expressed admiration for a slave's homicidal act in defense of his friend: "[A]re we not forced, in spite of stern policy, to admire, even in a slave, the generosity which incurs danger to save a friend?"[34]

Later that same year, in *Herring v. Wilmington and Raleigh Railroad Co.*, Judge Pearson explicitly stated an intuition of slaves that partially explains his opinion in the *Caesar* case. The case turned on whether a railroad company owed damages to a master for the death of one slave and serious injury to another, both of whom had fallen asleep on the company's tracks. The judge decided that the railroad was not liable because, as a matter of fact, "the negroes were reasonable beings, endowed with intelligence, as well as the instinct of self-preservation."[35] For Judge Pearson, the natural instinct for self-preservation among slaves was far from suspicious: it was an emblem that marked the race as capable of admirable conduct. Though the facts of record might be uncontested, judicial impressions could vary. Thus, Judge Pearson adopted the principle that preserving the life of a fellow slave could mitigate a slave's criminal culpability.

In legal terms, the disagreement among Judges Ruffin, Nash, and Pearson was related only obliquely to an 1840 opinion by William Gaston. Judge Gaston considered whether in his own defense, under any degree of provocation, a slave might strike out at a white man who was not his master. Again, in *State v. Jarrott*, personal intuitions were dispositive. The judge found sufficient provocation in the case under review, despite observing as fact "the habits of humility and obedience which belong to the condition of the slave."[36] A sentiment he had expressed in an 1835 speech was partially operative in his decision making: "Without freedom, man is a poor, miserable, abject thing, the sport and victim of his fellow man's rage."[37] A slave, the judge further observed in his opinion, has a duty "to submit—or flee—or seek the protection of his master; but it is impossible, if it were desirable, to extinguish in him the instinct of self-preservation."[38] In other words, the slave did not necessarily have to suffer being "the sport and victim of his fellow man's rage." As he had announced thirty years earlier in a broadside, Judge Gaston formed his political creed "upon reflection, confirmed by experience, and endeared by habit."[39] He formed his judicial creed along the same path. Reflecting on his experience in 1840, the judge expressed admiration for a slave's "instinct of self-preservation," finding in it a plausible and desirable premise from which to reach a decision—just as Judge Pearson would do.

Similar to colleagues elsewhere in the Upper South, North Carolina's judges relied on their intuition to resolve the complex cases under review. The judges were not thoroughly convinced about the economic benefits of slavery, addressing instead the natural fit of slaves into a degraded social condition. In this regard, the judges reflected on the slaves' instinct of self-preservation. The judicial mind pondered to what lengths slaves should be permitted to defend themselves against whites' violence. Not all of the judges interpreted their plantation experiences in the same way. Thomas Ruffin, for one, seemed more suspicious of slaves than his colleagues. However, regardless of differences in their intuitions, the judges commonly applied them to the crafting of their opinions.

Cultivating social and professional relationships with colleagues in Virginia and North Carolina, Tennessee's judges shared a common narrative technique in composing their opinions. However, William B. Reese felt obligated to apologize for reaching a decision "by the aid rather of principle than authority." In *Henderson v. Vaulx*, the judge determined that slave property of Henderson's estate should not be removed to Mississippi because the slaves' value would decline outside the control of Tennessee's court system. Lacking authority, the judge followed his intuitions and contrasted the lives of slaves in Tennessee and Mississippi on several counts. He assessed differences in legal treatment: "We have a mild penal code." He drew contrasts in physical welfare: "Here . . . [the slave] may not be over-worked." Dedication to preserving the integrity of slave families was another difference between the states: "Here . . . mothers and children are tenderly treated." Even the climate was different: "Here we have a temperate, healthful climate."[40] By his own admission, the judge lacked authority for his opinion other than the accuracy of his perceptions.

These same perceptions influenced Judge Reese's opinion on the administration of another estate in *Kennedy v. Williams*. Estimating the "value of slaves . . . upon physical strength, upon intellectual capacity, upon mental culture, upon moral worth, as fidelity, honesty, obedience, etc., and upon handicraft skill," the judge condemned lesser methods of evaluation as used in "the wretched market of the mere slave-trader."[41] Again, he relied for authority on his narrative of the facts of life in the Old South. Not a risky technique, the judge cannily anticipated his fellow planters' agreement with his perceptions.

The accuracy of his perceptions formed a similar basis for William B. Turley's judicial confidence. Affirming a trial court's avoidance of a Memphis ordinance in *Mayor of Memphis v. Winfield*, the judge cited indisputable facts opposing restrictions on the free movement of free negroes after ten o'clock at night. He baldly announced: "Every one knows that in cities, very often, the most profitable employment is to be found in the night." Then he supported his bare assertion with equally subjective impressions of black laborers' "loading and unloading steamboats and other craft, waiting about hotels, theatres, places of amusement, both public and private, wood-cutting, fire-making, shoe and boot-cleaning, not to mention the various handicraft employments such as that of the barber, etc."[42] This judicial narrative is a rich source of firsthand information about the positions available to blacks in a thriving southern city as well as a model of judicial advocacy. Secure in his detailed grasp of urban lifestyles, Judge Turley dismissed the city's appeal of a rebuff to its lawmaking power.

Nathan Green expressed a noteworthy assessment of the nature of slaves in *Ford v. Ford*—the basis for acclaiming him "one of the most enlightened judges in regard to the rights of slaves."[43] His intuition told him that "[a] slave is not in the condition of a horse or an ox." In fact, a slave "has mental capacities, and an immortal principle in his nature, that constitutes him equal to his owner but for the accidental position in which fortune has placed him."[44] Rare among contemporaneous judicial narratives, this assertion confirms that Judge Green eschewed "Politics," perhaps because he was unwillingly to compromise his "strong feelings, and strong passions."[45] In any event, the judge's narrative should be compared with his earlier observation in *Wright v. Weatherly* that slaves constituted an "unfortunate, degraded, and vicious class of our population,"[46] as well as with his later assertion in *Nelson v. State* that the white and black races possessed "different habits of feeling, and modes of thought."[47] In each case, he argued for distinctive civil and criminal treatments of persons at least partially on the basis of his intuition of slavery and race. Whether saint or sinner by current standards of social justice, the judge applied oratorical form smoothly to his professional discourse.

Though reaching a legal decision that might have pleased the enlightened Nathan Green, John Catron was unusual among his Tennessee colleagues for his explicit repudiation of intuitive jurisprudence. He harbored a possessive attitude toward his own slaves, declining to free any of them at his death.[48] Expressing related feelings in *Fisher's Negroes v. Dabbs*, a case in which slaves were attempting to gain the freedom devised to them by their deceased owner, the judge declared: "I feel satisfied that I have no sympathies which would have misled me in this matter; for, when permitted to indulge my feelings and opinions as an individual, I find them in strong and direct hostility to all schemes for emancipating slaves."[49] Thus, the appellants in this case were lucky to receive a favorable ruling from Judge Catron. He, unlike his colleagues, desired more than "the feeble and unsustained character of judicial power" that relied on "the reason of the community."[50] He felt deeply that public opinion was grossly inaccurate and subject to stereotypes. Reflecting on his experiences as a westerner transplanted to Washington, D.C., he observed that "Eastern people are more ignorant of us generally than they are of the people of England, or even France; they suppose us a wild horde emerging from the hunter state, and cane-brake."[51] For Judge Catron, judicial opinions must flow from more durable premises than those derived from intuition.

Apart from John Catron, Tennessee judges addressed the nature of slaves in a narrative mode. They did not share the abiding concern of their North Carolina colleagues over the lengths to which slaves should be permitted to defend themselves against whites' violence. Rather, within a relatively generous perspective on the spiritual character of slaves, they addressed the economic value of slave property and how to conserve it.

Regardless of their special focus, though, the judges maintained a consistency between the factual premises in their opinions and their recollections of life in the Old South.

Arkansas judges addressed slavery from the same perspective as colleagues in other states, that is, from a planter's point of view. Somewhat "reticent and disposed to attend to his own business," Thomas Johnson farmed land near Little Rock.[52] Townshend Dickinson also lived on his farm near Batesville although, as one of only two practicing lawyers in the vicinity, he had an office in town.[53] Whether town or country ruled his perceptions, Judge Dickinson derived a sense of authority from his experience. In reviewing *Pyeatt v. Spencer*, for example, he editorialized about a slave named Sophia: "[S]he walked faster, and looked wild, *as negroes usually do*, when threatened."[54] Lacking the statistics that would sustain his claim and sensing no need to cite specific examples, the judge relied on experiential authority he shared with other members of his class.

In similar fashion, Edward Cross drew authority from his extensive experience with "plantation & negroes."[55] After reviewing the constitutionality of an Arkansas statute barring free blacks from emigrating to the state, the judge gratuitously developed an argument on the "impracticability" of black citizenship in *Pendleton v. State:* "The two races, differing as they do in complexion, habits, conformations and intellectual endowments, could not nor ever will live together upon terms of social or political equality."[56] As a representative of the planter class, Judge Cross was well qualified to describe the facts of life in a way that was persuasive for the members of his "social and political" group.

Judges Johnson, Dickinson, and Cross were easily distinguishable by professional reputation from colleagues in Virginia, North Carolina, and Tennessee. Yet these judges—excepting John Catron—embellished or edited the facts of record to justify their opinions. The economic facts of slavery were most often in need of repair. Even judicial concern about blacks' rights to self preservation in North Carolina can be interpreted as flowing from an economic incentive to protect slaveowners' property. Beyond finances, though, the judges expressed their intuitions of those characteristics that should entitle slaves to legal protection or bar them from such safeguards. Especially in North Carolina and Tennessee, several judges articulated mildly favorable estimates of the character of slaves. And in each case the judge spoke as an advocate by fashioning evidence or innovating a principle that was attractive to other members of his class.

Judicial narratives illustrate intuitions of slavery that were shared among members of the gentry in the Upper South. Despite their intended functions as persuasive evidence and embellishment, judicial narratives were not intended to startle audiences. At the time of its composition, this judicial discourse performed a maintenance role. Judges frequently used this discourse to introduce or conclude their opinions, often using no other argument in the same opinion. They disclosed by their narrative choices what they saw as a priority: the need to reaffirm a community of planters. Although it is tempting to search for an address to opponents of the southern system in the North, and opponents of slavery at home, the judges gave little if any indication that they viewed these groups as audiences.

Not the ideas but the saying of the ideas makes narrative a useful tool in analyzing jurisprudence on slavery. Their discourse reveals that the judges were not disinterested. They explicitly cited their personal experiences and intuitions to justify their opinions. Disclosing a homogenous judicial experience through their narratives, the judges spoke with enough unanimity to sustain an image of solidarity in their professional culture as well as a bond with their fellow planters. Above all, the judges took a supremely authoritative stance. They were sources as well as arbiters of the facts of slavery. Indeed, their narratives supplanted the testimony of slaves—frequently excluded as it was by statute and the rules of evidence "to assure the property interests of slave-owners, and the domination of whites over blacks."[57]

More theoretically intriguing, and potentially damaging to the professional culture, is the use of narrative to construct both premises and evidence in judicial opinions. The comparative levity of oratorical form, its loose structure and opinionated content, is traditionally excusable in politics. But tradition dictates that judicial decision making should illustrate a relentless logic. In their reviews of the legal treatment of slavery and race, however, the judges relied as much on the oratory they endorsed as on other, more professional resources. Expressing their thought in enthymemes, or what ungenerous critics might say are the hollow shells of syllogisms, the judges fashioned opinions that were both artistic and suitable for publication in law reports. Engaging rather than compelling, judicial narrative relied on personal example and societal custom. Except in those cases where relevant statutes, precedents, or other authorities were available, the judges had no use for legal logic. They needed no abstract principles as guides. They did not need someone else's recollection of plantation customs. What they needed was narrative.

Chapter Three

INTUITION IN JUDICIAL ADVOCACY
OF THE DEEP SOUTH

Judicial narratives differed subtly but meaningfully between the Upper
South and Deep South. As expressed in their opinions, the judges
perceived southern life to be much the same wherever one travelled
in the Old South. But judges in South Carolina, Georgia, Alabama, Mississippi, Florida, and Louisiana implied that they possessed especially
keen insights into the nature of slaves and the dynamics of the master-
slave relationship.

Perceptual accuracy aside, the oratorical functions of judicial narrative
in the Deep South remain distinct from the historical and legal functions
of analogous discourse in law reports. William Harper, for example, declined to speak from intuition and explicitly cited the historians from
whom he borrowed his chronicle of slavery.[1] Pierre A. Rost did not speak
in a narrative tenor when citing the legislative history of Louisiana.[2] In
this respect, it made no difference whether a judicial narrative was composed in North Carolina or South Carolina. Dedicated to the pursuit of
humanism, judges used this mode of discourse as a prelude to advocacy.

Peering down from the Upper South, Tennessee's William B. Reese did
not paint a flattering picture of the conditions under which slaves labored
in certain areas of the Deep South.[3] The judge's portrait also partially explains judicial intuitions of slavery in that region. Under relatively severe
conditions, slaves found it more difficult to act in a manner perceived judicially as human, much less noble.

Abraham Nott distinguished himself on the bench by his fluent as well
as clever speech.[4] An experienced planter, he shared in the perception of
slaves as valuable but troublesome commodities. He believed that, in ad-

dition to their natural penchant for mischief, slaves were also vexing because of their weak minds. The judge elaborated on his perception of
slaves as weak, fickle creatures in *Smith v. McCall.* Reversing an award of
damages to the buyer of a slave addicted to running away, Judge Nott observed: "The character of a slave depends so much upon the treatment he
receives, the opportunities he has to commit crimes, and the temptation
to which he is exposed, that we can form but a very imperfect opinion of
it, abstracted from those considerations."[5] According to the judge, a court
should strictly interpret the language of a sales warranty when the merchandise was a slave because the soundness of this property fluctuated
from moment to moment. Slaves had no innate ability to regulate their
behavior, and masters faced a very difficult task in isolating their slave
property from temptation. His decision did nothing to dissolve ambiguity
in commercial law, but Judge Nott correctly anticipated that his premise
would be acceptable; his own experiences in the marketplace matched
those of fellow planters.

Sustaining his brethren's attention to the economy, Henry W. DeSaussure also applied his perception of slaves to refuting the idea of emanici-
pation. Judge DeSaussure had revealed his financial interest in the peculiar institution long before his election to the Court of Appeals in 1824:
"The state of our market is dreadful. There is a perfect stagnation of
everything but the importation & sale of new negroes, which continues in
full activity. It is sad most of them are sold to the upper country people.
Many do certainly go that way."[6] Concerned about the disposition of a
valuable commodity, particularly the sales commissions he might lose, the
future judge preferred to see the bulk of imported slaves remain in the
Charleston area. Furthermore, though admitting the unsavory character
of slavery, he saw no practical way of abolishing it in 1822. Indeed, "the
citizen would be entitled to civic crowns and everlasting gratitude, whose
wisdom could devise a plan for getting rid of the evil."[7] Dismissing colonization of the slaves as impractical and too costly, he also dismissed complete or partial emancipation as both costly and vicious:

The two races never can assimilate perfectly. The mixture will be
partial, and incomplete—sufficient perhaps to do much evil, and no

good. The whites can never forget that they had been masters; and
could never lay aside the tone of superiority. The blacks could never
forget that they had been slaves; and they would retain either the
base and crouching spirit of slaves, or would attempt to throw the
cloak of oblivion over their origin, by assuming a pert and bragga-
dacio air of defiance and insult, as a substitute for that calm self respect which they could never feel.[8]

Judge DeSaussure's argument rested on perceptions he shared with fellow
members of the planter class. He equated "whites" with "masters," viewed
slavery as fundamental to the southern economy, and decried the debased
nature that slaves could not escape even when technically freed. The
judge intuited that former slaves, incapable of self-respect, would either
act no differently than before their emancipation or they would mask
their self-image by acting in an uppity manner. In all these respects,
Judge DeSaussure affirmed perceptions that ruled the decision making of
his colleagues.

Feeling similarly empowered by his intuitions, Charles J. Colcock declared that former slaves could own property—though they lacked most
other rights of citizenship in South Carolina. In essence, blacks lost most
of their value when freed from bondage and could be denied various
rights enjoyed by white neighbors. Judge Colcock was once quoted as
saying: "In deciding a case I always look for the justice of it, and having
ascertained that, I am very sure that I can find the law to sustain it."[9] And
so, when an appellant of African ancestry sought title to real estate in
Hardcastle's Estate v. Porcher, the judge cited legal authority as secondary in his opinion.

First he asked: "[W]hat is the fact with respect to these persons?"
Supplying the answer through his personal knowledge, he asserted "as a
general position" that "in all ages . . . there have been distinctions made
between the citizens or subjects of every country, and that that distinction has, by a kind of common consent of all, been applied with more
right to the class of persons to which the claimant belongs than to any
other."[10] Relying on the operative phrases "as a general position" and "by

a kind of common consent," Judge Colcock sought the assent of a like-minded audience for the premise that civil rights may be withheld from certain "citizens or subjects."

Feeling secure in the premise he had posed, the judge continued in a more strident tone. "There is no instance," he declared categorically, "in which they [former slaves] have been admitted to a full participation in all the rights of subject or citizen." As a matter of fact he observed that "even among those whose pretended sensibilities have been most awakened in their behalf, they continue to be considered and treated as a distinct class, unworthy to be incorporated in the general mass of society."[11] If he had recognized as evidence only the commonly accepted opinion that free people of color lack "sensibilities," then Judge Colcock could have ruled against the appellant as similarly "unworthy." However, he also cited as evidence his "earliest recollections" of such people being "entitled to hold lands" in South Carolina.[12] Then, and only then, did he cite two statutes that had also persuaded Judge Nott of the appellant's right of ownership. Notable, of course, was the judicial reliance primarily on perceptions and recollections. Judge Colcock's disposition of the case indicates that the facts he narrated were fundamental to his statutory construction.

David Johnson further illustrated the fundamental role of judicial perception in crafting opinions. He first studied law in Judge Nott's office, reluctantly accepted a seat on the appellate bench in 1825 (preferring that his friend Henry W. DeSaussure be appointed). He eventually succeeded Judge Colcock as president of the Court of Appeals before being elected governor.[13] Judge Johnson was well versed in plantation life—whether issuing orders about the cultivation of a sugar crop and operating a mill, directing the inoculation of "the little negroes" against smallpox and securing food for his slaves, or approving the dismissal of an overseer.[14] The judge underscored his personal expertise in *Perry v. Dunlap*, citing his "own experience and observation . . . especially with respect to slaves hired for field labor."[15] Whether interpreted as a personally honest disclosure or a judicially unforgivable slip, David Johnson's explicit reference to his "experience and observation" is striking.

During the same term, again asserting personal knowlege to justify his opinion in *Nowell v. O'Hara,* Judge Johnson observed that the "owners of slaves frequently send them off from amongst their kindred and associates as a punishment [often to the areas decried by Tennessee's William B. Reese], and it is frequently resorted to, as the means of separating a vicious negro from amongst others exposed to be influenced and corrupted by his example."[16] Six years later, in *Rainsford v. Rainsford,* he again relied on self-reference to identify an accurate method for estimating the value of slaves.[17] In both of these latter cases, he confidently balanced the practical worth of slaves against their penchant for mischief. His confidence, of course, was based on the same perceptions and experiences he confessed in *Perry v. Dunlap.*

Judge Johnson's opinion in *Young v. Burton* survives as the most substantial example of his narrative. The case turned on whether a slave might have peculiar value. Justifying the transfer of a peculiarly valuable slave in the specific performance of a contract, the judge distinguished American and British legal principles largely on the ground of his personal knowledge of slaves. He applied rhetorical questions, argument from analogy, and hyperbole to his task.

"Is there any thing in a barren sand hill that could attach a purchaser to it, and give it a peculiar and special value that may not be found in an able, honest, and faithful slave?" he queried rhetorically. Proposing a standard by which "you put their intrinsic value in competition," he concluded that "it will be found to be as a thousand to nothing in favor of the slave." The judge asserted personal expertise while elaborating on his theme through an imaginative comparison: "In every well organized plantation, you will find a carpenter, a blacksmith, a driver, a wagoner, a hostler, &c., &c.; and these are as necessary to successful planting, as four wheels, instead of three, are to a wagon. Remove one, and every thing is in disorder." Expressly mentioning his audience of planters, he then issued a challenge: "I put it to every planter to answer, whether he would not find it difficult, if not, often, impossible, to supply their places." Not content with citations of tangible worth, the judge continued in the same tone to discuss intangibles—each of which was a "well known fact." "But there are other considerations," he asserted, "which enter largely into this question. I mean the ties (which all who know any thing of the relations of master and slave, will appreciate) by which the master and slave are united." Specifically complimenting the personal worth of "the faithful and kind old nurse," the "body servant," "the honest, diligent, and faithful old slave," and "the more humble but equally faithful and devoted field slave," Judge Johnson insisted that his choice of examples was "not imaginary, but cases arising out of real life."[18]

Expounding a favorable image of slaves when it suited his judicial ends—unlike his earlier evaluation of slaves—David Johnson explicitly addressed fellow planters with evidence lacking in the record. But he was not a rare judicial specimen. Baylis J. Earle, Josiah J. Evans, Edward Frost, Thomas J. Withers, and David L. Wardlaw all made similar contributions to South Carolina law reports.

Judge Earle lived comfortably in a large home at Greenville and enjoyed the services of many slaves.[19] As a successful prosecuting attorney, his arguments had been "plain, perspicuous, and most cogent."[20] As an experienced but unsuccessful entrepreneur, his business acumen as well as his powers of argumentation were tested in *Chartran v. Schmidt*.[21] The trial court had set aside the affidavit of a free black plaintiff—allowing the white defendant to retain, without posting a bond, slave property sought by the plaintiff. Equal to his task, the judge asserted simply: "It would be gross injustice to allow a free person of color to bring an action, and withhold the means of making it effectual."[22] Regardless of race, the judge sensed, business cannot properly be conducted unless courts of law sanction fair dealing.

Like Baylis J. Earle, Judge Evans was concerned about the business climate. In his case, good business meant preserving slave assets. The judge's early biographers, at least, claimed that he treated his own slaves well despite their large number: "The tribute of tears when they followed his body to his garden, and saw him laid alongside of their loved mistress, and at the head of his bodyservant, Randolph, was all as slaves which they could pay."[23] Again, "[h]e was a large slave-owner, but a kind and most indulgent master."[24] In fact, the judge once complained of his slaves' abuse at the hands of Bristow, a neighbor, because he thought a complaint was "indispensable for the preservation of [his] property."[25] Reluctant to indict his neighbor, the judge was driven to drastic action by the potential loss of capital assets. As he explained in a speech to the United State Senate, fellow planters generally recognized the value of slave property:

> [I]n relation to the African, no man in this House, and no man out of it, can say that there is any corner of this earth, upon which the African race are as well off, as well provided for, with more of the elements of happiness, than in the slave part of these United States. I assert it without fear of contradiction. I know not from whence it has come; but this I know, that the Africans were slaves in the days of the Pharaohs; that nine out of ten of them are slaves in their native land; and that in no country of which I am aware are they received upon an equality with the white race. . . . Many of the negroes at the South are intelligent, although they have not much mental culture—certainly very little that is derived from books. They are an improving people—improving in intelligence and morals.[26]

Judge Evans explicitly cited his personal knowledge of the facts at issue in the slavery debate. More specifically, he lionized the care given to slaves by their masters despite inherent differences in the nature of blacks and whites. As a matter of fact, the judged claimed, slaves received treatment surpassing what their nature merited but which served well the master's investment in his property.

Edward Frost shared his colleagues' interest in finance, most notably as president of the ill-fated Blue Ridge Railway Company and acting secretary of South Carolina's Treasury.[27] More specifically, life at "Fairfield" plantation taught him the value of slave assets.

In regard to the economic facts of life and care of valuable assets, the perceptions of Thomas J. Withers matched those of his colleagues. As the Civil War approached he enjoyed the good life at "Gander Hill," an estate including "many little houses" for his thirty slaves. He made annual trips to Charleston to buy "the material for the dresses, shoes and other wearing apparel of the darkies," and disparaged criminal charges against his slaves by poor whites as lies born out of self-interest.[28] Driven by economic motives, the judge would not have failed to recognize the benefits in housing, clothing, and protecting his slave assets. Thus, in *State v. Boozer*, he instructed each of his peers to behave as a "discreet, sedate, intelligent and humane owner of slaves" while serving on patrols (the nightly mounted efforts to prevent slave revolts) and "to recognize what is eminently the negro's quality, the love of social intercourse, with no object beyond it, and no time to indulge it but the night."[29] Heedless of the judge's warning, patrollers might mistake innocent camaraderie for nocturnal plotting and might needlessly damage or destroy valuable slave property.

During the war the judge suffered enough to seek repeated exemptions from army requisitions.[30] By war's end he wrote: "I am in a very inconvenient condition to discharge judicial duties outside of my house. I have not a dollar and know not where to get one."[31] Surviving the excesses of patrollers, the judge fell victim to other armed forces.

The personal experience that informed Judge Withers also became the teacher of David L. Wardlaw. In reviewing *Parris v. Jenkins*, for instance, he remarked intuitively that the "words of a negro are at least as significant as the cry of a brute animal, or any sound proceeding from inanimate substances. . . . We all daily begin and quit and change occupation, command and countermand, resolve and act, according to the information received from negroes."[32] Based solely on perceptions of slave talk that he shared with his audience ("We all . . .") the judge resolved an evidentiary dispute. In *State v. Chandler*, he used related intuitions to support his dissenting opinion. "It is a great abuse," he conceded to the majority, "for an overseer to corrupt slaves by selling liquor to them." But, he went on to contest, "sometimes it may be commendable for an overseer to let the slaves confided to him have liquor, and even to stimulate their industry."[33] In each case, as his colleagues routinely did, Judge Wardlaw translated personal experience into premises and evidence.

Using the same judicial technique, but addressing issues prominent in the 1822 pamphleteering by Judge DeSaussure, John S. Richardson manufactured evidence about emancipation in *Vinyard v. Passalaigue*. "[L]aying aside all legal rules," he suggested, while respecting "our knowledge of the subject," the judge asserted that "the white Caucasian and the black African races cannot live together upon terms of equality." Whether on the African coast or in Jamaica, Illinois, New York, or Philadelphia, "Africans become, and do, as fully as in Charleston, constitute the contented menials, or other subordinate servants of white men."[34] The persuasiveness of this "probable truth"—the traditional limit of oratorical power—impressed Judge Richardson again three years later when resolving an evidentiary dispute in *State v. Belmont.* Holding that the testimony of Indians is credible because they are inherently distinct from blacks, the judge relied greatly on intuition: "All history assures us that the negro race thrive in health, multiply greatly, become civilized and religious, feel no degradation, and are happy, when in subjection to the white race."[35] Though he also cited testimony from a Mississippi author, from "a book destined to enlighten the public mind," Judge Richardson inserted personal intuition—under the guise of historical research—between the premise and conclusion of his argument.[36]

As illustrated in John S. Richardson's discourse, the perceptions of South Carolina's judges were based on a prejudice articulated by Elihu H. Bay and his colleagues in 1802.[37] Narrative discourse by William Harper, Andrew P. Butler, and John B. O'Neall—three frequently noted legal and political authorities of the period—reaffirms the shape of society previously endorsed by colleagues.

In one speech, Judge Harper declared that duties associated with maintaining slaves actually strengthened the character of masters. Lacking more tangible support, he asked rhetorically: "Were the Grecian and Roman republics wanting in energy?"[38] Two years later, turning his attention to the character of slaves, he asserted: "That the African negro is an inferior variety of the human race, is, I think, now generally admitted, and his distinguishing characteristics are such as peculiarly mark him out for the situation which he occupies among us."[39] The judge's reliance on a deferential attitude toward classical civilization, and on general admissions derived from that deference, punctuated his oratory with a humanist flavor.

At the same time, but as a judge rather than a lecturer, Judge Harper confidently estimated the social gap between freedom and slavery in *State*

v. Cheatwood. Fully thirteen years after the state code provided for criminal prosecutions in cases where whites killed slaves, the judge reviewed
"the first instance of conviction under the act" and noted a typical lack of
murderous feelings in "the relation of the freeman and the slave."[40] The
chasm between the two classes made personal conflict rare enough, so the
judge felt, that murderous intent should be imputed to whites who killed
slaves. In another case, *Sarter v. Gordon,* the judge further addressed the
specific "tie of master and slave," asserting that "unless there be something very perverse in the disposition of the master or the slave, in every
instance where a slave has been reared in a family there exists a mutual attachment."[41] In the respective cases, Judge Harper's decision making on
social conflict and economic value was entirely consistent with his oratorical assessments of character—white and black.

More knowledgeable in matters of planting than William Harper, Judge
Butler made several factual statements on slavery and race while rep-
resenting South Carolina in the United States Senate.[42] His discourse,
filled with self-references, should not immediately be discounted as in-
sincere because its author was speaking for political constituents. For
example, in attacking the aid given to fugitive slaves by northerners,
Judge Butler declared his statements to be "commended to the approval
of [his] own judgment by the force of reason."[43] He cited his personal
belief again when asserting: "There are not three millions of Africans
upon earth equal in condition with the slave population of the United
States. There are scarcely three millions of laborers of any kind equal
in their condition—certainly not better."[44] More intensely yet, he asked
"Who ever heard of the African astronomer, statesman, general, poet?
Who ever heard of the African soaring in those regions in which the Caucasian race have made their greatest developments?"[45] In any event, the
judge also expressly cited "the common practice in my district" to support
his claims that slaves were "a happy, contented, intelligent, and reformed
people."[46]

As William Harper had also done, Judge Butler relied on personal experiences and feelings to inform his judicial discourse on the nature on
slaves. In *Felder v. Louisville, Cincinnati and Charleston Railroad Co.,* he

asserted that "a slave is like his owner; he is a moral being of volition and intelligence, capable, by his foresight, of avoiding danger, or of extricating himself from it by consulting his reason."[47] Attributing limited human ability to blacks, the judge nonetheless compared them unfavorably with whites in terms of civilized achievements. Thus, while speaking to both political and legal issues of the day, Judge Butler told the same story of the Old South.

Judges Harper and Butler, despite their influence, have not received the acclaim for "greatness" attributed to Judge O'Neall nor the counter-vailing criticism of this judge for sustaining "the white consensus."[48] Looking out from his manor house at "Springfield," Judge O'Neall saw a substantial role for himself in southern society. Later in life, he auto-biographically claimed considerable success in writing and speaking about "temperance, education, Sunday Schools, and rail-roads."[49] Equally noteworthy, though, was his oratorical treatment of slavery. Among other items in his 1842 speech to the state agricultural society, Judge O'Neall instructed fellow planters on caring for their most valuable property:

> South Carolina is to become less a planting and more a farming State. That this will add to her greatness and her happiness cannot be de-nied. In this effort she has, it is true, one peculiar difficulty to en-counter, in the carelessness of her operatives. Still, our slaves are capable of more, much more, than we have hitherto had credit for. It is only necessary that they should be taught habits of regularity, economy, and thrift, to make them the most effective laborers in the world. . . . To my brother farmers, intelligent and experienced as you are, I need not add, you cannot succeed with negroes, as operatives, as you desire to do, *unless you feed and clothe well.* Make them con-tented, and then "Massa" will be, as he ought to be, the whole world to them.[50]

Neatly summing up major facts in his colleagues' discourse, Judge O'Neall addressed the inherently flawed but economically significant condition of slaves. According to the judge, the planter class was capable of making slavery profitable. This same story resonated throughout the discourse of

South Carolina's judiciary. Just as significantly, Judge O'Neall explicitly identified his audience as "brother farmers" and flattered them as "intelligent and experienced." Or was he speaking of himself?

Nearby in Georgia the same facts of antebellum life were memorialized in judicial discourse. For example, Hiram Warner earned his planter's credentials near Greenville and prompted one discerning eulogist to write: "To agricultural pursuits he is much devoted, and, unlike most professional men, makes good crops."[51] After the Civil War, losing "over one hundred slaves" to emancipation, he had to be innovative in his agricultural pursuits.[52] In *Nelson v. Biggers*, reviewing a trial court's instruction that warranting slaves as "healthy" expressed both physical and mental soundness, he relied on personal expertise despite the several precedents identified by attorneys for the parties: "Does the warranty that the negroes are 'healthy,' extend to soundness of mind? We think not, when taken in the common acceptation of the term."[53] To Judge Warner's mind and, he assumed, by the "common acceptation" of his fellow planters, sales warranties must assert "soundness" in order to exclude both physical and mental defects in slave merchandise. Perceiving that this premise was acceptable to his audience, the judge confidently inserted his opinion in the Georgia law reports.

Joseph H. Lumpkin contributed more narrative artifacts than Judge Warner simply because Judge Lumpkin authored many more opinions—over half of the reviews of criminal appeals between 1846 and 1860.[54] Both publicly and privately he confirmed his role in sustaining the myth of paternalistic masters.[55] For example, writing to his daughter, the judge decried "bad times" during which "[n]o negro now calls their own master or mistress or themselves—by their owner's name—and daddy and mamma—are obsolete words in their vocabulary."[56]

The judge's opinions illuminate his preoccupation with the parental disciplining of slaves. In *Scudder v. Woodbridge*, he analyzed the question whether the owner of a riverboat should compensate the owner of a slave who had been killed by the negligence of the boat's crew. Affirming the trial court's award of damages, Judge Lumpkin made liberal use of rhetorical emphasis and questioning to emphasize his argument:

They [slaves] dare not interfere with the business of others. They would be instantly chastised for their impertinence. It is true that the owner, or *employer*, of a slave is restrained by the Penal Code from inflicting on him cruel, unnecessary and excessive punishment; and that *all others* are forbidden to beat, whip or wound them, *without sufficient cause or provocation.* But can any one doubt that if this unfortunate boy, although shipped as a carpenter, had been ordered by the captain to perform the perilous service in which he lost his life, and he had refused or remonstrated, that he would have received prompt correction? . . . No! . . . Whether engaged as carpenters, bricklayers or blacksmiths—as ferrymen, wagoners, patroons or private hands, in boats or vessels in the coasting or river navigation, on railroads, or any other avocation—they have nothing to do but silently serve out their appointed time. . . . As it is, the guards thrown around this class of our population are sufficiently few and feeble. We are altogether disinclined to lessen their number or weaken their force.[57]

The judge revealed an intimate knowledge of slave labor in his society, especially the complexities of applying the fellow-servant rule in American jurisprudence.[58] More specifically, he addressed dual needs in the Old South related to slave labor. Black submission was essential: "[T]hey have nothing to do but silently serve out their appointed time." And so was white vigilance: "[T]he guards thrown around this class of our population are sufficiently few and feeble." Personal and intuitive endorsement of these dual needs was the sole basis for rejecting the legal authorities and case law relied on by attorneys for the boat owner.

Three years later, in *Mayor and Council of Columbus v. Howard,* Judge Lumpkin used similar intuitions in addressing municipal liability for the death of a hired slave. According to the judge, the city was liable to the slaveowner for damages because the slave had been "used for a different purpose from that which was intended by the parties" (for "blasting wells, pulling down old walls, . . . levelling dangerous and precipitous embankments" instead of working "*on the streets* of the city"). This time the judge was in a position to cite volumes of legal authority, but this advantage did

not bar his collateral use of oratorical embellishment. "The want of discretion in our slave population is notorious," he declared. "They need a
higher degree of intelligence than their own, not only to direct their labor,
but likewise to protect them from the consequences of their own improvi-
dence."[59] Not to be denied, Judge Lumpkin addressed the nature and
needs of southern society. He told a story of strong backs and weak minds
in the slave population that demanded fatherly concern among his fellow
planters.

Slave labor and its social implications inspired several of Alabama's
judges to craft their own narratives. As a planter, Anderson Crenshaw was
necessarily concerned over the quality of cotton crops and the supervision
provided by overseers.[60] As a judge reviewing *Brandon v. Planters' & Merchants' Bank*, he did not readily discard the belief based on firsthand experience that slaves existed for the benefit of their masters. He maintained
that "in this country, a slave is in absolute bondage," and he further
asserted that "his master is his guardian and protector, and that all his
rights, acquisitions, and services are in the hands of his master." More
generously, the judge also admitted "that a slave is not a beast, but is a rational human being, endowed with volition and understanding like the
rest of mankind."[61] Henry B. Goldthwaite, in reviewing *State v. Wisdom*,
later appraised the nature of slaves similarly by granting them "volition,
and the power of locomotion, but also intelligence."[62] Expressed in a
personal form of address without legal citations, this discourse functioned
as plausible narratives of slavery.

Unlike Judge Crenshaw, John M. Taylor failed in his business affairs.
And he earnestly hoped that his personal failure would educate federal
legislators when drafting a bankruptcy statute: "Among the many subjects which will probably occupy the time of Congress, there is one in
which I feel the deepest interest, I mean the passage of a bankruptcy
law." Forthright about his own failings, the judge felt that he could "no
better elucidate the subject, than by making myself & my own situation
the subject of my remarks." He confessed that he had been "unfortunate
in busines & failed, after having certainly been of considerable advantage to my Countrymen," and he bemoaned having "relinquished to my

Creditors the last cent that I was worth."[63] But several years later, in *Caldwell v. Wallace*, Judge Taylor put aside his personal failings and confidently analyzed the language of warranties in selling slaves, reaching the same decision on "soundness" as Judge Warner.[64]

More successful than Judge Taylor, Reuben Saffold was fluent in the words and figures associated with the antebellum cotton market.[65] As the master of "Bellvoir," Judge Saffold also expressed an appreciation of the intangibles of slaveowning. "There is usually some attachment for negroes raised or long used in a family," he observed in *Moore v. Dudley*, "and the sale of such property by legatees is often distressing to their relatives and friends, and indicative of embarrassment."[66] A knowledgeable planter, he recognized that the "embarrassment" caused by financial straits could defeat one's personal feelings toward slave assets.

When this issue was raised again in *Baker v. Rowan*, the judge explicitly cited personal opinion to guide his opinion:

> We freely concede, that slave property is, in general, distinguishable from other chattels, in this respect; that family slaves to which owners are attached, should be preserved in specie, by the interposition of the Chancery court, rather than leave the party to seek reparation in damages, by suit at law.[67]

In both cases, the judge addressed a contested issue matter-of-factly: slaveowners and their beneficiaries placed special value on family heirlooms, including longtime or particularly cherished servants. In neither case did legal authority exert as much influence on the judge's opinion as oratorical form. Because of widely known customs and practices in plantation life, the judge could forcefully cite facts that all parties would predictably affirm.

Henry W. Collier, born and raised on his father's Virginia plantation, spoke with as much personal confidence as Judge Saffold about the nature of slaves. In a gubernatorial address, Judge Collier asserted as "universally conceded," that "slaves are reasonable beings, with the moral feelings, it is true often obtuse, but susceptible of improvement." Moreover, he declared: "Our interest in slaves cannot be regarded in all respects similar to that we enjoy in mere beasts or inanimate objects."[68] He used the personal pronouns "our" and "we" properly—in view of his substantial "planting interest."[69] He also relied heavily on an intuition that his assertions were "universally conceded." And he extended this oratorical mode of discourse in his judicial opinions.

As governor, Henry W. Collier asserted that slaves had a flawed but tractable nature. Earlier in his judicial role, he made allied claims. Before citing any other authority in *Gillian v. Senter,* the judge narrated his personal impression of the need to enforce a set of plantation rules. He considered that "it is very difficult to define, yet there are some points in respect to the government of slaves, in which perhaps all of us are agreed."[70] Discussing the need to enforce industry and obedience—the "good principals and industrious habits" he would later acclaim as governor—the judge expressed his approval of both "moral suasion" and "corporal punishment."[71] He risked little in assuming universal agreement with his perceptions because his audience was comprised of fellow planters.

Like Judge Collier, the man he replaced, Silas Parsons experienced plantation life outside Alabama. After resigning his seat on the bench in 1851, he moved to Texas.[72] Judge Parsons also learned about law and order through personal experience, having served as a county sheriff early in his public life.[73] Widely experienced, he addressed criminal issues related to skin color intuitively without apparent tension when reviewing *Thurman v. State*—a case that turned solely on the nature and definition of a "mulatto."[74]

Edmund S. Dargan expressed an equally high level of confidence in his opinions, though addressing factual issues other than complexion. In *Carroll v. Brumby,* for instance, he rhetorically questioned whether a slave would always opt for freedom if given a choice.[75] In *Marshall v. Gantt,* he simply declared that juries were susceptible to being misled by the physical appearance of a slave. This tendency was another good reason, he considered, for barring slaves from trials.[76] Even more suggestive of his perceived command over the facts of life, the judge felt free to interpret the trial record of a slave's misdeeds with scant references to external authorities in *Baalam v. State.*[77]

John J. Ormond was at least as confident about his intuitions as other members of Alabama's high court. A successful planter, Judge Ormond sought a federal pardon shortly before his death because he had "[a]cqui-esced in and participated in rebellion by selling cotton to Conf. S. & furnishing money and clothing to soldiers." At war's end, he remained wealthy and had "150 Bales Cotton in possession of U.S. Taken from him under protest."[78] His judicial opinions attest to his recognition of slaves' human natures, although the oratorical portions of these opinions imply a devotion to impersonal principles when business transactions might be compromised by surrendering to sentiment. In *Hardeman v. Sims*, he de-nied the remedy sought by "an owner, who for peculiar and sufficient rea-sons, sought the recovery of a slave in specie." Instead, the judge approved "the cheaper and more convenient remedy afforded by the Courts of com-mon law." He gave his approval despite recognizing that slaves "are intel-lectual, moral beings, and attachments of the strongest kind, sometimes grow up between master and slave, having its origin not unfrequently in early infancy, and strengthened in after life by dutiful service and obedi-ence, on the one hand, and care and protection on the other."[79] For this no-nonsense judge, slaveowners should not be granted the more creative remedies offered in courts of equity—personal sentiment notwithstand-ing—when slave assets could be readily administered by courts of law.

Judge Ormond saw himself thoroughly in command of the facts of plan-tation life, relying on firsthand experience to guide his opinions. "The as-certainment of the value of a slave," he recalled in *Bethea v. McColl*, "is a matter of some difficulty, as it depends upon the ability of the slave to per-form labor—the quality of the soil upon which it is employed—the skill with which it is directed—and the price of its product." To his mind, "the hiring of slaves for agricultural purposes, is generally ruinous to the hirer, and not unfrequently also, injurious to the owner."[80] Confidently narrating the problems attached to assessing a slave's value, the judge also asserted as a general premise that certain business practices were "ruinous . . . inju-rious." Although he spoke in a less severe tenor when addressing the issue of punitive damages for slave abuse in *Wheat v. Groom*, Judge Ormond ex-pressed ambivalent feelings about the personhood of slaves. "The slave, although property, is also a moral agent, a sentient being," he conceded. He further conceded that, because a slave "is capable of mental, as well as corporal suffering, . . . vindictive damages, may be given." Finally, since a slave's "master is his natural, as well as legal protector," the master "may recover for an injury to the slave, considered either as a person or as property."[81] Allowing recovery on either of two legal theories, the judge implied that he himself favored justice for the master rather than the slave. In any event, the opinion concludes with an intuitive reflection rather than a citation of more legally binding authority.

Given Judge Ormond's earlier advocacy, his reversal of a slave's conviction for a capital offense—partially biting off the ear of an armed overseer with whom he was fighting—is striking in *State v. Abram*. "To hold otherwise," he insisted, "would indeed be to reduce the slave, to a level with the brute creation." Before injecting an alternative view of "the circumstances of the case," the judge opined that "there may doubtless be cases, in which the slave obeying the mere instincts of his nature, and from his impulses as an animal, rather than from the exercise of his will as an intellectual being, might inflict an injury of this description." However, in this case, the judge argued that lawful self-defense was equally probable:

> Slave though he be, . . . he is nevertheless a human being, and when engaged in mortal strife, his adversary armed with a deadly weapon, and he defenceless, the law, in compassion to the infirmity of our nature, and to the instinctive dread of death, common alike to the bound and the free, would attribute such a mutilation of the person of a white man to the instinct of self defence, in which the will did not co-operate.[82]

In both content and form, the narrative tenor in this opinion is remarkably different in its degree of certitude from prior examples.

Substantive differences in *State v. Abram* may quickly be explained away as a result of the type of law being administered. In criminal cases, especially when death rather than imprisonment was at issue, a judge would have considered the slave's appeal from a mindset most favorable to the prisoner—who had "a good character, as an obedient servant." But noteworthy formal differences remain. The judge spoke of a human nature shared by slaves and masters ("our nature"). He also spoke of a fear "common alike to the bound and the free." He used these intuitive flourishes not to express a general change of heart but to add intensity to the substance of a specific argument. So used, the language transcends mere ornamentation. It is a tactical device. It also affirms the constancy of a jurist who had remarked several years before in *State v. Jones* that the "record is a narrative of what took place at the trial." As such, he insisted, the factual record should "be construed according to its plain and obvious import, and not by those rules which would make it necessary that it should state those facts it purports to detail, with so much precision and certainty as to exclude every other conclusion."[83] On this point Judge Ormond communed with his colleagues across the Deep South—most certainly with Judge Dargan—in relishing the judicial prerogative to interpret and narrate facts so that a legal conclusion might be less than predictable.

Mississippi's judges were no exceptions to the rule followed in Alabama. They assessed the factual setting of cases in relation to personal recollection and intuition. Joshua G. Clarke was able to rely on his experiences at "Claremont."[84] William L. Sharkey was able to generalize from his experiences on a large plantation near Vicksburg.[85] Alexander M. Clayton also counted on his experience as a planter—from the time he initially relied on slaves to clear his land of timber, through wartime concern over the destruction of his cotton crop, to postwar despair over the destruction of his house, plantation, and personal property.[86] In his opinions, the judge relied on experiential learning as much as factual review to justify his conclusions.

In *Murphy v. Clark* Judge Clayton analyzed "the peculiar nature and character of slave property," citing prior reviews of the same issue by colleagues such as Tennessee's William B. Reese and South Carolina's William Harper. However, Judge Clayton ultimately relied on a whimsical tale to justify his own analysis: "I recollect a case in my practice, in which a bill was filed to recover what is called a mad stone; that is, a stone supposed to be a specific and talisman against the bite of all poisonous and rabid animals." Concluding with a specific application to slave property, the judge asserted: "It could not well be said that a man had a peculiar affection for this stone, and yet it will scarcely be doubted, that, whether its extraordinary properties be real or imaginary, the true owner would have, in equity, a right to recover it in specie."[87] If a "mad stone" should be treated as having peculiar value in transfers of property, the judge decided, then any slave not previously assessed as commonplace merchandise could also have peculiar value. Although the suit for recovery of a mad stone was factual, Judge Clayton's application to the case under review added a tangy rhetorical flavor to his jurisprudence.

More generous in his assessment of the character of slaves while reviewing *Lewis v. State,* Judge Clayton observed on his own authority that "simple, elementary truths of christianity, the immortality of the soul, and a future accountability, are generally received and believed by this portion of our population." His declaration indicated the judge had seen "this portion of our population"—including, perhaps, his own slaves—attend religious services where they "hear these doctrines announced and enforced, and embrace them as articles of faith."[88] Asking fellow planters to search their own memories, the judge anticipated their agreement that slaves were fundamentally unlike mere stones and brute creatures.

The relative scarcity of judicial narratives in Mississippi is provocative because Judge Clayton's latter assessment was among the most flattering depictions of slaves in the Old South—or in the North. But lacking a baseline for measurement, his attribution of religious belief to slaves remains no more compelling than his less flattering reference to the mad stone. Moreover, even the minimal composition of judicial narratives in Mississippi surpassed the amount of related discourse in Florida, as neither Thomas Baltzell nor George S. Hawkins applied personal intuitions to their dispositions of cases involving slaves.

Not surprisingly, in keeping with their distinctive legal heritage, Louisiana's judges had different experiences and at least several of the judges told related stories. Pierre A. C. B. Derbigny, for instance, had fled from the French Revolution and resided in Pennsylvania, Missouri, and Florida before establishing legal and political roots in Louisiana. He put down family roots on a fifteen-hundred-acre plantation.[89]

Alexander Porter also cultivated thousands of acres, employing hundreds of slaves. A visitor to "Oaklawn" recalled that Judge Porter, along with his neighbors, assessed slaves as less than "morally responsible beings" but treated them "liberally and kindly." Charles Stewart, the slave who managed Judge Porter's stable of thoroughbreds, recalled: "He was 'jes as open-handed an' gin'rous, but he wouldn't stand no foolin' neither."[90] As a political representative, Judge Porter unleashed narrative that he shunned on the bench. Early in 1836, joining the Senate debate over abolition petitions, he attacked the credibility of abolitionists by describing slaveowners in glowing terms:

> I wish . . . that those who denounce them would visit their country before they poured out these effusions of ignorance and malignity. They would find these men imbued with as lofty and disinterested patriotism as the world can exhibit, and the love of the union in these States so entwined with every fibre of their heart as to constitute, as it were, a part of their being. They would see women as pure and as gentle as the earth holds or the sun looks at; and they would behold homes and hearths consecrated by the practice of every domestic and Christian virtue. Instead of oppression and tyranny displayed to slaves, they would see kindness practised to those whom Providence has placed under the care of the inhabitants of this region.[91]

In modest defense of Judge Porter's idealized portrait of southrons around their hearths, it should be noted that he bequeathed emancipation to two of his own slaves. Yet the hundreds of other slaves he owned remained in bondage, and he never used the bench as a pulpit to endorse treatment of slaves that belied "oppression and tyranny."

A central figure in the legal history of Louisiana, Francis-Xavier Martin established models for applying intuition to judicial opinions. He authored a state history in which he observed matter-of-factly the reason behind importing "five hundred negroes" early in the eighteenth century:

> Experience has shewn the great fertility of the land in Louisiana, especially on the banks of the Mississippi, and its aptitude to the cul-

ture of tobacco, indigo, cotton and rice; but the labourers were very few, and many of the newcomers had fallen victims to the climate. The survivors found it impossible to work in the field during the great heats of the summer, protracted through a part of the autumn. The necessity of obtaining cultivators from Africa was apparent.[92]

For the narrator, simple "necessity" obviated the need for further explanation or justification of slavery in the region. A painfully frugal bachelor, the judge valued necessity in his personal affairs as well. He implied this value in instructions to his small household staff of slaves: "I intend to be a generous master; I will permit you a room, but you must feed yourselves and supply my table with decent fare, besides cleaning the house in which we all reside, and which is yours as well as mine." Perceiving his house rules as generous, the judge continued: "This is all I require of you. The rest of the time is yours, and whatever money you make and save after you have nourished me and kept my clothes in a good state of repair, is your absolute property."[93] Judge Martin articulated no-nonsense pragmatism in his household management and applied the same standard to his professional duties. Viewed as eccentric and difficult by contemporaries, he established a simple, need-based scale for interpreting the factual record of cases under review.

Perhaps adopting a line of argument established earlier by Judge Martin, Alonzo Morphy asserted in *Taylor v. Andrus* that "[a]n intelligent being like a slave, cannot be assimilated to a horse or an inanimate object."[94] Reviewing a breach of warranty in a slave transaction, Judge Martin had noted that "the habit of running away" was a statutorily defined vice, though proof of this vice in some slaves did not necessarily violate the warranty attached to an entire consignment of slaves and did not void the entire transaction. As introductory material, the judge incorporated an analogy cited by attorneys for both parties: "[The slaves] did not constitute a whole, as a company of comedians or a span of horses, in which the value of each of the component parts is increased by its union to the rest."[95] Though folksy on the surface, this analogy requires careful scrutiny to understand the judge's narrative rhetoric. The references to valuable teamwork among comedians and horses is adapted from a text by Pothier on contract law, translated for American lawyers by Judge Martin in 1802.[96] Whether flattered by the references or impressed by the analogy itself, the judge nonetheless uttered a factual comparison that identified slaves with comedians—a suspect class at the time—and beasts of burden.[97] As introductory material, the identification set a tenor for judicial review of the facts.

Always mindful of efficiency and economy, regardless of how it might affect his tenor, in *Palfrey v. Rivas* Judge Martin reviewed practical limits on a citizen's duty to assist in the capture of runaway slaves. Interpreting an 1816 statute (contained in his own *Digest* of state laws), Judge Martin emphasized the factual basis of his decision making. "The act requires a person who takes up a runaway slave to carry him before a magistrate," the judge reported accurately, "but it does not fix any particular time for doing so." Then, resorting to personal intuition and common sense, Judge Martin observed: "The taker-up cannot be expected instantly to abandon his own work and go accompanied by his own negroes to the justice. A reasonable time must be allowed for that purpose. And this is a *matter of fact*."[98] For Judge Martin, the reasonableness of his decision could be measured on a factual scale. He had a clear vision of the scale. Although members of the planter class might resist limits on their recovery of property, they must bow to "a matter of fact." After all, as he illustrated in *Poulard v. Delamare,* his view of facts could as readily sustain the planters' views as oppose them: "[T]here is hardly any difference between an emancipated slave and a slave which cannot be compelled to labor."[99] Louisiana's planters and the judge alike would agree that slaves were valuable only as servants, not fellow citizens.

Supplementing Judge Martin's perceptions with his own, George Mathews revealed his personal intuitions of slavery and race. "Slaves, being men," he declared when reviewing a title action in *Johnson v. Field,* "are to be identified by their proper names, which distinguishes them one from another; and where there are two or more of the same name, by some other, which distinguishes them in relation to physical, or, perhaps, moral qualities."[100] Although he was addressing a technical problem in titling property, the judge entered the realm of intuition by declaring that, by their nature, slaves had moral as well as brutish qualities.

Addressing this issue again in *Bruce v. Stone*, Judge Mathews embellished his expression of the same intuition with an aside about the degraded nature of slaves: "Men free and men who are slaves, (perhaps not much in accordance with the dignity of human nature,) are distinguished, one from another, by names arbitrarily given, as well as by their different physical and moral qualities."[101] His earlier allowance of moral qualities to slaves, though modest, was unqualified. His later opinion, featuring a parenthetical remark on the indignity of slavery, was more elaborate. Just as striking was his opinion in *Landreaux v. Campbell*, where he held that a slave should not be considered insane simply because he or she exhibited a feeble constitution, laziness, and an aversion to work.[102] These behaviors, he sensed, were perfectly natural to the species.

Pierre A. Rost and George R. King added related perceptions of fact to those underlying Judge Mathews's opinions. The master of Destrehan Manor and a leader in Louisiana's sugar industry, Judge Rost decided that a taste of freedom reduced a slave's value.[103] After a slave named Felix had been permitted to work freely in Illinois and Iowa, the judge observed in *Spalding v. Taylor* that "he must have been utterly worthless."[104] For his part, Judge King took up a theme narrated by colleagues across the Deep South and asserted in *State v. Nelson* that slaves "would naturally look for protection" from their masters.[105]

Judges Rost and King summarized implicitly the intuitive premises used across the Deep South. Slaves were adjudged as valuable but troublesome assets. They were at least as valuable as good land and domesticated animals. Though their value might fluctuate wildly—depending on their natural vices as well as unnatural brushes with liberty—slaves were essential to the cultivation of staple crops. The judges also agreed that slaves possessed naturally intelligent and moral qualities, though the notion of a pluralistic society to be shared with blacks by whites was fantastic. For one thing, slaves naturally looked to their masters for protection—much as adoring children might do—and this emblem of servitude could never be expected to disappear.

Judicial narratives illustrate intuitions of slavery that were generally shared in the Upper South and the Deep South. For example, similar to

North Carolina's Thomas Ruffin, Georgia's Joseph H. Lumpkin expressed a paternalistic stance toward slaves that achieved mythic status across the Old South. These judges' views of life were nearly uniform, though the members of North Carolina's judiciary uttered mildly favorable stories about the intellectual and moral capacities of slaves. Then again, Mississippi's Alexander Clayton attributed a capacity for formally religious belief to slaves that stood out from the estimates rendered by his colleagues. Here and there, other judges reported perceptions of slaves as individuals rather than faceless members of a class.

As in the Upper South, judicial narratives essentially summarize antebellum proslavery arguments. Indeed, South Carolina's John S. Richardson explicitly deferred to "the well considered discussion of the whole subject by Dr. Matthew Estes, of Columbus, Mississippi, entitled 'a defence of negro slavery, as it exists in the United States.'"[106] Judicial narratives also served the dual ends of persuasive evidence and embellishment.

However, judicial narratives in the Deep South imply a more penetrating insight into the mental and physical abilities of slaves than judges in the Upper South could manage. The differences are subtle, but Judge Clayton's anecdote about the "mad stone" illustrates the type of experiential base and interpretive power that a judge in Mississippi did not readily attribute to a judge in Tennessee—even if that judge claimed to be as perspicacious as William B. Reese. Moreover, the richness of detail in judicial narratives of life in South Carolina surpassed quantitatively if not qualitatively the narratives related by judges in North Carolina, or any other pairing of jurisdictions in the Deep South and Upper South. The judges addressed clearly and distinctly the tension between conserving property and conserving life. By judicial accounts, slave property was extraordinarily valuable and merited close, personal management. Yet the business of slavery was extraordinarily dangerous. The peculiar institution required constant vigilance in order to preserve life—whether master or slave.

Chapter Four

EQUATIONS OF HUMANITY
AND INTEREST
IN THE UPPER SOUTH

onfident about their intuitions, judges still faced a daunting task in applying a humanist perspective to their advocacy. They seldom warmed to this task of equating humanity and interest, following the dictates of their professional culture and preferring to address the law as distinct from morality and politics. Some judges explicitly disavowed related appeals in their opinions. Appeals to morality, much less to Providence and scriptural revelation, could mock the secular authority by which the judges found a legal basis for slavery in the United States. Appeals to policy and arguments from necessity could be demeaning—even embarrassing—because they implied judicial powerlessness in the face of larger forces.

Equations of humanity and interest remain skeletal in terms of humanist substance and oratorical form. In only a handful of instances did judges define sociopolitical interest or explain the meaning of humanity in depth. Appeals to policy and morality in the law reports take the shape of baldly stated premises that lead abruptly to legal conclusions. Sparsely developed as they were, each species of judicial discourse required pairing with the other to achieve persuasive force. In this sense, the prevailing interpretation of jurisprudential style in the Old South is wrong; the judges never intended to promote a choice between humanity and interest. These issues were meaningless except when linked. For the judges themselves, the humanist tradition established a meaningful link: a morally good orator always reflected on the welfare of the state.

Blended appeals to the conservation of life as well as property became more valuable in the Upper South as sectional strife became more intense. However, since many judges also had political experience at the state and federal levels, and since talk of secession—serious talk—had been going on since the nullification controversy of 1832, judicial discourse contains traces of the blended appeals long before civil war erupted. Fulminating on sectional interest and meditating aloud on humanity, judges in the Upper South addressed their opinions to partisans as well as to southrons who were becoming disaffected with slavery. Paranoia was growing and proslavery advocates, many of them "leaders of the bar and bench," appreciated the persuasive tools afforded them by these blended appeals.[1] Indeed, "a judicial secession" can reasonably be asserted to have taken place between the North and South on matters such as comity a decade after 1850.[2]

Virginia's judges, recognizing an age-old tension between legal and moral principles, authored widely disparate opinions. But, when pressed, the judges resorted to blended appeals. Joseph L. Fry addressed this clash in *Commonwealth v. Garner,* though only in a figurative sense, when he analyzed a dispute over the free passage of slaves on the Ohio River. The judge insisted that his state exercised dominion over the entire waterway rather than losing jurisdiction at its midpoint because "it is impossible oftentimes to avoid crossing the middle line of the river; sometimes to avoid collisions with other boats, driftwood, ice, to avoid sandbars and ripples in low stages of water, and from many other causes which may arise." Then, as any good advocate would do, he assessed the opposing argument: "If [the opposing] view could be sustained in law, it would be lamentable indeed. It would make the Ohio river in truth what it has been said that its name signifies—the river of strife—the war river—the river of blood." More specifically, the judge speculated that "people on one side would attempt to free the slaves on the river: the people on the other would regard it as mere robbery, and would defend their property."[3]

In hindsight, Judge Fry might have applied his analysis to the debate over slavery itself: references to strife, war, and blood were prescient. In the flood of competing arguments, where one current ran against slavery (often relying on appeals to humanity) while the other carried slavery along in its flow (relying on appeals to interest), a dangerous maelstrom occurred. Civic leaders like Judge Fry—in hopes of avoiding the legal equivalents of riparian snags and collisions—steered clear of appeals to morality or policy.

Anticipating Judge Fry's sentiments, John W. Green uttered a disclaimer of "moral and political considerations" in *Maria v. Surbaugh*. He decreed that his court was duty-bound not to be influenced "by considerations of humanity on the one hand, or of policy (except so far as the policy of the law appears to extend) on the other."[4] Judge Green clearly expressed his resistance to considering most policy issues—and all moral issues—when reviewing cases of slavery.

In *Commonwealth v. Turner*, William A. G. Dade composed an alternative version of Judge Green's disclaimer. Judge Dade asserted that his court should not consider "what may be expedient, or morally, or politically right" in reaching a decision. Yet he ultimately depicted the act under review—a master's abusive punishment of a slave—as a "reproach to humanity."[5] The judge's declaration was entirely consistent with his earlier instructions to a grand jury. "The social intercourse of man," he declared, makes legal regulations necessary. In fact, only where "the state of man has ever been found the least dignified and the least happy"—the status of slaves—have laws been dispensed with.[6] Like John W. Green, Judge Dade preferred his legal duty to be clear and simple and dreaded the political and moral misdeeds that came under his review.

A successful career in state politics made William H. Cabell's avoidance of appeals to policy all the more noteworthy. He restricted these appeals exclusively to his private correspondence, while analyzing acts of "inhumanity" in *Randolph v. Randolph*.[7] He saw his way clear to distinguish law and politics, but he perceived no flaw in interrelating law and morality.

Briscoe G. Baldwin was similarly active in the political arena, until he saw this conduct as "unseemly" after ascending Virginia's highest bench in 1842.[8] As a state representative the judge had inveighed against restrictions on slavery in Missouri, citing the "sovereign character" and the "sovereign rights reserved to the states."[9] As a judge, he did not engage in appeals to interest.

Despite the resistance to policy-based appeals by Judges Cabell and Baldwin, several colleagues addressed both humanity and interest in hopes of enhancing their suasory power on the bench. Francis T. Brooke, speaking as president of the court in *Allen v. Freeland*, asserted that slaves were "entitled to the humanity of the Court, when it can be exercised without invading the right of property."[10] Trying to accommodate the competing demands of interest and humanity, the judge clearly expressed an equation that became commonplace in the Old South: conserving wealth was as moral as conserving life.

As sectional tensions grew, Judge Brooke amplified his sentiments in *Anderson's Ex'ors v. Anderson*. "[I]f the humanity of the court is to be appealed to," he objected, "the rights of the master must be controlled, the moral influence that subjects the slave to the master disregarded, and a spirit of hostility engendered while they continue to be slaves, calculated to diminish their value while slaves." Worse yet, he continued, "the property of the master [would] be invaded in a manner subversive of the institution of slavery, and likely to have an influence on those who are slaves for life; and the next step may be to interfere with the master in their case also."[11] The judge curtly dismissed appeals to humanity after speculating on the social and economic injuries that would happen if such appeals were entertained by the court. He doubtless hoped that his own appeals—including references to anticipated declines in peace and prosperity—enhanced his persuasiveness.

Reviewing two cases of slave abuse, William Brockenbrough lacked the intensity of Judge Brooke but shared his technique of measuring morality against policy. Judge Brockenbrough rejected the appellant's claim in *Commonwealth v. Carver* that, as a free white, he could not be criminally prosecuted for maiming another man's slave. Justifying his decision, the judge cited both the "interest" of the master and the safety of the slave.[12] Later that same year, dissenting from Judge Dade's opinion in *Commonwealth v. Turner*, Judge Brockenbrough insisted that his court should consider as norms both "the peace of society" and "humane treatment" when reviewing acts of slave abuse.[13] Remarkably, in both of his opinions, the judge merely announced political and moral norms without fully developing an argument. The sketchy character of these appeals indicates judicial difficulty in articulating a humanist perspective on slavery—in this case alleviated a generation later through statutory means.[14] Nonetheless, Judge Brockenbrough's inchoate appeals endorse the two objects of conservation—property and life—that imbue his opinion with a humanist tenor.

Dabney Carr shared the perspective of Judge Brockenbrough. When reviewing a manumission statute in *Manns v. Givens,* he first asserted the property interest at stake and then opined: "It is clear that the legislative will was in favour of suffering every man to exercise his benevolence, or satisfy his scruples of conscience, in respect to freeing his slaves."[15] A decade earlier, he had punctuated his opinion in *Allen v. Freeland* with an exclusively moral appeal by expressing relief that "[n]o sacrifice of feeling" was made and "no considerations of humanity" were omitted.[16] At the same time, in *Dabney v. Taliaferro,* he remarked with pleasure that the "genius of our law is not so cruel and unfeeling" as to ignore the suffering of slaves. "Non obtusa adeo gestamus pectora."[17] Modestly improving on Judge Brockenbrough's inchoate appeals, Judge Carr uttered his humanist perspective in more fully developed oratorical form. He argued that his state's policy was inherently moral, and underscored this humanist theme with a relevant Latin proverb.

Judge Carr's advocacy should have been well developed. He drew on prior experience, peppering his *Old Bachelor* essays with appeals to both humanity and interest. "[I]n a country and under a government like this," he observed, "the *political* condition of the people must ever depend upon their *moral* and *intellectual.*"[18] The shifts in this judge's appeals over time—first blended, then discrete, and finally blended again—suggest that the youthful Dabney Carr did not yet feel comfortable with playing the role of advocate on the bench. He had reserved his blended, humanist advocacy for political essays in 1814—ironically attributed to an "old" bache-

lor. By 1836, a more mature Dabney Carr felt no restraints on melding political and moral principles in his opinions, however sketchily drawn. He
finally permitted himself to express his political and moral vision regardless of the forum.

Successors echoed Judge Carr's sentiments and extended his techniques. On the one hand, John J. Allen characterized an increase in the
population of free blacks as contrary to policy in *Wynn v. Carrell*.[19] On the
other hand, in *Martin v. Martin*, he decreed that humanity opposes the
separation of slave children from their mothers.[20] Unlike Judge Carr, however, he did not articulate blended appeals in arguing a single issue. Moreover, in composing a fiery preamble to an 1860 resolution favoring secession—an indictment of "pharasaical fanaticism prevailing in the North"
and a refusal to surrender "to a barbarous race"—he disdained to consider
morality altogether.[21]

Embedded in the private correspondence of John T. Lomax was the
thought that southern interest enjoyed both religious and legal sanctions.
He agreed with his daughter, for example, that the slaves' failure to rally
around John Brown at Harper's Ferry was not meaningful in terms of
"the fidelity of the slave population."[22] A reluctance to rise in that particular revolt scarcely demonstrated an affirmative allegiance by slaves to
their masters. The next day, addressing both humanity and interest, the
judge expressed contempt for "the shreaks & yells & whoops of northern
fanatics" and predicted a war "frightful in its ravages" that would mean
"the days of our prosperity are numbered." Nonetheless, he insisted, "We
can not compromise rights which we hold under the sanctions of religion
and the constitution and our laws, or expose our safety to the caprices of
fanatical delusions." Rather, the "tremendous recoil upon northern interest, which abolitionism must produce" might bring the North to its
senses.[23] Although morally defensible, thought Judge Lomax, the institution of slavery would survive if only because northerners would recognize
their own interest in rejecting abolition.

Presaging this notion in *Bacon v. Commonwealth*, the judge used similarly blended appeals to policy and morality to reverse the conviction of a

minister for preaching against slavery. Tracking statutory language and its legislative history, he argued in oratorical form:

> To dissuade a member of a Christian flock from merchandizing in slaves, or taking and keeping human beings in slavery, may be done by a pastor, without any denial of the right of owners to property in their slaves. A spiritual law, apart from human law, might be inculcated by him upon their consciences for their peculiar government, according to their creed, without exciting, or intending to excite, any spirit of rebellion against the law of the land; which, according to Christian doctrine, all are bound to obey. With the fullest sense of the sanctions with which the rights of owners to property in their slaves have been clothed by the law of the State, and the law of nations, and the law of the scriptures, and with the most profound submission to these sanctions, he might innocently urge an abstinence from the enjoyment of these rights, as not being expedient, or as inconsistent with the professions of a peculiar religious faith.[24]

One of the most intricate blends of these appeals in antebellum case law, Judge Lomax's joint invocation of property rights and moral righteousness articulates the humanist perspective that most of his colleagues struggled less successfully to express. Nonetheless, the substance of the judge's opinion—approving the accused's deference to criminal statute, natural law, and scriptural canon—appears meretricious. The gross artifice in his opinion, favoring the devices of parallelism and polysyndeton ("the law of the State, and the law of nations, and the law of the scriptures"), scarcely enhances an impression of spontaneity in the judge's expression. Perhaps overwhelmed by the legal morass of social-political sentiment, statutory rigor, and religious vocation, Judge Lomax simply threw up his hands and did the best he could.

Of course, Judge Lomax was not alone in seeking refuge among moral canons rather than civil and criminal codes. In concurring with Judge Carr's opinion in *Manns v. Givens*, Henry St. George Tucker referred obliquely to morality by declaring that the authors of a manumission statute "looked upon the existence of slavery among us not as a *blessing* but as a national misfortune."[25] However, because Judge Tucker's address to morality is metaphorical, it may not constitute a substantive guide to his priorities.

The judge had earlier expounded sectional interest more substantively, though not in a judicial capacity. In writing to Senator James Barbour, he had decried the Missouri Compromise—a "compromise which gives up the fairest & largest portion of the Western territory." Consideration of interest prompted the future judge to complain about slaveholders' being left with "a narrow slip" of territory that was "intersected with Mountains in one direction, destroyed by Earthquakes in another and interspersed in a third with Swamps & bayous & infested with mosquitoes & bilious diseases."[26] Several years later, he once again stressed sectional interest while lecturing at the University of Virginia. "I do not question the right of revolution," he stated, "when either the government through all the branches, or the members of the confederacy itself, shall concur in gross and intolerable oppression and usurpation."[27] In another series of lectures he further insisted:

> Where the interests, the feelings or even the prejudices of two different sections of a confederation are distinct and conflicting, where one regards as essential, what the other looks upon as ruinous, and where the line of demarcation is as plain territorially as it unfortunately is in point of interest or opinion, it may be confidently pronounced that the union of the respective portions must speedily be dissolved, unless there be co-existing causes of an opposite tendency more than adequate to control the repellent principles. Take for example, the subject of abolition, which unfortunately now stands forth so prominently on the canvass. . . . Such a state of things places the two large divisions of the union in dire hostility to each other. They stand in the position of separate nations.[28]

His partisanship, clearly stated and repeatedly affirmed, distinguishes his isolated use of moral appeals on the bench. The lure of moral appeals was evidently powerful enough that even champions of sectional interest found it difficult to resist them entirely when executing judicial duties—the sole accommodation being a sketchy development of these appeals.

More than Judge Tucker or any other colleague, Richard E. Parker emphasized humanity in his opinions. Exclusively pursuing this type of appeal in *Commonwealth v. Boone,* he asserted that assaults by masters on their slaves become criminal when they show "inhumanity."[29] In *Aldridge v. Commonwealth,* he argued that poorly drawn criminal statutes must be saved from "gross inhumanity" in their application to the conduct of blacks.[30] Despite a lapse of thirteen years, the judge continued to insist in *Spencer v. Pilcher* that "Humanity to the slave" demands judicial attention to working conditions.[31] And in *Ruddle's Ex'r v. Ben,* Judge Parker declared that "the dictates of humanity" as well as justice should be applied to cases involving a recision of emancipation.[32] Distinctive in his choice of appeals, Judge Parker shared his colleagues' scant development of them. His frequent yet curt references to "humanity" suggest that Judge Parker was determined to express the morality of his state's interest in slavery, despite the considerable difficulty attached to this line of advocacy.

Virginia's judges, despite their forebodings, failed collectively to resist appeals to civics and morality. As individuals, the judges may have favored one type of appeal over the other but, as a group, the judges addressed slavery's moral as well as political foundations. In their judicial opinions—illustrated prominently by Judge Lomax's dissertation on "spiritual law"—they favored appeals to morality. But the relatively flimsy development of this type of appeal indicated that the judges found it difficult to accommodate the southern way of life with the humanist tradition.

The judges of North Carolina invoked policy and assessed the moral quality of slavery in much the same ways as their brethren in Virginia. Though acknowledging mitigating provocations in *State v. Tackett,* such as "turbulence and insolence" on the part of slaves, in *State v. Hale* John Louis Taylor was convinced that "the march of benignant policy and provident humanity" in North Carolina—as well as the "light and influence" of Christianity—substantially removed any legal justification for slave abuse.[33] Several years earlier, he had embellished this perspective while instructing a grand jury: "Among the accusations for capital crimes, none occur more frequently in the courts than that for the murder of slaves. . . . the dictates of humanity, as well as the character of the country, make a strong appeal to the Legislature to revise the laws on this subject."[34] When it came to physical injury or death, at least, this judge adopted a humanist perspective on slavery. He explicitly deferred to Christian principles, but he also endorsed the conservation of property.

Sustaining the argumentative flexibility displayed by colleagues across the Upper South, Judge Taylor favored policy considerations over "the dictates of humanity" in opinions composed after *Tackett* and *Hale*. He supported strict regulation of the peculiar institution in *Trustees v. Dickenson*, fearing that "slaves, . . . would naturally excite in [freedmen] discontent with their condition, encourage idleness and disobedience, and lead possibly in the course of human events to the most calamitous of all contests, a *bellum servile*."[35] In his discourse, Judge Taylor identified the contrasting feelings that excited much of the southern gentry: love of material prosperity versus fear of slave revolts. In the face of servile insurrection, only the conservation of white lives was salient.

Dissenting in *Trustees v. Dickenson*, John Hall recommended that the majority of the court, including Judge Taylor, "take a step into the moral world and contemplate the unbiased principles of our nature."[36] Though less expansively than Judge Taylor, Judge Hall demonstrated in other opinions a similarly wavering allegiance to sociopolitical and moral principles.[37] Close on the heels of Judges Taylor and Hall, three other colleagues also expressed their overriding allegiance to civic policy. Leonard Henderson, William Gaston, and Frederic Nash devoted the bulk of their advocacy to considerations of interest.

By customary standards, Judge Henderson devoted considerable space to a moral meditation in *State v. Reed*. Responding passionately to counsel's argument that the common law did not recognize murdering a slave as a crime, the judge declared: "This is argument the force of which I cannot feel, and leads to consequences abhorrent to my nature." Indeed, he considered this argument to be "abhorrent to the hearts of all those who have felt the influence of the mild precepts of Christianity." In conclusion, he expounded "as an additional argument, that if the contrary exposition of the law is correct, then the life of a slave is at the mercy of any one, even a vagabond."[38] The combination of appeals to natural kindness and supernatural precepts was emotionally powerful. Pushing the opposing argument to its absurd extreme was logically compelling.

More typically, Judge Henderson composed succinct, policy-based analyses of slavery cases. Adding his opinion to *Trustees v. Dickenson*, he upheld legal barriers to slaves' hiring themselves out because he assumed that reasonable southrons recognized the "pernicious effect" of this practice. Based on this assumption of shared interest, he asserted that "no one, I think, can for a moment doubt the policy of these [prohibitive laws]."[39] More intensely yet, in *Stevens v. Ely*, he declared his agreement with "the stern policy of the State, necessary to support our institutions in regard to slaves," and his belief that judges were properly sensitive "to whatever may interfere with or laws on the question of slaves."[40] Other than ideological shifts that occurred because of an abominable tariff and other prompting events, only the distinction between criminal and civil causes of action accounts clearly for the differing stances taken by Judge Henderson between 1823 and 1830. Yet it remains unclear whether differences in the forms of action account for his inconsistency in the forms of address to humanist ideals. Facing knotty probems, the judge supplemented his legal logic with whatever oratorical form seemed useful.

As collateral evidence of Judge Henderson's technique, Judge Nash was equally flexible in composing his reviews of criminal appeals. Keenly attuned to politics, he appealed to interest when approving a statute that barred free blacks from carrying firearms.[41] "From the earliest period of our history," he observed in *State v. Newsom*, "free people of color have been among us, as a separate and distinct class, requiring from necessity, in many cases, separate and distinct legislation."[42] On the contrary, five years later in *State v. Caesar*, he mused on "the degraded state of slaves." According to the judge, "what would arouse to phrensy a white man, he is brought up from infancy to bow to." Recounting that he was "told that policy and necessity require that a different rule should exist in the case of a slave," the judge fulminated that "Necessity is the tyrant's plea, and policy never yet stripped, successfully, the bandage from the eyes of

Justice."[43] Unaccountably diverging from his earlier defense of a statute on grounds of civic necessity, the judge derided the force of necessity in attacking a proposed rule of law. Short of dismissing this inconstancy as a flaw in professional competence or personal integrity, critics may find the key to Judge Nash's oratorical form in judicial discomfort over the equation of humanity and interest. Though judges like Frederic Nash were adept in both species of appeals—in 1838, for example, he blended his political and moral sentiments in a speech on Masonry—they struggled with a fluent adaptation of humanist ideals to practical needs.[44]

Responding to the tension between the ideal and the practical, William Gaston demonstrated rhetorical dexterity. As a correspondent, he addressed friends about both national and state politics, including his reactions to Nat Turner's revolt.[45] After the nullification crisis of 1832, he expressed profound reservations about secession:

> There has been for several years, and there is now, a settled design among some of the leading bold and artful politicians on this side of the Potomac to establish a separate Southern Confederacy. Of this there is no doubt. The Tariff and Nullification were seized on as means for this end. These have failed, but the design has not been abandoned. It will be prosecuted with unabated perseverance, and the honest fears of the Southern Slaveholders and the fanaticism of the Northern abolitionists are relied on to bring about a conviction that the interests and feelings of the different sections of our country are too contradictory to render the union consistent with the good and harmony of the whole.[46]

The judge was a unionist and, despite seeing "honest fears" in slaveholders' complaints and "fanaticism" in the abolition movement, he deferred to peace and prosperity. His speechmaking underscored these interests. In 1832, he decried "the detestable suggestion of *Disunion!*" as born out of "sneers, menaces, reproaches, and recriminations" that all would lead to "parricide—the dismemberment of our 'father-land.'"[47] Finally and poetically, Judge Gaston proclaimed his sociopolitical interests in the five stanzas of "The Old North State," a paean to his jurisdiction. In its concluding stanza, he stated lyrically:

Then let all who love us, love the land that we live in,

As happy a region as on this side of heaven,

Where plenty and freedom, love and peace smile before us.[48]

In both prose and poetry, this judge wanted to make clear his civic devotion.

The judge's public appeals to morality were less frequent. In 1835, he declared that "the man who would excite hostile feelings between the different classes of society, . . . commits treason against social happiness, and does what in him lies to frustrate the message of divine beneficence."[49] This particular oratorical flourish, in which the judge granted equal priority to human and divine norms, is a rarely fluent expression of the bridge he envisioned between political and moral appeals. For him, the political treason of endorsing secession frustrated a divine plan.

More typically, in his judicial role, he expressed an overriding concern for domestic peace and prosperity. In *State v. Jarrott*, for instance, he opposed legal punishment of slave misconduct that was "unsuited to the state of our society, and incompatible with the subordination of ranks essential to the safety of the State."[50] His undivided attention to policy in this opinion is noteworthy. As a Roman Catholic, he had called for an end to religious bigotry, becoming for many a champion of religious toleration through speeches such as the one he delivered on June 4, 1835.[51] The judge suffered only modestly in public life from his Roman Catholicism, but he may have feared undue reactions to moralizing in his opinions. He expressed this "fear to err" in *State v. Will*, when reviewing a case "where reason and humanity plead with almost irresistible force on one side, and a necessary policy, rigorous indeed, but inseparable from slavery, urges on the other." Resolving this clash between law and morality with an oratorical flourish, he found a slave guilty of felonious homicide but not murder:

In the absence, then, of all precedents directly in point or strikingly analogous, the question recurs: if the passions of the slave be excited into unlawful violence by the inhumanity of his master or temporary owner, or one clothed with the master's authority, is it a *conclusion of law* that such passions must spring from diabolical malice? Unless I see my way clear as a sunbeam, I cannot believe that this is the law of a civilized people and of a Christian land. I will not presume an arbitrary and inflexible rule so sanguinary in its character and so repugnant to the spirit of those holy statutes which "rejoice the heart, enlighten the eyes, and are true and righteous altogether."[52]

Availing himself of rhetorical question and simile, Judge Gaston contributed one of the rare appeals to morality ("the law of a civilized people and of a Christian land. . . . those holy statutes") that were substantially developed in antebellum slavery cases. Hardly an accident of composition, the appeal is made within a shower of consciously rhetorical devices.

Because of his notorious religious affiliation, Judge Gaston could be excused for feeling less comfortable than his colleagues in issuing moral appeals. In *State v. Manuel*, for example, he reviewed a court's power to sentence convicted former slaves to forced labor. He introduced his opinion as having been reached through "diligence and care, and if the conclusion to which we have arrived be not right, the error will not have resulted from the omission of our best efforts to form a correct judgment." Then, defending the morality of his opinion, he declared that "the principles of humanity sanctioned and enjoined [in the bill of rights] ought to command the reverence and regulate the conduct of *all* who owe obedience to the Constitution."[53] Though curt, Judge Gaston's moral appeal underscored his belief that all citizens should agree with his definition of humane principles regardless of religious affiliation.

Untouched personally by the religious intolerance faced by William Gaston, Thomas Ruffin freely uttered a full equation of humanity and interest. Writing to his children, Judge Ruffin consistently adopted a moral tone whether in reference to formally religious devotions or personal ethics. To his daughter, Catherine, he stressed traditionally religious devotions: "Neglect not your *private* prayers and read the Scriptures daily. Give your *Heart* to God and he will reward you."[54] To his son, William, he ventured beyond private devotions and issued a question and answer about tensions between the ideal and the real. Addressing conflicts between virtue and vice, the judge asked whether "the former [should] yield, because their dictations are, for the present, the less agreeable and the latter [should] triumph, because they may afford some temporary respite from reproof or pain?" So that his son would form a right mind, the judge then answered: "It is the part of every good man to sustain his uprightness through every adversity, and maintain truth at every peril of present opposition or future pain."[55] To Sterling Ruffin, he further insisted that piety is "the only principle, which, ever the same in itself, gives identity to the person, thro' the longest period of time and under all circumstances, adverse or propitious. The religious man only is he, who, as our Scriptures beautifully express it, 'can *overcome the world.*'"[56] According to Judge Ruffin, virtuous people—sustained by religious practice—must resist the allure of transitory pleasure and, by doing so, become inured to the pain of everyday life. However, progress toward perfection is arduous and uncertain. In his later speechmaking, for example, Judge Ruffin failed to demonstrate resistance to worldly interest in addressing the institution of slavery. Speaking to the State Agricultural Society in 1855, the judge expressed a policy-based perspective on leading issues of the day.[57]

Most of his comments on slavery in his 1855 speech address the South's economic interest, but he also imaginatively sketched the personal and moral attachments between masters and their slaves. "Often born on the same plantation, and bred together," declared Judge Ruffin, "they have a perfect knowledge of each other, and a mutual attachment"—seldom parting company "but from necessity." "The comfort, cheerfulness, and happiness of the slave," he continued, "should be, and generally is, the study of the master; and every Christian master rejoices over the soul of his slave saved, as of a brother." After having established to his own satisfaction the morality of slavery, the judge then attempted to defend the institution on other grounds. He acknowledged that the "condition of a slave denies to him, indeed, opportunities of education sufficient for searching the Scriptures for himself, and working thereout his own conversion." But, he interjected, "God forbid that should be necessary to salvation! It is not; for to the poor and unlettered the Christian graces are promised and given in an especial manner, because they have less pride of intellect, more simplicity of faith, and more singleness of heart." Moreover, the judge claimed, "slavery in America has not only done more for the civilization and enjoyments of the African race than all other causes, but it has brought more of them into the Christian fold than all the missions to that benighted continent from the Advent to this day have."[58]

Restating assertions made by southern partisans, Judge Ruffin attributed civic and religious improvement of the African race to slave laws. He did not deny that property interest was foremost for the master class, but he insisted that the lot of slaves—including their formal exclusion from an education—did not deprive them of happiness here on earth and salvation in the hereafter. His oratorical effort to accommodate political and moral agendas illuminates a humanist's approach to judicial decision making.

Addressing both humanity and interest in the legal treatment of slaves, Judge Ruffin spoke from the bench in the same way that he spoke from the political rostrum. In scrutinizing the line of cases stemming from his opinion in *State v. Mann*, where the court upheld "the full dominion of the owner over the slave," analysts have accounted for much of the judge's technique.[59] What critics have not traced is the inconsistency between the judge's opinion and contemporaneous declamations on morality addressed to his children.

Critical attention to introductory remarks in the published opinion of *State v. Mann* has obscured the judge's appeals to humanist ideals in his rough draft: "This is one of those cases which a Court will always regret being brought into judgment—One in which principles of policy urge the Judge to a decision in discord with the feelings of man."[60] (The second draft conforms more closely to the published opinion.) Having introduced rhetorically the clash between interest and humanity, he cited the lack of precedential and statutory guidance. Then, arguing in his rough draft that intelligent slaves could never be expected to obey their masters through a sense of duty, knowing as they must that slavery itself is unjust, the judge asserted logically that "submission of [the slave's] will can only follow from the power of the Master over the Body—a power which the Slave must be made sensible is not usurped, but conferred at least by the law of man, if not of God." In both his second draft and published opinion, the judge revised his claim to state: "The power of the master must be absolute to render the submission of the slave perfect." Thus, although he exhorted his children not to compromise their moral principles, he did not follow this advice in the superheated atmosphere of reviewing *State v. Mann.* Using oratorical form almost exclusively, he ranked policy over morality as the warrant for his opinion.

Venting personal feelings about the consequences of his ruling, Judge Ruffin explicitly confessed his "sense of the harshness of this proposition." Similar to the language in the published opinion, the judge declared in his second draft: "I feel it as deeply as any man can, and as a principle of moral right every one in his retirement must repudiate it and condemn it." However, he stood far from retirement. Moral right was extraneous. Acceding explictly to "the actual condition of things," he acknowledged the rights only of the white race to peace and prosperity. Moreover, he lashed out at opposing points of view—including the abolitionist perspective—by denigrating "a judiciary tainted with a false and fanatical philanthropy, seeking to redress an acknowledged evil by means still more wicked and appalling than even that evil." This final utterance—nowhere to be found in early drafts of the opinion—was necessary if Judge Ruffin was to hold together a majority. Similarly, he reasserted that "slavery is fundamentally wrong" twenty years later in *State v. Caesar.* Again he insisted that judges must be "cautious against rash expositions, not suited to the actual state of things and not calculated to promote the security of persons, the stability of national institutions and the common welfare."[61]

His resolution of the tension between interest and humanity in subsequent opinions was consistent with Judge Ruffin's choice of premise in *State v. Mann.* Several times, when addressing interracial sexual relations, he granted socially normative power to the "stigma" of color.[62] He regretfully but fully endorsed the policy of barring slave marriages.[63] With similar expressions of regret, he affirmed the servile condition of a slave's offspring: "There is a natural inclination in the bosom of every Judge to favor the side of freedom; . . . and if we were permitted to decide this controversy according to our feelings, we should with promptness and pleasure pronounce our judgment [differently]."[64] Yet, despite his feelings of regret, he later endorsed statutory restraints on emancipation because freed slaves were "burdensome as a charge on the community."[65] Moreover, throughout the 1840s Judge Ruffin expressed comfort with legal prohibitions against trading with slaves in the absence of their masters' consent, and comfort with racially discriminatory legislation in general.[66]

At odds with the moralistic advice to his family to resist worldly interest, the judge's opinions were nonetheless consistent with other expressions of his priorities. He expressed an active consciousness of political affairs in early letters to Bartlett Yancey and James Iredell, Sr.[67] In later correspondence with Welden Edwards, he agonized over developments that might injure the planter class.[68] As sectional strife became more intense, his policy statements became more strident. In his speech to the State Agricultural Society, he asserted the constitutionality of slavery as well as the South's readiness to "cut off a right hand or pluck out a right eye" whenever unconstitutional behavior could be detected. Moreover, he denied any ill effects of the peculiar institution on free labor. He argued that "there is not a country on earth in which honest labor and diligence in business in all classes and conditions, is considered more respectable, or more respected." Furthermore he observed: "We, like every other people, have the idle and the vicious amongst us. But they are chiefly those who have the least connexion with slaves." Having defended southern interests on these grounds, he ultimately lambasted abolitionists as "those who do not know our slavery." "Why should this propitious state of things be changed?" he asked. "Why should any wish a change? Especially, why should persons who have no concern in it, who are not of us, and know not what they do, officiously interfere in a relation so entirely domestic and delicate?" Such meddlers, he felt, should take notice of what happened to the Cherokee and Creek tribes when they captured or purchased slaves.

They immediately developed the arts of civilization and prospered: "Such works hath American slavery wrought upon those tribes!"[69]

During the war, he wrote proudly of supplying the troops with clothing. He condemned "the devils from Yankeedom," urging his son, Thomas, to "[d]efend Richmond to the bitter end, and if the Demons should *burn* it, yet never let them *occupy* it."[70] Insisting elsewhere that he had not originally favored secession, by 1863 he wrote: "I deprecate, if possible to avoid them, all names importing offensively party designations: 'Originial Secessionists,' 'Destructives,' 'Unionists,' or the like." These formal affiliations were ruinous, according to the judge, because they "only serve to heat and to divide—to make heat *without* light. We are all Secessionists *now*."[71]

After the war, in his petition for pardon to Andrew Johnson, Judge Ruffin recited his loyalty to the Constitution and his fervent efforts to conciliate North Carolina with the North. Failing that, he denied becoming a secessionist or traitor, claiming his constitutional right to revolt from an unjust government. On more practical issues, he attested to the personal loss of more than one hundred slaves and $250,000 in investments.[72] Repeatedly decrying the postwar destruction of constitutional liberty despite being pardoned,[73] the judge wrote of his fervent hope that former slaves, as women before them, would be denied the vote in favor of protecting the interests of "the most numerous, intelligent, virtuous, and valuable portion of the population."[74] Thus, his civic concerns overshadowed his moral concerns with but one exception: six months before his death, he attacked the program of the Ku Klux Klan as "a horrible heresy in Religion, morals, and public polity."[75]

Thomas Ruffin was a complicated person and a skillful judge, making it difficult to assess simply his opinions. In general, however, legal issues related to slavery and race fell outside the strict adherence to moral principle this judge preached to his family. Despite his judicial prowess, Thomas Ruffin struggled oratorically to accommodate humanist ideals and southern realities.

Likely to be overlooked in a professional comparison with Judge Ruffin, Richmond M. Pearson was nonetheless a skillful advocate. Unlike Judge Ruffin, though, he expressed no discomfort whatever with the dominion of interest over humanity.[76] Judge Pearson's opinion in *State v. Jowers*, reversing the conviction of a white man who battered a free black for being insolent, is an encomium of southern culture that rests on oratorical device rather than legal logic.[77] The judge bemoaned the existence of free blacks and held that they could be punished for their insolence—as Jowers had done—under common-law principles. The "perfection of reason" he saw in the common law rested on its flexibility: "[I]ts principles expand so as to accommodate it to any new exigence or condition of society, like the bark of a tree, which opens and enlarges itself, according to the growth thereof, always maintaining its own uniformity and consistency." The cultivated grace of this woody simile masks raw speculation on the judge's part about the legal "uniformity and consistency" with which slaves were treated.

Off the bench, Judge Pearson also crafted his discourse to address practical needs with scant regard for ideals. Pardoned in 1865, he had petitioned Andrew Johnson on the same grounds as Judge Ruffin.[78] Three years later, he appealed to conservative friends to exploit reconstructed politics to their advantage. "[C]oncede to the freedmen political equality," he urged because resistance "makes them 'pull together.'" Instead, he advised, "remove the pressure and their vote will be neutralized." Indeed, unless he was prone to "mistake the power and effect of the superiority of the white man, aided as he is by education, and the possession of the wealth of the country, in a few years they will vote as before 1835."[79] This discourse reflects speculation as raw as the judge's views on the common law. Playing the role of seer as well as judge, Richmond M. Pearson crafted a stylish appeal founded on the postwar interest of his fellow planters.

Judicial advocacy of slavery in North Carolina illustrates that humanist ideals were endorsed inconsistently and unevenly. The judges who developed arguments for the conservation of property were unlikely to endorse as frequently or fully the conservation of life—leaving it to exceptional judges such as Thomas Ruffin to make skillful accommodations of the peculiar institution and the humanist tradition. The judicial advocacy of slavery was robust but the equation of humanity and interest was frail.

In Tennessee, with practical needs similar to those in Virginia and North Carolina, the judges also struggled to compose a link between humanity and interest. John Catron provided a notable exception in *Loftin v. Espy*. Reviewing a case in which a master's unpaid debts and shady deals had led to a sheriff's sale of a family slave (as distinct from a field hand), Judge Catron asserted his state's policy "to encourage and promote" a special bond between master and slave. Without this encouragement, he predicted, "they will live enemies, and in a scene of domestic strife, the slave acting from fear for good, and through revenge for evil; the master protecting himself as well as he may by violence, but too often brutal." For this judge, imbedded within state policy was a moral concern for the humane treatment of slaves:

> Nothing can be much more abhorrent to these poor people, or to the feelings of every benevolent individual, than to see a large family of slaves sold at sheriff's sale; the infant, children, father and mother to different bidders. To treat them as other domestic animals would be to declare, that, as a people, we had, in reference to this class, sunk all feelings of humanity, and that the slave is not elevated in his sensibilities over the lower classes of animals, which are allowed to have none worthy of the protection of man. As a fact, and as a theory, this is untrue. . . . the mutual feelings of dependence, affection and humanity existing between master and slave have no cash price and cannot be compensated in money.[80]

His depiction of the moral ties between classes in plantation society is vivid enough to draw a casual reader's attention away from the overall argument the judge was crafting. In theory, he agreed that slaves should be treated humanely and their attachment to masters should not be destroyed at any price. But, he further argued as a matter of fact, the mutual interests of master and state already ensured this treatment. In other words, the policy sustaining his legal interpretation was eminently moral.

In other texts Judge Catron did not subjugate humanity to interest. He ignored moral concerns entirely. His opinion in *Fisher's Negroes v. Dabbs*, for example, illustrates an overriding concern with policy when reviewing the testamentary manumission of slaves. He stated that, as a matter of "public policy" not to be disturbed by a testator, "free negroes are a very dangerous and most objectionable population where slaves are numerous; therefore no slave can be safely freed but with the assent of the government where the manumission takes place." Expanding his focus to sectional policy, he then declared that each state must consider the "injustice of forcing our freed negroes on our sister states without their consent, when we are wholly unwilling to be afflicted with them ourselves." This interstate dumping of former slaves would be unjust and cruel, not to the former slaves but to neighboring states. "To treat our neighbors unjustly and cruelly, and thereby make them our enemies, is bad policy and contrary to our interest."

With equal confidence he announced that both "society" and "the negro" suffers by manumission. In the North, for example, "people are less accustomed to the squalid and disgusting wretchedness of the negro, have less sympathy for him, earn their means of subsistence with their own hands, and are more economical in parting with them than him for whom the slave labors." Exiled to the North, former slaves endured the same social degradation that was characteristic of their lot in the Old South. For the former slave, "his fancied freedom is a delusion."[81] Unlike lesser colleagues on the bench, Judge Catron addressed policy considerations incrementally—exploring the full range of local, sectional, national, and international interests. Concluding that African colonization was the only method whereby emancipation could be permitted in Tennessee, the judge laid a political foundation for his later elevation to the United States Supreme Court and his notable concurrence in the *Dred Scott* case.

Judge Catron's incremental strategy did not arise in a vacuum. Over the years he consistently uttered appeals to interest on various levels. In 1820 he had joined several other concerned citizens in seeking the release of John Fry, a free black convicted of horse stealing in Davidson County, because the county could not afford his imprisonment.[82] As a Jacksonian, Judge Catron had also stressed economic interest in opposing the charter of the Bank of the United States.[83] As a faithful unionist, he emphasized the need for domestic tranquility in correspondence during the nullification crisis.[84] Confident about his grasp of both law and policy, Judge Catron was predictably reluctant to admit in *Dred Scott* that "he had been all the while acting in mistake, and as an usurper."[85]

Colleagues of Judge Catron reluctantly addressed policy and morality in their opinions. Nathan Green singularly and baldly declared in *State v. Claiborne* that free negroes made up "an inferior caste in society, with whom public opinion has never permitted the white population to associate on terms of equality, and in relation to whom the laws have never allowed the enjoyment of equal rights."[86] Political advancement of himself and his son was a more pressing concern.[87]

Appeals to morality were rare enough to suggest that they were considered to be unworthy or irrelevant. Only in *Werley v. State* did Archibald W. O. Totten condemn slave abuse in a moral tenor: "We utterly repudiate the idea of any such power and dominion of the master over the slave. . . . Such doctrine would violate the moral sense and humanity of the present age."[88]

Jacob Peck's earlier opinion in *Fields v. State* was more striking but equally isolated. Judge Peck rejected on moral grounds the argument that, since slavery was unknown in the common law, manslaughter could not be charged when the victim was a slave. "Law, reason, christianity and common humanity" pointed to a different conclusion. More specifically, he questioned the claim that civilized, religious Americans could kill slaves with impunity because this was the rule in the slaves' homeland. "I have been taught that christianity is part of the law of the land. The four gospels upon the clerk's table admonish me it is so every time they are used in administering oaths," the judge fumed. Simply because southrons had property rights in "pagans or savages," pious and civilized gentlemen must not "retire more into the dark, and become in government partly christian and partly pagan."[89] For this judge, religious principles were interwoven with legal ordinances in all but the unenlightened nations. Judge Peck's discourse is striking because he did not spice his private papers with similar assertions and because none of his colleagues felt as free to cite scripture as readily as their law books. Moreover, in developing a free state of Frankland in East Tennessee, the judge later claimed equal benefits of interest and humanity for a fellow investor in the project—"a business which may result in profit to himself and humanity to others."[90]

William B. Reese, a contemporary of Judge Peck, was nicknamed "Old Strictissimus" because of his avowed program of applying the law strictly without regard to any hardships created as a result.[91] True to his sobriquet in *Henderson v. Vaulx*, the judge observed curtly that "humane philosophy" had been applied only recently in Tennessee to adjudicating "the peculiar nature of slave property, and of the relation between master and slave."[92] Three years later in *Elijah v. State*, he equated appeals to humanity and appeals to interest in reviewing the conviction of a slave for assault: "On the grounds of public policy, of common humanity, of absolute necessity, the master must be held to be competent as a witness for or against the slave."[93] Strict or not, with these words Judge Reese contributed to the submersion of humane concerns within state interest that Judge Catron had expressed in 1833.

Like their brethren in Tennessee, Arkansas judges confined their remarks about the humane treatment of slaves to their legal opinions. Townshend Dickinson led the way in *Pyeatt v. Spencer* when reviewing a verdict on the insanity (and unmarketable condition) of a slave named Sophia. Among other episodes of plantation discipline by her new master, she had been whipped with a fifteen-inch buckskin lash, and had salt applied to her wounds, after being "*stripped,* and *staked down* on the ground; her feet and hands extended, and fastened to stakes; and her face downwards." She then exhibited distracted behaviors and ran away repeatedly. Judge Dickinson refused to conclude that Sophia's conduct provided grounds for avoiding her sale to her abusive master. "It is with pain and sensibility," he explained, "that the court feels itself constrained to remark that whatever seeming wildness and aberration of mind might be perceived in the slave, it is but reasonable to suppose, was caused by grief and the excessive cruelty of her owner."[94] An accomplished state legislator, Judge Dickinson ignored in this one instance the countervailing policies of contractual freedom, restraint of trade, and the like, to emphasize personally his abhorrence of slave abuse.[95]

Again in an isolated instance, Thomas Johnson extended Judge Dickinson's reasoning to include abuse by the state. Vigorously denying the constitutionality of punishing slaves more severely than free whites for the same crimes, the judge asserted in *Charles v. State* that the provision for equal punishment "was doubtless inserted in the constitution from a feeling of humanity towards the unfortunate African race, and in order to secure them against that barbarous treatment and excessive cruelty which was practiced upon them in the earlier period of our colonial history."[96] Judge Johnson was scarcely apolitical—having enjoyed family influence "to promote his advancement"—and his address to humane principles stands alone among his relevant opinions.[97]

Like Judges Dickinson and Johnson, Edward Cross did not frequently attempt to express a humanist perspective. He contributed lengthy service as a Presbyterian church elder and delegate to church synods, but moral concerns did not dominate his decision making about slavery.[98] Rather, his concerns as a bank officer and railroad president prompted him to defend economic interest. Affirming the constitutionality of a state law requiring free negroes to post a bond if they wished to remain in Arkansas, he declared in *Pendleton v. State* that the "constitution was the work of the white race; the government, for which it provides and of which it is the fundamental law, is in their hands and under their control." Moreover, he declared that white legislators "could not have intended to place a different race of people in all things upon terms of equality with themselves." Only incidentally, the judge added, "protection of their persons and the right to property is provided for to a humane and just degree."[99] Echoing John Catron's argument, Judge Cross merged concern about the humane treatment of African Americans with state interest.

In Arkansas as elsewhere in the Upper South, judges grudgingly addressed matters of morality and policy when reviewing cases involving slavery and race. Professional duty discouraged the judges from reviewing anything other than matters of law and fact. When exceptional reviews were made, the issues of humanity and interest were frequently addressed together—denying to auditors of weak or weakening partisan views the chance to consider policy apart from morality. Moreover, several judges'

strategy of locating humane concern within state interest was well designed to bolster partisanship.

The judges' invention of narratives as premises and evidence was preliminary to the more difficult task of equating humanity and interest. The
challenges of composing blended appeals to morality and civics—applying
humanist ideals to the pragmatics of slavery—resulted in varying levels of
individual success. As members of a professional culture, however, judges
of the Upper South articulated an innovative argument that state interest
was inherently humane, that policy was innately moral. In theoretical
terms, this judicial discourse illustrates the argumentative process of association, or bringing separate elements together in order to evaluate
them positively by means of one another. But, in theory at least, the advocate using an association of ideas must recognize and account for the
equal and disunifying force of dissociation. "The two techniques are complementary and are always at work at the same time."[100] Opinions in which
one type of appeal was favored to the exclusion of the other illuminate the
judicial struggle to advocate slavery while revering the humanist tradition.

In isolation, each type appeal has the gaunt look of a reluctant foot
soldier pressed into service more often than tactically desirable. Acclaiming the art of oratory if not always mastering it, the judges recognized
this argumentative flaw and mated the appeals to policy and morality in
order to achieve cogency. Thus, the judges never planned to force a
choice between interest and humanity. In the classical age, under the
auspices of civic humanism, moral virtues like prudence were applied oratorically to political intiatives. The judges composed artifacts of their
own reverence for humanism when using moral and political appeals to
discharge their civic duty.

Many judges were active in the political arena. As political agents, they
clearly relished opportunities to address domestic peace and prosperity.
But their careers off the bench do not account for their remarkable
appeals to interest. As professional judges, they looked first for other
premises to justify their opinions. However, even when statutory or precedential authority was available for citation, the judges appealed to socio-

political interest. They could reasonably be expected to favor this appeal because, from the humanist perspective, interest was compatible with the dictates of humanity. Particularly in the Upper South, the judges expressed or implied sensitivity to the effects of abolitionist crusades on citizens of the border states. For these audiences, the link between policy and morality was theoretically comforting. More important for the judges, to partisans in the Upper South the equation of humanity and interest was likely to be persuasive.

Chapter Five

EQUATIONS OF HUMANITY
AND INTEREST
IN THE DEEP SOUTH

In comparison with colleagues in the Upper South, judges of South Carolina, Georgia, Alabama, Mississippi, Florida, and Louisiana did not articulate as uniformly their allegiance to a professional culture. Their intuitive base was roughly identical, but fractured appeals to morality and civics in judicial advocacy of the Deep South reveal a greater struggle to accommodate humanism and slavery. Only in Georgia and Alabama did blended appeals to humanity and interest thrive. Elsewhere, appeals to policy tend to dominate the oratorical passages in law reports. In the language of the judges, conserving the property rights of planters was more important than conserving the life of this or that slave.

An early biographer claimed that South Carolina's William Harper renounced his father's Methodism and antislavery views.[1] Judge Harper's opinion in *Tidyman v. Rose*, at least, contains language discounting a link between morality and the laws of slavery. "It is little that legal decisions can do to enforce humanity," he reflected; "this must depend on public opinion."[2] But three years later, in *Fable v. Brown*, he mused that "the true state of the slave must be ascertained by reference to the disabilities of an alien enemy, in which light the heathen were anciently regarded; though certainly modern humanity, the progress of opinion, and positive legislation, have greatly modified their condition."[3] For this judge, moral improvement had to be measured along with political change if the peculiar institution was to be truly appreciated. Unlike his father, Judge Harper faced no moral dilemma in endorsing the political process and he articulated his perspective in speechmaking during the nullification crisis.[4]

In later speechmaking, he summarized leading issues in the minds of his judicial colleagues. His summary offers an invaluable guide to a perspective that was expressed less regularly and fully by other members of the state's judiciary. Slavery, he asserted, was forever woven into "all the habits and relations of society" and determined for the Deep South "the character of our people and our government." Southrons would never willingly abandon the institution because it reflected "our most essential interests—our humanity and consideration for the slaves themselves." Slavery provided "a bond of common interest, for maintaining the security of property and the peace and order of society," the judge observed, but slaveowners must not forget the "advantage in the practice of humanity."[5] The twin deals of conserving property and life are prominent among the judge's assertions. Two years later, in an 1837 lecture, he reasserted his position axiomatically: "Slavery anticipates the benefits of civilization, and retards the evils of civilization."[6] From a humanist perspective, nothing could be more civic-minded than this joint promotion of property rights and moral righteousness.

Summarizing a perspective that prior colleagues had developed and later colleagues would endorse, Judge Harper insisted that civilization itself was at stake in the struggle over slavery. His concerns were presaged by Elihu H. Bay, Henry W. DeSaussure, Charles J. Colcock, Abraham Nott, and to a lesser extent, David Johnson.

According to a colleague, Judge Bay was descended from Presbyterian ministers and was himself an "orthodox Christian . . . profoundly versed in the Bible."[7] Perhaps encouraged by the judge's background, a venireman once wrote to him requesting exemption from jury duty on religious grounds.[8] And indeed the judge tried to accommodate both morality and policy. In *Gist v. Cole*, addressing the relative power of patrols—the night watch on horseback for which masters were responsible—Judge Bay declared the patrol law to be "one of the safeguards of the people of South Carolina, for the protection of their dwellings and habitations, and for the prevention of the unlawful assembling of a particular class of our population, and as a security against insurrection." Slave rebellion in particular "never can or ought to be lost sight of in the southern States."[9] Prompted in 1820 by a fear of slave revolts that was soon to grow more intense, the judge acknowleged the preeminent value of conserving the peace.

A decade later, in *Kinloch v. Harvey*, he acknowledged that slaves were entitled to legal protection under "the rights of humanity, and the principles of benevolence and natural justice"—so long as these rights were not interpreted as "absolute." Indeed, the judge observed, "the humanity and kindness of his master" combined with "the interest he has in the preservation of his health and bodily labor" is the slave's best hope of "security and happiness."[10] Thus, in addition to distinguishing the type and scope of "security and happiness" to be pursued by slaves and masters in the South, Judge Bay eventually blended appeals to humanity and interest. His attention to both appeals was noteworthy. Ten years had gone by since *Gist v. Cole*, and sectional tensions certainly had not subsided, but the judge succeeded in expressing a humanist perspective.

Like Judge Bay, Henry W. DeSaussure was "devoutly religious."[11] Outspoken in political affairs, Judge DeSaussure oratorically endorsed the South's interest in protecting slaves from abuse while providing them with adequate food and clothing.[12] Yet he denied them education because "knowledge is power."[13] Moreover, appeals to humanity had little place in the judge's conception of legal process. In *Frazier v. Ex'rs of Frazier*, for example, he reviewed a case of emancipation using politically ominous tones. "[N]either the State nor its authorities, nor any of its citizens," he insisted, "would ever permit the interference of that government with that subject, on which the government of the United States has no right to intermeddle." Furthermore, he warned, if the federal government "made any attempts directly or indirectly, a disruption of the bonds which bind and unite the States, would necessarily take place." For this judge, emancipation was a "noli me tangere subject. . . . Any intermeddling by the government would be the immediate death of the Union (however valued and cherished on other grounds) by the general consent of the citizens."[14] There was no moralizing from the bench in his opinion. Pragmatically envisioning "the immediate death of the Union" if states rights were invaded, Judge DeSaussure was motivated to address only the civic half of the humanist vision.

Though nurtured in formally religious climates, Judges Colcock and Nott avoided appeals to morality in their opinions.[15] Rather, they stated on grounds of policy that runaway slaves were a menace that justified fear about public safety. Judge Colcock opined in *White v. Helmes* that the degraded condition of slaves justified depriving them of a wide range of political favors.[16] "I do not know," remarked Judge Nott in *Richardson v. Dukes*, "but instances might occur where runaway negroes may become so dangerous that every person in the community might be considered as acting on the defensive against them."[17] Clearly for these judges, conserving white security was a greater good than conserving black life.

Judge Johnson, the son of a Presbyterian minister, was politically unpredictable.[18] Elected governor in 1846, he had earlier opposed nullification but later vigorously attacked abolition.[19] Judicially unpredictable as well, he articulated a rare appeal to both humanity and interest in reviewing *Gordon v. Blackman*. This was a case of testamentary manumission, "another of those cases, multiplying of late with a fearful rapidity." The judge first complained that legacies of freedom were spawned by "the superstitious weakness of dying men, proceeding from an astonishing ignorance of the solid moral and scriptural foundations upon which the institution of slavery rests." Moreover, testamentary manumission contradicted "the indubitable and declared policy of the State" and reflected "a total inattention to the shock which [former slaves'] conduct is calculated to give to the whole frame of our social policy."[20] In addition to support it derived from "social policy," the institution of slavery rested securely on "moral and scriptural foundations" for Judge Johnson. For him, the humanist perspective was both ideally attractive and legally persuasive.

Presaged in the opinions, speeches, and letters of colleagues, Judge Harper's focus on the politics of slavery underwent modification in the opinions of John B. O'Neall and elaboration in the extrajudicial discourse of Andrew P. Butler. Along with several contemporaries, Judges O'Neall and Butler relied almost exclusively on appeals to policy.

Judge O'Neall made noteworthy contributions to the temperance movement, Bible societies, and other programs of moral improvement. However, his 1848 *Digest* of laws affecting South Carolina's people of color merits special attention as a guide to the argumentative limits of interest in his opinions on slavery. His legal digest did not please "prejudices of the day," he recalled, saddling him with "the unpopularity of doing right."[21] In the same spirit, he did not hesitate to dissent in *Ex Parte Boylston* from an otherwise unanimous finding of criminal behavior in slaves' insolence. Complaining that "insolence is but another term for sauciness," he asked rhetorically: "[W]ho has ever dreamed that an open-mouthed, saucy negro, is the deep intriguer calculated to raise, or attempt to raise, an insurrection?" Moreover, fearing too much power in the hands of those who dispensed local justice, he warned: "Clothe them with the power to try slaves for insolence, and the result will be that passion, prejudice, and ignorance will crowd abuses on this inferior jurisdiction to an extent not to be tolerated by slave owners."[22] These remarks were crafted to alert slaveowners to the threat posed by trial judges rather than insolent slaves. By granting unlimited power to these judges in punishing deviant slaves, slaveowners would surely suffer the destruction of their property interests. When deviant slaves were legally executed, both property and lives were lost. Thus, in a curious twist of standard argumentation, the judge applied a humanist perspective to negate criminal law.

Judge O'Neall expressed his humanist dedication to the conservation of a master class early in his career on the bench. In *State v. Hayes*, for example, he declared that "distinctions between our white and colored population are founded upon policy; and although it is a rigorous, it is at the same time, a wise, and a necessary policy." He felt "that the negro and his descendants should never, in any shape, be put upon an equality with the white man."[23]

The judge never retreated from his dedication to this policy—later treating mastery over slaves in *Tennent v. Dendy* as analogous to the government of citizens. He asserted that, "consistent with good policy," slaves had surrendered their natural right of self-protection by becoming slaves and ceded this right to the master. He elaborated further that the "slave ought to be fully aware that his master is to him what the best administered government is to the good citizen, a perfect security from injury."[24] Masters deserved this power, according to the judge's opinion in *Carmille v. Carmille's Adm'r*, because "[k]indness to slaves . . . is the true policy of slave owners, and its spirit should go (as it generally has) into the making of law, and ought to be a ruling principle of its construction."[25] Indeed, as the judge opined in *Bowers v. Newman*, the subservient relationship of slave to master is so complete that, even when a slave acquires property, the acquisition benefits the master: "For if it either feeds or clothes [the slave], it so far relieves the master from expense on his account."[26]

The property interest of the master, not state interest and certainly not the fuzzy notion of humanity, dominated Judge O'Neall's thinking on the laws of slavery. This definition of interest antagonized his contemporaries and colleagues, especially when it sustained opinions favoring emancipation. Dissenting in *Vinyard v. Passalaigue*, Judge O'Neall asked rhetorically: "What is there in the policy of the law of South Carolina to forbid emancipation, by an owner, of a faithful, honest, good slave? Have we anything to fear from such a liberal and humane course?" In answer, he stressed his long-standing policy: "I should be sorry to believe that our domestic institution of slavery required any such restriction upon the rights of owners. Indeed, when anything is pushed to extremes, injury is done by it."[27] The judge's stylistic flourishes can be explained by the traditional latitude given to dissenting opinions, but the content of his ideas merits close attention for its modification of Judge Harper's perspective. The interest he was addressing had been narrowed to that of individual masters.

Judge Butler may or may not have been "intimately acquainted with Bible truths," but he routinely invoked God and the scriptures in his political speechmaking.[28] With this device and others he constructed elaborate arguments on behalf of slavery, defending the position Judge Harper had announced earlier. In 1840, in the House of Representatives, Judge Butler attacked the "barefaced and reckless falsehoods" of abolition petitions. Setting the fully humanist tenor of his remarks, he described a battle "for the security of our firesides, and the sanctity of our domestic regulations." First, though, he claimed "that slavery was coeval almost with the existence of the human race; that it was fully recognised under the Old and New Testament dispensations; and that to us it is a political blessing, instead of an evil."[29] By 1850, he was decrying in the Senate various attempts at political compromise by the South and predicting a wreck for the ship of state.[30] That same year, at the Convention of the Southern Rights Associations, he reported simply that "slave and nonslaveholding states cannot long remain together. . . . That is as certain as if it were written on the wall."[31] Later, as his prediction came closer to being fulfilled, his oratory became even more impassioned.

Addressing the Kansas-Nebraska Act, he described a divine plan in which "[i]nequality pervades the creation of this universe." Racial discrimination "seems to characterize the administration of the Providence of God." Accordingly, the judge claimed that "Abolitionists cannot make those equal whom God has made unequal in human estimation."[32] As a "ripe orator, who is proud of the reputation of his state," rather than a "vapid rhetorician," he later opposed a repeal of the Fugitive Slave Law.[33] This "ripe orator" spiced the national debate over slavery with his elaboration of Judge Harper's position.

Several colleagues of Judges O'Neall and Butler seconded their advocacy of slavery.[34] But the speaking and writing of Josiah J. Evans, David J. Wardlaw, Edward Frost, and John S. Richardson lack frequent appeals to religion or morality.

Joining his fellow senator, Andrew P. Butler, Judge Evans spoke against the Massachusetts Resolutions of 1856. His congressional speechmaking asserted the South's contentedness with "institutions as they are; . . . with that form of civilization which exists among them." Furthermore, he defended the social and political status quo by reciting the commonplace arguments that slaves were better off in the South than in their homelands—indeed, better off than in the "crime and pauperism" that greeted runaway slaves in the North. Like Judge Butler, he referred obliquely to the professional norms restricting his previous entry into public debate; yet he denied present fears that his stance on slavery would subject him to condemnation in "some future fourth of July speech, or some college oration."[35] Consistent with a humanist perspective on civic activism, Judge Evans expressed concern about his own treatment at the hands of future orators.

Judge Wardlaw was a codrafter of his state's Black Code and a honored guest at the capture of Fort Sumter.[36] In his judicial role he stressed policy considerations exclusively when writing the opinion in *Ex Parte Boylston* that drew Judge O'Neall's wrath. "The various Negro acts," he found, "contemplate throughout the subordination of the servile class to every free white person, and enforce the stern policy which the relation of master and slave necessarily requires."[37] Like it or not, Judge Wardlaw observed, necessity dictated a harsh legal treatment of slaves.[38]

Necessity also played a major role in one of those rare instances when the law favored slaves over their master. In *State v. Bowen*, drawing on his experience as attorney general, Judge Frost dismissed an appeal from a criminal conviction for denying slaves adequate food and clothing. Hardly magnanimous in expressing his opinion, the judge cited "public sentiment"—not personal feeling—and identified as grounds the protection of "property from the depradations of famishing slaves" rather than the welfare of the slaves themselves.[39]

Equally pointed was Judge Richardson's opinion in *Vinyard v. Passalaigue*. Off the bench, the judge had spoken vigorously against nullification and disunion.[40] But he had few qualms about asserting a "moral justification" of state interest in slavery while executing his judicial duties. "Our slave code," he allowed, "is consistent and essentially suited to the natural endowments of the white and black man; and in no way is it regardless of just humanity to slaves."[41] His opinion in *State v. Chandler*, addressing an overseer's trading with slaves, was less embrasive of the humanist tradition. He rejected commerce between overseers and slaves on the grounds of "policy and prudence, not to say the necessity of avoiding so great a temptation to abuse the trust." The overseer in question had committed "a foul abuse," but the stench arose from a political sin rather than a moral transgression.[42]

Judicial idiosyncrasies make it barely passable to say that William Harper spoke for his colleagues on slavery. Nonetheless, he illustrated a typical preference for appeals to policy. His avoidance of moral defenses and resignation to necessity generally reflected the minds of his colleagues.

Playing the role of Judge Harper's counterpart in Georgia, Joseph H. Lumpkin addressed moral norms as synonymous with state interest. According to an early biographer, Judge Lumpkin was a "religious man" who had "abandoned politics."[43] Various reflections he penned in 1827 sustain this impression. Meditating on a sabbath morning, he questioned whether he had accepted his salvation: "Do I rejoice with joy unspeakable of the thought that my sins were nailed to the Cross on Calvary and my pardon purchased there? Do I indeed love the Lord for what he has done for me?" And later in the same document he mused: "A man's private life is the best commentary on his public acts."[44] But private and public concerns tended to merge in Judge Lumpkin's mind—from national campaigns on behalf of temperance and biblical study, to a final remedy for "the errors & abominations of Romanism."[45]

As early as 1837, he endorsed the training of "men thoroughly disciplined, to vindicate our peculiar institutions in our State, and Federal councils, and ecclesiastical judicatories." Fearing a world in which church was separated from state "by our misguided assailants, which we deprecate as the greatest of all evils," the judge thought that properly trained advocates of the status quo "would be able to appeal successfully to the judgment of mankind, as well as the searcher of hearts, to show that we were blameless."[46] Advocating with fully humanist fervor the "peculiar institution" was thus reasonable to the judge. In this regard, he preferred his state to be found blameless in the court of public opinion as well as in private meditation.

Judge Lumpkin pursued the goals of popular and moral acceptability in reviewing *Vance v. Crawford*, a case of testamentary manumission. Endorsing the emancipation of slaves only if they were colonized in Africa, he expressed deep concern over the rapid increase in the American slave population since 1790: "It has grown from a molehill to a mountain." To justify his concern, the judge invoked both human and divine authority. "Neither humanity, nor religion, nor common justice," he declared, "requires of us to sanction or favor domestic emancipation; to give our slaves their liberty at the risk of losing our own." He denied that slaves, if freed, were capable of sharing in government with whites. As authority, the judge invoked his personal vision of righteous world order: "To set up a model empire for the world, God in His wisdom planted on this virgin soil, the best blood of the human family. To allow it to be contaminated, is to be recreant to the weighty and solemn trust committed to our hands."[47]

While judges in other jurisdictions were struggling to articulate a blended perspective on humanity and interest, Judge Lumpkin proclaimed explicitly that God had created American government as a model of moral politics. From this perspective, tampering with absolute dominion over the slaves amounted to frustrating a divine plan. As his prior meditations reveal, he had been reflecting on the marriage of policy and morality for many years: "The condition of the human race is most prosperous and happy when governed by absolute power under the guidance of wisdom and virtue."[48]

Eugenius A. Nisbet agreed wholeheartedly with Judge Lumpkin. Judge Nisbet was characterized by an early biographer as a model of "the principles of the Christian religion."[49] So too he rejected politics (but held elected office for several years thereafter): "I am disgusted with the Georgia Legislature. No honesty, or *tallent* can do anything here, against the corruption, ignorance & prejudice of the majority."[50] In fact, he once wrote to Judge Lumpkin that he was "no politician," and merely "a lover of my country."[51] Like Judge Lumpkin, he endorsed "the Bible, the Catechism, the Sunday School Tract, the Temperance document, and the Religious biography." Commending to his wife the "wise & merciful" deity, he insisted that "Christianity comes with her commission from God, and adding human means to divine power, asserts her empire over the heart and will. All human knowledge needs her guiding power, else it but bewilders and misleads."[52] To apply political or legal knowledge without recourse to first principles would be fruitless.

Appreciating Judge Nisbet's incorporation of moral and religious principles into the life of the state makes it possible to decipher his opinion in *Spalding v. Grigg.* Reviewing a case of testamentary manumission, the judge declared that "the policy of Georgia—a policy which pervades all her legislation, and of which she has a right to be proud, [is] to encourage the humane treatment of the slave."[53] An experienced politician, he was conversant with the issues of peace and prosperity. In 1840, endorsing Harrison for president at the expense of Van Buren, he cosigned with his fellow congressional representatives a circular stating: "The truth is, fellow citizens, looking abroad upon the vast interests involved in this great question, we believe that there is no adequate protection to slave rights, but in a stern, uncompromising maintainance of the limitations of the constitution."[54] He did not accept, though, that favoring the state's social, economic, and political interests taints a person's moral stature. Writing from Congress to his wife one year later, he reported a heated exchange with an advocate of higher tariffs. His oratorical victory was sweet, he said, but "more gratifying than any thing else" the victory was won "without any injury to my Christian character."[55]

In this judge's opinions there was no impassable barrier between policy and morality. For instance, in reviewing *Macon & Western R.R. Co. v. Holt*, he comfortably opined that the patrol laws "however necessarily stringent, operate humanely and beneficially for the slave, as well as the master, and the whole body of the community."[56] Criminal laws, as he declared in *Johnson v. State*, have the laudable goal "to suppress the demoralizing and impolitic practice of gambling with slaves or free persons of color."[57] The judge's review of these laws describes a zone in which he felt morally comfortable with decisions based on policy.

Indebted to Judge Nisbet in more ways than one, Hiram Warner easily commingled sociopolitical interest with morality. He once exhorted an academic community: "Having faithfully performed all your moral and social duties, to God and your fellowmen, contributed to the improvement and elevation of your race, morally, socially, and politically . . . then you will have *successfully* fought the great battle of life."[58] Borrowing, perhaps, from the combative atmosphere of the courtroom, he identified dual paths to victory in the execution of "moral and social duties." Earlier, he had harangued Congress that excluding slavery from the territories would violate that "American liberty; . . . which protects the citizen in the enjoyment of all his civil and religious rights." He declared that the members of Congress knew full well "the practical effect of the proposed restriction," and that it should be opposed pragmatically as well as in principle. Indeed, he insisted on the utter impossibility of the slaveholding states' giving up their rights "as coequal States": "There is a great, overruling, practical necessity which would prevent it. They ought not to submit to it upon *principle* if they could, and could not if they would."[59] Because it was spoken in his role as a political representative, Judge Warner's discourse bears the stigma of insincerity or bombast. And the same may be claimed of his academic speech. However, as a guide to personal consistency if not sincerity, both forms of address may be compared with his judicial discourse.

In *Cooper v. Mayor of Savannah*, Judge Warner merged political and moral norms. He felt strongly enough about "liberty" to locate it among the "personal rights" of free persons of color, though he agreed that such persons lacked all "political rights" in Georgia.[60] For slaves, he insisted on a marriage of political and moral principles in determining proper treatment. Reviewing *Hicks v. Moore*, a case in which the slave property of a judgment debtor was sold at a sheriff's auction, the judge concluded: "On the score of humanity, the Sheriff is bound, at his peril, to treat all slaves, while in his custody under levy, with humanity." Although begging the question by simply repeating his assertion about "humanity,"[61] the judge did identify a moral standard by which the actions of civil servants might be evaluated.

Like their counterparts in Georgia, Alabama's judges located humanity within the range of actions motivated by interest.[62] Henry W. Collier, for instance, was eulogized for a "moral and religious character" that was consistent with his speech at a Methodist Sunday School meeting in which he addressed "truth for the love of it."[63] Moreover, in a gubernatorial address, he declared that "it can be no violation of policy to conform municipal law to good morals."[64] Violating judicial decorum in reviewing *Sorrelle v. Craig*, the future governor of Alabama also used oratorical form to endorse the virtuous life: "Vice is certainly social, and my observation upon human character, persuades me, that a frequent indulgence in any of the grosser offences against morality and religion, weakens the force of moral principle." Warming to his task, Judge Collier continued his moral lesson by observing that each surrender to vice "renders less sensitive the conscience, and predisposes to a disregard of truth, not only where there is a temptation to speak falsely, but from the depravity of the heart itself."[65] On and off the bench, this judge expressed his unqualified love of "truth." Though sensitive to "moral principle" and "the depravity of the heart," he felt no pangs of conscience when subjugating humanity to interest in other opinions.

Judge Collier never personally endorsed secession but, as governor, he reluctantly announced the decision by his constituents—based on "a dissolution of the partnership as a lesser evil than degradation"—not to "merge our self-respect in the degree to perpetuate this hitherto glorious Confederacy."[66] His deference to the good of the polity extended to his review of *State v. McDonald*. "[I]ntegrity of motive," he declared, was no defense against inciting slaves to revolt by speaking openly of emancipation. He found obnoxious any "free person, whether white or colored, who seeks to sow in the bosom of our slaves, the seeds of dissaffection, and urges them to resist by force, the authority of their legitimate masters." Even those "professing to be prompted by the pure spirit of christianity," must risk criminal prosecution if they "proclaim to our slaves the doctrine of universal emancipation, and denounce slavery as incompatible with the sublime and elevated morality of revelation."[67] By negation, the judge left open the possibility that slavery did not violate the "pure spirit of christianity" or "the sublime and elevated morality of revelation." But by referring to "our slaves," he also rhetorically identified with slaveowners.

One year later, in *Trotter v. Blocker*, he again denigrated emancipators by announcing the salutary policy that opposed their efforts. "As a measure of expediency," he announced, "the State owes it to its citizens at large, to protect their interests, by throwing suitable guards around the institution of slavery." Decrying the "consequences disastrous to the quiet of the country" that would accompany emancipation, he speculated further that "the demoralizing tendency of such a policy would be such as should induce every christian and philanthropist to deprecate its toleration."[68] The judge magnified the strength of his argument by identifying "christian" priorities with civic "interests." As an index of his versatility in *Turnipseed v. State,* the same merger of values sustained his denunciation of conduct that violated a statute barring the cruel and unusual punishment of slaves—"even without bodily torture, in a manner offensive to modesty, decency, and the recognized proprieties of social life."[69] Slavery might be virtuous, in civic terms, but slave abuse was clearly a vice on the scale of secular values.

In *Brandon v. Planters' & Merchants' Bank,* Reuben Saffold sustained the example set by Judge Collier. Balancing "the peculiar policy of this government" with "the principles of humanity to slaves," Judge Saffold concluded that masters may seize things of value found by their slaves as long as the slaves were protected "from the violence and depredations of persons who might discover them in possession of articles which the master had not actually seized."[70] If a master wished to enjoy the benefits granted to him by public policy, he must own up to his corresponding moral duty.

Consistent with Judge Saffold's technique, John J. Ormond attempted a humanist juggling of concerns over humanity and interest when he reviewed *Black & Manning v. Oliver*—a case in which a jury voided the sale of a slave because the seller had originally bought her on the condition he would marry her and emancipate her. Judge Ormond reversed the jury's verdict on the grounds that "law, public decency, and good morals alike" did not sanction marriages between whites and blacks.[71] From this perspective, undesirable legal treatment of masters and slaves was eliminated by judicial attention to both social and moral standards. In other opinions the judge similarly cited "a moral and legal obligation" of masters to care for their slaves' physical health, as well as the legal remedies afforded masters when a slave's "morals" and "his value as property" were put at risk.[72]

William P. Chilton shared Judge Ormond's professional attention to blended appeals, just as he shared his personal devotion to the Confederacy. Judge Chilton admitted to a belated but unequivocal support for secession in his petition for amnesty—a posture attested to by one of his descendants.[73] In *Wilks's Adm'r v. Greer,* the judge also approved legal treatment of slaves as "human beings," though "deprived, doubtless for wise purposes, of their freedom."[74] In theory, the curtly expressed and thinly developed arguments by which Judge Chilton and his colleagues asserted that humane principles were imbedded in Alabama's policies regarding slavery could not have sustained persuasive addresses to audiences other than partisan southerners. Humanity and interest were code words that evoked predictable responses from parties, advocates, and occasional readers of law reports who shared the judicial mind on slavery.

Across the Tombigbee River in Mississippi, judges also favored simple declarations of policy and morality in reviewing the legal treatment of slaves. However, the two issues were intertwined even more closely than in the discourse of Alabama's judges.

Joshua G. Clarke, for one, suggested that the moral fiber of Mississippi's citizens and legislature assured slaves of justice. Reviewing *State v. Isaac,* one of the many early cases in which trial judges were unsure whether a white could be prosecuted criminally for killing a slave, Judge Clarke delivered a secularized sermon:

> In this state, the Legislature have considered slaves as reasonable and accountable beings and it would be a stigma upon the character of the state, and a reproach to the administration of justice, if the life of a slave could be taken with impunity. . . . in vain shall we look for any law passed by the enlightened and philanthropic legislature of this state, giving even to the master, much less to a stranger, power over the life of a slave. Such a statute would be worthy [of] the age of Draco or Caligula, and would be condemned by the unanimous voice of the people of this state. . . . shall this court, in the nineteenth century, establish a principle, too sanguinary for the code even of the Goths and Vandals, and extend to the whole community, the right to murder slaves with impunity?[75]

Unable to cite a relevant statute or precedent—other than judicial speculation in the Virginia law reports—Judge Clarke relied entirely on oratorical form. The quoted passages illustrate his integrated claim that political honor ("the character of the state") and moral conscience ("the unanimous voice of the people") prevented slaves from being murdered with impunity. Furthermore, the passages illustrate a typical reference to classical Greece and Rome—from whose cultures the judges derived authority and models for domestic bondage.

Whether Judge Clarke spoke from personal conviction or professional expedience remains moot. The same ambiguity surrounds William L. Sharkey's review of *Isham v. State*. In this case, Judge Sharkey had to assess the exclusionary rule as applied to a master's testimony in his slave's trial for murder. "What would be the condition of the slave," he queried, "if that rule, which binds him to perpetual servitude, should also create such an interest in the master, as to deprive him of the testimony of that master?" Condemning the "hardship" thereby imposed on slaves, the judge endorsed extending "humanity . . . to that race of people."[76] Although scantily developed, the judge's argument makes it clear on moral grounds that trial courts must allow masters to testify when their slaves are prosecuted for murder. Again lacking statutory or precedential grounds—aside from a parallel decision made by Tennessee's William B. Reese—Judge Sharkey relied on rhetorical question and an appeal to moral scruple.

Yet, on the same grounds, he had rejected a clever attempt to free slaves by taking them to Ohio and there executing a deed of emancipation (outlawed at that time in Mississippi). In *Hinds v. Brazealle*, he saw "an offence against morality, pernicious and detestable as an example."[77] A comparison of the oratorical form in both cases clarifies the judge's sense of morality. Permitting a master to testify was humane when slave assets were in danger of being destroyed by state action, but permitting masters to free their slaves was morally offensive. The judge stopped short of equating socioeconomic policy with morality, but he did equate endangering that policy with immorality. In tortured style, he wedded humanity to interest. Notorious for his opposition to secession, the judge's mode of argument may have been developed side by side with his method of expressing a controversial political stance that elicited the following editorial when Judge Sharkey led a delegation to the 1850 Nashville Convention: "From such an advisor or leader, in these times of peril good Lord deliver us and the South."[78]

Predictably drawing the concurrence of Judge Sharkey, James F. Trotter used integrated appeals to policy and morality when assessing the slave

trade in *Green v. Robinson*. Barred by the state constitution of 1833, continued trafficking in slaves "would entirely subvert the great object which
the [constitutional] convention had in mind," and it would resurrect the
"barbarities, the frauds, the scenes so shocking in many instances to
our feelings of humanity and the sensibilities of our nature." Moreover,
"the introduction of slaves from abroad of depraved character" would impair "the moral and orderly condition" of domestic stock.[79] Offensive to
the moral posture of both masters and slaves, as well as dangerous to peace
and prosperity, the slave trade was thoroughly objectionable from a humanist perspective.

Unlike his review of slave trading, Judge Trotter generally favored appeals to policy. For example, he agreed with appellee's counsel in *Ross v.
Vertner* that emancipation threatened "the safety of the owners of slaves,
and the security of the public peace." He could not deny that emancipation created "too great an increase of free negroes, whose example and
whose means too of sowing the seeds of mischief, of insubordination, perhaps of revolt, amongst the slaves in their neighborhood, was very greatly
to be apprehended and guarded."[80] Like many southrons, the judge wor-
ried about servile insurrection. And, after slavery had been abolished, it
was the "increase of free negroes" that elicited strident oratory from the
judge. Addressing the grand jury of De Soto County, he fulminated:

> [I]t is a melancholy fact, that the writ of *Habeas Corpus*, that great
> bulwark of human liberty is still suspended in our State, and the
> "Freedmans bureau" with its accompanyments of negro garrisons,
> still flaunts its flag in our faces, and openly sets our laws & statutes at
> defiance. . . . And so long as this badge of our slavery, this "im-
> perium in imperio," this foreign power which claims the right, and
> backs it with bayonets, to interfere at any moment, as it has done in
> many cases heretofore, with the civil authorities & set their action at
> defiance, we can scacely hope to do much towards correcting abuses
> & suppressing the disorders of which all complain so loudly.[81]

The judge died less than a month after delivering this charge, never
having come to terms, morally or politically, with emancipation.

Judge Trotter's successor on the high court, Alexander M. Clayton, expressed an even stronger stance on the politics of slavery and secession.
He represented his constituents at the Nashville Convention of 1850 (advocating resolutions too harsh for the tastes of most delegates); he attended his state's secession convention; he served as a delegate to the Pro-
visional Confederate Congress; and he lost his judicial office after the war
when he refused to take the "iron-clad oath" of allegiance to the Union.
As he exclaimed in his 1865 petition for amnesty, "I regarded slavery as
the greatest material interest of the world, & was desirous to save it."[82]

Judge Clayton's opinions reflect his priorities. In *Leech v. Cooley*, he
rejected the power of the federal government to enforce a will—void in
Mississippi—providing for the transportation and emancipation of slaves.[83]
He also endorsed the policy behind a statute barring the sale of liquor to
slaves without their masters' permission. In *Jolly v. State*, "the security
and well-being of society" was dispositive for Judge Clayton.[84]

Ultimately, again appealing to policy, he wrote an 1876 oration in
which he castigated the antebellum conspiracy of "anti-slave States" and
bemoaned "the prostrate condition of every branch of industry" during
the era of Reconstruction.[85] According to Judge Clayton, there was no
reason to merge political and moral issues. Peace and prosperity were sufficient motives to dispose of legal appeals and to advocate the southern
system off the bench.

A relatively harsh environment for slaves in the Deep South, and the
occasionally rebellious reactions to these conditions, promoted judicial
reliance on appeals to policy. In Florida, for example, George S. Hawkins
grudgingly upheld a trial court's decision in *Sibley v. Maria* to honor the
testamentary manumission of a slave. However, the judge restricted the
application of his decision to conditions under which the "good order" of
society and the "proper subordination" of the freed slave were maintained. Indeed, though referring to the testator's intent, he explicitly denigrated the "the impulsive principle of self-interest which so generally di-
rects and governs the actions of men."[86]

Thomas Baltzell was somewhat more generous in his judicial discourse
even though he had served on the legislative committee that had authored

a stinging rebuke to increased freedom of travel by Florida's black population. This committee reported that the 1832 law restricting the movement of "Free Negroes and mulattoes" was "extremely salutary." In fact, it was becoming "daily more and more necessary to the peace and well-being of this community." Amendments were undesirable because they "would at once open the door to the successful prosecution of the systematic warfare which a deluded and vicious fanaticism is now making upon the very existence of the Southern states."[87] Judge Baltzell, however, had presided over the trial from which the appeal of testamentary manumission had been taken to Judge Hawkins. And in his own review of *McRaeny v. Johnson and Moore*, Judge Baltzell opined that "American courts, by a spirit of enlightened humanity" had extended more protection to slaves than their legal status otherwise earned.[88] A stickler for legislative detail, it was unusual for him to remark on any feature other than the technical correctness of the decision.[89] To that extent, at least, moral concern was wedded to political expediency in his discourse.

Judicial disdain for anything more than a sketchy appeal to morality can also be traced in the opinions of Louisiana's Alexander Porter. In *Delery v. Mornet*, he applauded "a wise and salutary law" prohibiting the sale of liquor to slaves without their masters' permission, noting that such legislation was "founded alike on regard for the interests of the master and the slave."[90] Moral appeals were appropriate only in limited doses for a judge who was more concerned about the character of northern abolitionists—calling them "hypocrites and fanatics."[91] For example, reviewing *Markham v. Close*, Judge Porter encountered a case in which one master had sued another for cruelly abusing a slave—leading to forfeiture of the slave. Initially asserting how deplorable it was "that owners of slaves should abuse their authority and violate the duties of humanity," Judge Porter then nullified and reversed the trial court's verdict of forfeiture. "[W]hat in this instance was the suggestion of humanity," he observed, "might, in the next, be the promptings of envy, malice, and all uncharitableness."[92] Though important, humanity was not a dispositive issue.

Like Judge Porter, Thomas Slidell made selective uses of appeals to morality. Attributing substantial "humanity" to legislation on slavery in his review of *Hendricks v. Phillips*, Judge Slidell emphasized this issue in reviewing the liability of an overseer for cruel treatment of his employer's slaves. For Judge Slidell, the overseer's actions were "of a most revolting character, and exhibit conduct on the part of the overseer utterly indefensible."[93] One year later the judge invoked "natural justice and humanity" in *Bertrand v. Arcueil* to argue that slave families should be preserved at the time of sale.[94] No maverick, however, in *Oates v. Caffin* the judge readily upheld the policy behind Mississippi's fugitive slave law "to secure her own citizens against [fugitive slaves'] depredations or evil example."[95] For Judges Porter and Slidell, the twin ideals of humanism were desirable but not easily applied to the peculiar institution of slavery.

Francis-Xavier Martin extended his colleagues' primary attention to policy issues. Making state law as he wrote his opinion in *Heno v. Heno*, Judge Martin decided that a father who lived at home with a woman of color could be compelled to support his children who had moved out in protest. The father's "concubinage, with a woman of color" was a patently "good reason," declared the judge, "why the court should not compel his daughter, a white girl, to return into his house; neither can there be any propriety, though the reasons are not equally strong, in ordering the sons to return there."[96] In his manuscript opinion, the judge wrote "expect" rather than "compel."[97] The difference is significant. Before he phrased his opinion in terms of an institutional power to compel, Judge Martin recited a social expectation—a norm that was violated by the father's living arrangements just as clearly as his failure to maintain his family would violate a legal standard. Moreover, in the judge's mind, mere mention of the father's conduct was persuasive; his violation of public policy was "good reason" enough to find against him.

Judge Martin's also illustrated his confidence in the persuasive force of appeals to policy when he reviewed a claim for inheritance made by a testator's "adulterous bastard," a woman of color. He argued in *Jung v. Doriocourt* that "part of the population of this state has been placed by law under certain disabilities and incapacities, from which it is not the province of courts of justice to relieve them."[98] And again, in *Gardiner v. Cross*, when reviewing one planter's defense to a charge of assault and battery brought by another planter, the judge declared: "It is certainly true, that the attempt to excite slaves to insubordination, ought to be promptly and effectually suppressed."[99] In the first instance, the judge endorsed *a priori* his state's "courts of justice"; in the second instance, he invoked a "certainly true" policy against slave resistance. If not for the similarly crafted opinions of his brethren, Judge Martin's reputation as a curmudgeon might be sufficient to explain his discourse. His curtly policy-based appeals, though, echo in the antebellum law reports of Louisiana.

In one of these instances, *Martineau v. Hooper*, Pierre Derbigny affirmed a trial court's verdict that an overseer was not liable for damages when he killed a rebellious slave. The judge asserted simply that "the interest of the [slaveowner] himself and the community at large" excused the overseer.[100] Along with prosperity, peace on the plantations was a compelling factor in his decision making. By way of collateral evidence, several years later then Governor Derbigny promoted legislation that was designed to restrict the number of troublesome slaves being exported to Louisiana from other states.

Rice Garland and Pierre A. Rost confirmed off the bench what their brethren stated as a priority in judicial opinions: sectional interest must be served. Before his disgrace in 1845, Judge Garland promoted the Whig agenda in his correspondence and in his pamphlet endorsing a large standing army.[101] Later a Confederate commissioner to France and Spain, Judge Rost condemned northerners for being prone to "popular delusions" that blinded them from recognizing the "advantages of Slavery as a political institution in a Democratic republic"—advantages recognized presently by southerners and in antiquity by "the Athenian philosophers." More specifically, the judge attacked members of the Know Nothing party for echoing "the blind fanatics, sordid novel writers and ungodly divines, who have combined to make that institution hateful by concealing the benefits it confers upon the country and upon the slaves themselves."[102] As confident in their grasp of policy as Judge Martin, colleagues like Rice Garland and Pierre A. Rost spoke out on the desirable means and ends of preserving the peculiar institution. And like most of their colleagues, these judges felt that appeals to interest were sufficient if not preferable for justifying the laws of slavery.

In Georgia and Alabama the judicial equation of humanity and interest was vigorous, but it waned in South Carolina, Florida, and Louisiana. In Mississippi, judicial references to the twin ideals of humanism were uneven. As political agents, the judges relished opportunities to address domestic peace and prosperity. As pillars of their communities, the same judges were accustomed to proclaiming and interpreting moral norms. But these common factors do not explain differences among the judges' crafting of opinions.

Little evidence suggests that judges in Georgia and Alabama were more idealistic than their brethren in neighboring jurisdictions. Robust idealism, of course, might have sustained the humanist link between conserving property and conserving life. More likely, humanist accommodations in their opinions reflected the judges' respect for similarly blended appeals common to the Upper South's professional culture. These accommodations also matched the judges' adjustments to public debate over slavery and states rights. The resistance to purely sectional interest—illustrated by unionist and cooperationist sentiment in northern Alabama before the Civil War, and by tory activity during the war—suggests the disaffection that judges were addressing within their own jurisdictions. Political and cultural influences of these types would have prompted high-court judges to consult a fully humanist roster of appeals in order to justify the laws of slavery.

Despite a sketchy development, singular appeals to policy would have been satisfying for partisans who resented and feared outsiders meddling with an institution peculiarly adapted to the soils of South Carolina, northern Florida, and Louisiana. And for those citizens who were disaffected with the institution of slavery in these jurisdictions, judges supplemented their arguments with curt invocations of Christian authority. The constitutional separation of church and state—a flimsy arrangement at best in any event—suffered as judges invoked religious authority to justify policy. Nonetheless, mere discomfort over an abstraction such as argumentative validity would not have significantly bothered judges who composed opinions amid the legendary fire-eating that sparked public debate in South Carolina, the relative isolation of Florida physically and culturally, and the unique political and legal heritage of Louisiana.

Mississippi law reports, however, reveal another cause of judicial differences. If Jefferson Davis—evoked from Mississippi to administer the Confederacy—could not gain uniform adherence to the ways and means of ensuring the Confederacy's survival, then why in earlier decades should individual judges be expected to employ uniform methods of gaining adherence to the laws of slavery? The ways and means of advocating slavery that emerged within the professional culture of the Upper South did not prosper in the Deep South, despite the otherwise strong desire of southern judges "to be part of the national legal culture."[103] A personal idiosyncrasy, writ large as political sectionalism, explains the shifting tides of judicial opinions. Whether by design or circumstance, the equation of humanity and interest in the Deep South represented a greater struggle than it posed in the Upper South.

Chapter Six

JUDICIAL APOLOGETICS

The judges were not oblivious to bias in their intuitions or artifice in their equations of humanity and interest. Although the humanist urge was strong, it did not blind them to their struggle in advocating slavery. And so, within the same opinions that contain a humanist defense of slavery, the judges defended their efforts. These apologetics include considerations of professional status as well as complaints about working conditions. Collateral evidence in the judges' private letters confirms the sincerity of judicial concerns if not their accuracy.

The scope of judicial apologetics can be attributed partially to the ways in which state legislatures organized appellate courts. Antebellum southern society has occasionally been addressed as if it were unified, but this convenient generalization masks important distinctions in kind and degree of social cohesion. The same sentiment may be applied to variations in court systems.[1] The rich legal tradition of the Upper South embraced a complex evolution of state courts. As originial colonies, Virginia and North Carolina endowed their state courts with ancient common-law traditions. Tennessee courts, as the offspring of North Carolina's system, shared in these traditions. The Deep South embraced widely disparate court systems in terms of tenure and procedure, although the colonial heritage of South Carolina and Georgia also embraced common-law traditions.

In particular, the conference system (or committee system) of appellate courts fostered judicial discourse aimed at maintaining professional comfort and respect. In this judicial system, peers were required to review each other's jurisprudence—often at each other's elbows. The routines within the legal establishment also prompted judicial concerns over unsettled law, especially a lack of precedents. Another and equally powerful explanation for the scope of judicial apologetics is that the judges felt a pressing need to address the interpersonal dimensions of their careers.

UPPER SOUTH

Virginia's revolutionary constitution provided for the appointment of judges to four state courts: the Supreme Court of Appeals, the General Court, the Court of Chancery, and the Court of Admiralty. The state's jurisdiction over admiralty cases ended when the federal constitution was ratified, but the other three courts flourished in Virginia for over fifty years. The judges specifically appointed to the Court of Appeals were joined, as the cause of action dictated, by judges from the inferior courts. In addition to addressing their colleagues' social and professional reputations at a distance, judges of the Supreme Court had to address some of their colleagues' reputations at close quarters. Thus, judges of the highest court interacted closely with those judges from whose courts the cases had come on appeal, thereby stimulating a social-professional dynamic that was addressed in judicial apologetics.

Richard E. Parker came from a planter family of local prominence, served Virginia admirably in politics and war, and fathered the judge who tried John Brown in 1859.[2] Although he is not as celebrated as several of his colleagues, Judge Parker admirably illustrated apologetic tenor when he addressed the effects of his novel construction of an 1823 statute. In *Aldridge v. Commonwealth,* he denied the authority of all trial courts that had recently sentenced persons of color to be sold into slavery when convicted of minor crimes:

> [T]he Judges had, on the former occasion, considered the question [whether convictions carrying sentences of two years or less supported selling the free criminal of color into slavery], and it was granted, pretty much as a matter of course. Since then, we have, all of us, on our Circuits, and I amongst the rest, acted on these impressions in a variety of Cases, until it requires some effort to free ourselves (I speak at least as to myself) from the influence of these pre-

conceived opinions, and to examine the question as a new one. . . .
This opinion I should pronounce with confidence, but for the contrary opinions of so large a majority of my brethren, which admonish
me to distrust my own, however maturely formed or carefully examined.[3]

Judge Parker's language is striking. Self-references, including a parenthetical aside, inject a confessional tone into his opinion. Moreover, deferential language in the last sentence—a careful measurement of the judge's
competency in view of competing opinions—underscores professional dynamics at work in the state's court system.

Judicial conferees also shared weak precedents for their legal treatment of slaves. Personal ideals of humane treatment notwithstanding, William A. G. Dade expressed discomfort with precedents underlying criminal prosecutions of masters for assaulting their slaves in *Commonwealth v.
Turner.* Speaking for all but one of his colleagues, Judge Dade disclaimed
the "latitudinous doctrine" whereby judges fashion law from unexpressed
rights in the absence of statutes or precedents. He recited at length the law
of slavery among "the Theocratic Jews, and the polished nations of Greece
and Rome"; he distinguished American domestic slavery from English
"villenage"; and he concluded that, excepting cases of slave killing, the
court lacked jurisdiction over assaults on slaves by their masters.[4] This
judge's considerable efforts to defend his opinion in a criminal case was
matched by colleagues in civil causes.

Dabney Carr and William H. Cabell expressed mirror images of Judge
Dade's feelings when reviewing *Paup's Adm. v. Mingo,* a case in which
former slaves sought damages for illegal bondage. Judge Carr asserted on
his own authority that "[s]uits of this kind have been very frequent in Virginia, for more than a century past. . . . yet, in not one single case, have
damages for the detention been given."[5] Judge Cabell concurred. A popular former governor of Virginia who ultimately served for forty years in
the judiciary, Judge Cabell considered the issue to fall within "the settled
law of this country" and felt it was "unnecessary to inquire into its policy
or abstract justice."[6] Their perceptions of settled law comforted the judges

in a degree equal and opposite to that pain endured by Judge Dade when solid precedents were lacking.

Virginia's 1830 constitution abolished the General Court and Court of Chancery. For the remainder of the antebellum period, the Supreme Court of Appeals reviewed cases from district and circuit courts that were established from time to time by the state assembly. In this setting, John J. Allen was "comparatively unknown to the people of the district" upon his first judicial appointment in 1836.[7] Not surprisingly, Judge Allen attended to maintaining social and professional relations. In 1844, for instance, he advised an absent colleague, Briscoe G. Baldwin, that "[o]ur brethren of the general court are heartily sick of the Ct of Ap*ls*." Not prepared for appellate duties by their experience in trial courts, "They say they will never blame the court for not continuing in session more than three hours a day. They find themselves much more exhausted and worn down than by the most protracted sessions in the inferior courts."[8] To the same colleague, Judge Allen later announced naming his new son "Baldwin" ("we made free with your's").[9] By such discourse, Judge Allen not only attributed distinction to a colleague's judicial role but also commemorated personal excellence in choosing a name for his son.

Unlike Judge Allen, William Brockenbrough affirmed professional relationships that extended beyond their own jurisdiction. Before taking his place in Virginia's high court in 1834, he had corresponded with North Carolina's Thomas Ruffin (a distant relative) about the legal issues that prompted Judge Ruffin's famous decision in *State v. Mann*. Consulting the "Atto. General, and several other lawyers on the subject," Judge Brockenbrough reported that settled law in Virginia made it permissible for masters to testify for or against their slaves but that he could not report as authoritatively on other issues that had troubled Judge Ruffin. In addition, he reported that Virginia's "whole Judiciary system is now under the Anvil in the House of Delegates," but that "whether they will beat it out into anything valuable" he did not know.[10] Scarcely chatty, his correspondence addressed the legal establishment in a mode suited to the differences in rank of the correspondents.

However, after Judge Brockenbrough had taken his high court position, he addressed Judge Ruffin more as an equal while requesting help in finding a school in Raleigh for his youngest son. In fact, Judge Brockenbrough concluded: "Should you think proper to communicate freely your opinion, it will be received in a spirit of friendship, and of confidence."[11] William Brockenbrough's earlier letter did not necessarily alter Thomas Ruffin's approach to *State v. Mann*, and quite possibly had little influence on his perception of Virginia's legal establishment. Instead the letter illustrates how the judges consciously maintained professional relationships. Judge Brockenbrough's later correspondence underscores the scope of the communication network among judges in the Old South. In other discourse within the same network, the judges were prone to render informal verdicts on their working conditions.

Judge Carr indicated discomfort with his labors in Virginia's high court. "[H]aving neither time nor books for research," he recounted fashioning an opinion with a "few hasty remarks." He also described the "many cases" on his docket and how the "business of the Court so completely" absorbed his time that he had to deflect his attention from politics—despite his recognition that "signs of the times are dark, ominous, & discouraging."[12] Judge Cabell, cajoling his son to pursue his college studies diligently, speculated: "If you could see how incessantly occupied we are, from shortly after the dawn of day, to 10 or 11 oclock at night, without any intermission from labour, except at our meals, and a walk of half an hour about sun set, I think it would be of service to you."[13] The judge's Memorandum Book—an account of his travel, lodging, and self-doctoring for real and possibly imagined maladies between the years 1840 and 1850—contains more substantial evidence of life on the judicial circuit in Virginia.[14]

The evidentiary weight of testimonials by Judges Carr and Cabell can be evaluated on several scales and then rejected as mere whining or embraced as spontaneous declarations of important concerns. Whether or not the judges' complaints are entirely credible, they reveal perceptions. They illustrate the degree to which judicial apologetics express a felt need.

In 1799 the General Assembly of North Carolina provided for a meeting of all the state's judges twice annually to resolve legal and equitable disputes and discrepancies among the courts. Initially named the "Court of Conference" and later called the "Supreme Court of North Carolina," this court system was vulnerable to the same social and professional dynamics being experienced in Virginia. In their appellate roles, North Carolina's judges not only reviewed issues arising from trials conducted by members of inferior benches, they themselves occupied those benches. Treating a colleague's verdict less than respectfully when it was appealed could cause the appellate judge to suffer the same fate. Even after 1818, when the Assembly provided for a separate three-judge panel to staff North Carolina's highest court, the web of professional relationships remained influential.

The correspondence of Frederick Nash provides a valuable introduction to judicial apologetics in North Carolina. Commenting on his experience as a judicial conferee, Judge Nash addressed the hard feelings that arose from dutiful but unpleasant reviews of trial court decisions: "We sincerely regret that in the performance of what [the Supreme Court] considered right any thing should have been done calculated to hurt the feelings of an old friend & associate."[15] With colleagues' feelings having so prominent a place in the consciousness of an appellate judge, it is little wonder that high courts used similar premises in reviewing cases.

Judge Nash expressed related sentiments in *State v. Caesar*—from the perspective of one who was reluctant to disturb the decisions of his predecessors "upon the subject of homicide committed by white men on slaves, and by slaves on white men." "It is not my purpose," he insisted, "to sit in judgment, on this occasion, upon their correctness; they were made by able men and profound lawyers—by good men, who could not be seduced from what they considered the path of duty."[16] Elsewhere he meditated gloomily on a "treacherous treacherous world" that "spreads its pleasures before us, entices us with forgetfulness of higher duties, and when the hour of trial comes leaves us, to meet death as we may."[17] The judge's distaste for seduction of various types is noteworthy. His concerns about treachery, especially the pitfalls along his own "path of duty," would have colored his advocacy.

Unlike Judge Nash's psychological woes, John Louis Taylor's financial woes constituted a focal point of professional dynamics for North Carolina's judges. In an 1823 letter he acknowledged his "incompetence to manage negroes" and desperately sought advice from a brother-in-law and later supreme court justice, William Gaston: "I am constrained to write you however reluctantly concerning my private affairs, which have become so perplexed as to threaten speedy and irretrievable ruin."[18] Judge Taylor's plan for counteracting "the depression of property and the expensive family of negroes" he was maintaining was modestly successful. In 1827 he wrote to James Iredell about plantation matters and, again in 1828, wrote to William Gaston about success in mastering both "white servants" and "the blacks."[19] By 1829, however, shortly before his death, Taylor's finances had bottomed out. William Gaston wrote of the collapse to Thomas Ruffin, an interested colleague:

> The melancholy event which has brought me to this place will I fear occasion you some embarrasement. The Chief Justice had conveyed his house and adjoining possessions in trust to secure the payment of his bank debts. A sale will necessarily take place, but at what time I can not at present tell. Should I become the purchaser (and this I do not propose to do except to prevent a sacrifice) I shall take pleasure, if you desire to occupy the place to make an arrangement with you for that purpose.[20]

By this point, three present or future judges of the high court were deeply enmeshed, both socially and professionally, in Judge Taylor's personal problems.[21] A sitting judge sought personal and financial advice from a future judge, his brother-in-law, who in turn tried to make related arrangements with another sitting judge. Not unusual or shocking, due to the modest size of the ruling class, this type of financial concern represents a typical distraction from the pursuit of humanist ideals.

In a counterpoint to William Gaston's 1810 campaign broadside, in which he proclaimed his vision of "a Judiciary, wise, virtuous, and dependent on their good conduct alone for continuance in office," his brother-in-law additionally relied on professional connections.[22] Indeed, Judge

Gaston observed more accurately in an 1835 speech that legal professionals had "long since discovered the necessity of courtesy and deference" with their peers.[23] So too, Judge Ruffin remarked in a timely letter
to James Iredell: "I am convinced that a man [Iredell] overwhelmed with
debt is not only unhappy but that he is so, often, because he can not do
what he believes to be right. His choice lies between evils & not between
good on one hand & evil on the other."[24] Thus distracted, Judge Ruffin
might have gone on to say, his colleagues should not be held accountable
for flawed defense of slavery.

A related concern emerges from Judge Ruffin's solicitous letter to his
colleague, Leonard Henderson. "You know," Judge Ruffin asserted, "without any open profession now to be made, the affection, the respect and
reverence with which my intimate knowledge has inspired me towards
you." The judge then assured his colleague that he should "not be sur-
prised at the uneasiness I shall suffer while ignorant of your convalescence
or at the earnestness with which I urge for frequent and explicit accounts
of your health."[25] In addition to financial woes, Judge Ruffin noted, concern over the poor health of a colleague might impair clear thinking and
eloquent advocacy. The judge's dual attention to wealth, or property, and
health, or life, is consistent with his pursuit of humanist ideals.

Beyond relational concerns, the lack of precedents for slave law be-
deviled North Carolina's judges. William Gaston, for one, expressed his
related discomfort in *State v. Manuel:* "Whatever distinctions may have
existed in the Roman law between citizens and free inhabitants, they are
unknown to our institutions."[26] In this case, a free man of color had been
fined for criminal assault and Judge Gaston needed to determine the constitutionality of the sentence. Enhanced by his eminent credentials and
social standing, the judge's use of oratorical form ensured his clear ar-
ticulation of a genuine uneasiness over the relative novelty of American
slave laws.[27]

Presaging Judge Gaston's uneasiness, Leonard Henderson grappled
with the same feelings in a case of slave killing. Judge Henderson was one
of the original three appointees to his state's Supreme Court, becoming its
chief justice in 1829.[28] Transforming his underlying legal argument into an

expression of moral sentiment—a technique he might have taught in the law school he founded at Williamsboro—Judge Henderson observed in *State v. Reed* that "with me it has no weight to shew that, by the laws of ancient Rome or modern Turkey, an absolute power is given to the master over the life of his slaves."[29] In this instance, the lack of precedent forced a judge to look far and wide for legal authority.

North Carolina's judges measured their legal reasoning against the best efforts of their colleagues, affirming a professional culture in which the peculiar institution was advocated in uniform ways. And when this relationship was put at risk, the judges reacted predictably. For example, Richmond M. Pearson reflected on his personal debt to Thomas Ruffin when writing to him upon his retirement from the bench:

> Judge Nash and myself lose the aid of one, who lessened our labors more than one half: For myself; I can say, my labor was lessened much more than one half; If after examining a subject, the conclusion to which I had arrived, agreed with yours, I rested upon it with entire confidence, and it gave me no further trouble; If we differed, the free and full discussion which followed, either produced a concensus of opinion, or I then rested upon my own judgment, entirely satisfied, that by your aid, everything that could be suggested on the other side had been brought to my notice and been duly considered.[30]

Judge Pearson, whose license to practice law had been approved personally by Judges Taylor and Henderson in 1829, became a distinguished educator in the law school he established on his Richmond Hill plantation. No sycophant, he irritated Confederate partisans during and after the war with his political stances and associated activities.[31] His remarks to Thomas Ruffin should be taken seriously for their illustration of the judicial network that sustained North Carolina's judges in their hour of need—and whose maintenance required the judges' constant attention.

Also relevant as an apologetic commonplace were the difficult working conditions. Shortly before resigning from his Superior Court bench, Thomas Ruffin described conditions on the judicial circuit to his son, William, that matched the descriptions rendered by judges throughout the Old South. "I am now on my Spring Circuit . . . so long a tour, rendered the more severe from my being very unwell."[32] Two years later, after accepting a position on his state's highest court, Judge Ruffin again reflected on caseloads that might cause judges to lose sight of their priorities. "I am very busy—but my mind is not so much occupied in the affairs of the Court as to make me forget our dear children or my dearer wife or my dearest Saviour."[33] By all accounts, Thomas Ruffin was a remarkable judge who kept his wits about him. However, his self reflection—including mention of the possibility of witless neglect—implied situations that could cause judges of a lesser rank to ply their trade poorly.

Later in life, Judge Ruffin summarized his feelings on this issue. "I have many times very seriously regretted having yielded to the persuasion of my friends to assume again, so late in life, judicial labours and responsibilities." He did not abandon his regrets, "though the duties have become less irksome than at first." Despite recalling that his judicial "associations" were "very agreeable," he found duty on the bench "a labour—not of love."[34] The strain on judicial attention and commitment in a well-established legal system such as North Carolina's, affecting a well-respected judge, suggests the pervasiveness of this problem across the Old South.

By 1811 trial court judges in Tennessee were banned from sitting on the state's appellate bench. Thus the conference or committee system did not prevail in Tennessee, but the strain of maintaining a deferential stance toward colleagues still took its toll. This strain can be seen in discourse contributed by Jacob Peck, who gained positions in both the state Senate and Supreme Court after emigrating from Virginia.[35] In *Fisher's Negroes v. Dabbs*, Judge Peck declared that "whenever judges in this country cannot stand up as firmly and independently before the people as the judges of England did before their sovereign, then there is an end of the administration of law, and a reign of terror at hand."[36] However, judges also had to stand up to their colleagues. Judge Peck demonstrated his related technique when, in 1829, he asked Governor Sam Houston to extend clemency to a convicted murderer. In his petition, Judge Peck asserted as the lone dissenter that he followed "higher reason" rather than emotion in finding "all the proceedings as erroneous and void" (based on an illegal search and seizure of evidence). He declared that he "could not yield to the opinions assailing me" and that, "with all due deference to the opinions of others," the murderer deserved clemency.[37] In Judge Peck's mind, at least, professional deference should not cover up flawed jurisprudence. Nonetheless, in these instances, polite discourse about one's colleagues was the rule.

Perhaps it was undue concern over deference to colleagues that prompted John Haywood to portray Tennessee's Supreme Court in unflattering terms. Judge Haywood had left North Carolina after gaining prominence as a superior court judge and law reporter. A controversial and occasionally obnoxious figure, he served on the high court of Tennessee from 1812 until his death.[38] In an undated letter written between 1810 and 1824, he decried a "weakness of intellect" among the judges that resulted in decisions "so made and tinged with inexperience and real ignorance of legal precepts as to be a disgrace to the State."[39] Judge Haywood's complaint, however, may also be traced to a routinely callous treatment of fellow professionals. For example, according to one account, he interrogated an applicant to the bar rudely and at length while lying on a bull's hide under the shade of an oak tree on his estate. The judge, who weighed as much as 350 pounds, repeatedly called his slaves to haul him into the shade as the day-long interrogation continued.[40]

More commonplace among Tennessee's judges were expressions of concern about their working conditions. Late in the antebellum period, Archibald W. O. Totten apologized to a colleague for some delay in responding to his request for the court's opinions in a case of special importance. The judge explained that "[t]he opinions were out being delivered near the close of the term when in the rush of business, it was too late to write."[41] Although not a catastrophe, the situation in which Judge Totten found himself was repeated over and over again.

A generation earlier, Spartan provisions for his state's highest bench drew the attention of John Catron. Judge Catron later gained notoriety for his concurring opinion in *Dred Scott* while an associate justice of the United States Supreme Court.[42] In the 1830s, though, he made no memorable revelations of his perspective on slavery from the bench. Rather, he was intensely concerned about the legal establishment in his state. Writing to the Judiciary Committee in Tennessee's House of Representatives, Catron bemoaned the delays in administering justice to the "weak & virtuous" as a result of overcrowded dockets. At the same time, he revealed his political sensitivity by appealing tactfully to "that friendly feeling, between the Legislative & Judicial departments that should always be maintained."[43]

In equally passionate tones, Judge Catron prefaced his opinion in *Fisher's Negroes v. Dabbs* with a complaint about working conditions. He recounted that the "motion to set aside the decree in the case of Fisher's negroes was brought before the court on yesterday, the last business day of the term." At this late stage of the term, he confessed that his "mind was too depressed with recent over-exertion to take that strong view of the subject its intricacy and importance demanded." Indeed, he felt himself "wanting in vigor. However, there is no time left."[44] Judicial exclamations of this intensity ("there is no time left") are rare, and Judge Catron's outburst underscores the potentially devastating effect of extraneous pressure on the crafting of judicial opinions on slavery. Considering that Judge Peck injected his rhetorical flourish about judicial independence into the same report, John Catron's complaint takes on added significance. That is, Jacob Peck may have made his assertion precisely because he too was "wanting in vigor" at the time.

Although populated with lawyers and judges from other jurisdictions in the Upper South, Arkansas never accepted the conference system. Instead, a three-judge Supreme Court, including a chief justice, was authorized by the constitution of 1836, and none of the lower or circuit court judges served on the high court bench.

Despite the absence of conferees, Townshend Dickinson found himself embroiled in controversy during the 1842–43 term because his concurring opinion in *Conway, ex parte* irritated the governor. After deciding not to rehear arguments in a case involving the Real Estate Bank favored by Governor Archibald Yell, and fearing that the governor would sabotage his career, Judge Dickinson sought external endorsements from respected jurists James Kent of New York and Joseph Story of the federal Supreme

Court. "Personal and political capital are endeavored to be made," claimed the judge, "by destroying the independence of the judiciary for the purpose of defeating the re-election of one of us to the Bench."[45] As a source of distraction, Judge Dickinson's problem with the governor of Arkansas was distinctive in form but similar in substance to the professional dynamics attested to elsewhere.

On the frontier, one might expect less sophisticated problems—such as those suffered by Edward Cross. Judge Cross, according to one biographer, routinely faced the perils of "swimming rivers, crossing creeks on rafts, camping and traveling twenty or thirty miles without seeing a house on his way to court."[46] Whether psychological or physical, though, the difficulties faced by Arkansas judges made for poignant apologetics.

Strains on professional status and equally strained working conditions provided grist for the mill of judicial apologetics across the Upper South. Addressed as a priority in communications with their colleagues, similiar complaints that were voiced in the Deep South reflect a comparable degree of vexation.

DEEP SOUTH

Judges of the Deep South addressed somewhat different issues in their self defense. The organization of court systems partially accounts for this difference. The degree of judicial confidence and comfort—based on self-perceptions of how settled was the legal treatment of slaves—accounts for the remainder.

Distinctive in the tenor of its politics, South Carolina also was notable for its deference to tradition in organizing appellate courts. Strictly following the British model, appeals arising in equitable cases were heard by one court while legal appeals were heard by another. Both courts were staffed through the conference system that required judicial peers to review the disputed outcomes of each other's trials. The legislature temporarily replaced South Carolina's bifurcated system in 1824 by providing for a three-judge court of appeals but, in 1836, restored the earlier arrangement. After 1836, however, a combined conference of law and equity judges was authorized to review constitutional disputes and to resolve all other appeals that were not finally adjudicated in the separate conferences. In this court, remarked one expert observer, "[C]onsultation was almost interminable, and . . . harmony of views could no more be expected than in a Jury room."[47]

Intrigues within the conference system were not the only source of stress for South Carolina's judges. Several years before assuming judicial duties, Andrew P. Butler served on a legislative committee charged with investigating a circuit court judge. Although two-thirds of the representatives voted for the articles of impeachment endorsed by Judge Butler's committee, the representatives then unanimously awarded a year's salary to the disgraced judge.[48] This experience understandably may have impressed Judge Butler—who later served on the Judiciary Committee of the United States Senate—with the need for delicacy in his professional relationships.

The judges were more apt to articulate their concerns about the legal establishment in general than about individual colleagues. William Harper, successful in law and politics in both South Carolina and Missouri, orated in 1835 that the South "is an aristocracy, and we by our position are *conservatives;* and it is our business to show that conservatives are the truest reformers. We will not overturn the fundamental institutions of society; but we will improve them to the utmost where they are capable of improvement."[49] In the same year that he oratorically expressed his conservatism, Judge Harper propped up his opinion in *Fable v. Brown* (denying to slaves the right of inheritance) by asserting that interested parties should recognize the tradition behind his decision: "But it is unnecessary to multiply facts which are perfectly known to any one having the slightest acquaintance with history."[50] Revealing the strength of his feelings by measuring "the slightest acquaintance" with his topic as a sufficient ground to agree with his opinion, the judge endorsed a conservative frame of mind in language that smacked of the humanist agenda.

The legal establishment may not have been perfect but avowed conservatives like Judge Harper committed themselves publicly to preserving the integrity of all fundamental institutions. Abraham Nott had also addressed this issue several years earlier by expressing the sentiment: "I am always opposed to innovation when I can not see any good to be attained."[51] However, traditionalist judges were uncomfortable with the vague legal authority available to them in reviewing cases of slavery. "This unfortunate species of property," Judge Nott declared in *Wingis v. Smith*, "is constantly presenting us with cases involving considerations of policy rather than law, and in which little assistance can be derived from authority."[52] In this regard, William Harper's appeal to the acknowledged facts of history also acknowledged the struggle faced by judicial devotees of humanism. Although it was eminently moral to invoke considerations of policy, professional judges were reluctant to ignore entirely statutes and precedents.

The judges hearing appeals in Charleston and Columbia did not readily agonize in public over their working conditions. Perhaps "the gallant zeal and uncalculating chivalry" so dear to the hearts of South Carolinians like Judge Butler may have discouraged apologetic discourse that could be interpreted as a sign of weakness or pettiness.[53] These sorts of disclosures would erect barriers on the humanist path to recognition as a civic hero. Nonetheless, John S. Richardson cited an undue workload when defending himself against charges he should be dismissed.[54] When asked to provide biographical details for publication, Josiah J. Evans made it clear that the "life of a judge in South Carolina is very laborious."[55] His mild complaint is consistent with his earlier and private mention of "a very busy circuit."[56]

Additional apologetics may be culled from reflections like that by John B. O'Neall in his biography of Judge Harper:

> Mr. Harper had married the daughter of David Coulter, Esq. . . . He removed with Mr. Coulter to Missouri in 1818. He there soon rose to eminent distinction; he was elected Chancellor, and fulfilled the onerous duties of that office until the poverty of his compensation forced him to resign. After the death of his father-in-law, he returned to South Carolina, in 1823. . . .
>
> In 1830, Chancellor Harper and the writer were placed on the Appeal Bench. My commission as a Law Judge was a few days older

than his as Chancellor, and so it happened that I received a few more votes than he did. These gave me position as second in the Appeal Bench, although he was three years my senior in age. No Judges ever encountered a heavier portion of duty than then fell to our lot. We entered the Court of Appeals the first Monday of December, 1830, and with short intervals of rest were employed until the first Monday of July.[57]

By Judge O'Neall's self-interested reckoning, a truly dedicated judge's workload was "onerous." His personal experience was highly informative. In 1818, when he voted to raise judicial salaries as a member of the state's House of Representatives, he lost his seat for the next two terms.[58]

Moreover, in the special circumstances of South Carolina, the process by which one ascended the bench was riddled with peculiarities. In addition, caseloads were overwhelming. A planter himself, Judge O'Neall was eminently successful in law and politics. He was appointed a trustee of his alma mater and eventually rose to the rank of major-general of militia. He wrote and lectured widely, heading Bible societies, temperance leagues, and agricultural associations.[59] Despite the breadth of his accomplishments and public agenda, though, he could not restrain himself from criticizing the working conditions with which a South Carolina appellate judge had to contend.

Georgia cases were decided in the courts of ten judicial districts, where the presiding judge issued the last word in every proceeding. Not until 1845 did the legislature actually establish the Supreme Court authorized several years earlier in the state's constitution.

Judge Lumpkin candidly described to his daughter the conditions under which attendance at the Supreme Court of Georgia might reflect extraordinary judicial devotion, even in a relatively civilized Atlanta:

We have between 40 & 50 cases, we shall get through here this week. Yesterday morning Governor McDonald went home on account of his health, which is very bad, and Judge Benning and myself, heard the arguments in eleven cases & decided them last night. Was not that a days work? The town has been enveloped in a cloud of dust, ever since

I have been here, yesterday it began to sleet & turning warmer, it commenced raining. . . . So now we shall have to plough our way to the Court House, which is some distance from the Hotel.[60]

In their own minds, a record of faithful attendance was flattering to the judges. At this purely functional level, Hiram Warner pointed with great satisfaction to his unblemished record while serving in the Superior Court. Moreover, he was reported to have stated with pride "that during the four years he had been on the bench of the Supreme Court, he always presented himself at every term which had been held in the State, making, in the aggregate, a period of sixteen years, within which time he was punctual in his attendance."[61] For Judges Lumpkin and Warner, simply staying on the job was a praiseworthy accomplishment not to be ignored when assessing the humanist quality of their jurisprudence.

The court system in Georgia, lacking the conference format of the Upper South, did not foster as much judicial attention to professional alliances as in other jurisdictions. Personal relationships were another matter. Judge Warner, for instance, had to work out financial as well as professional debts to his colleague, Eugenius A. Nisbet. Mailing payment of his $200 debt to Judge Nisbet, Judge Warner thanked him "for the favors extended to me."[62]

Also in contrast with other jurisdictions, the settled character of statutory and common law in Georgia preempted related apologetics. As early as 1809, for instance, Thomas U. P. Charlton was able to rebut easily the objections to a judicial order for a new trial in *Bank v. Marchand*, on the issue of whether a marriage settlement had been fraudulent. "I shall only briefly observe," he declared, "that as to all legal consequences there is no distinction in this state between one species of chattel and another, or between real and personal property, and if slaves can be the subject of a marriage settlement, so (may) bales of merchandise."[63] In 1822, the same superior court judge confirmed in *Spencer v. Negroes Amy and Thomas* the relative comfort afforded the judiciary by settled law: "I always feel happy, when I can decide upon the plain expression of the law itself, without travelling beyond its context into a field of unnecessary superogatory learning."[64] Judge Charlton's sentiments reflect a commonly shared feeling.

Judge Warner enjoyed the comfort of settled law. And he felt no need to transcend it. In *Mayor of Columbus v. Goetchius*, an 1849 case testing the rules of evidence, the judge placed no dispositive weight on facts of the grisly and unnecessary death of Crawford, a slave. Instead, Judge Warner focused on objections to the trial court's admission of testimony. Reciting the underlying facts for the record, he observed:

> Crawford was attacked with confluent small pox, while on the lot, and there died. During his sickness he was in a small house, sixteen by twenty feet, with one door and one window, but no chimney. . . . The negro was lying on blankets, and the pustules breaking, the oozing matter caused the hair or nap of the blanket to adhere to the flesh, and thus the negro became one mass of filth and corruption.[65]

Judge Warner obviously possessed a strong stomach. The grisly and undisputed facts of Crawford's demise did not disturb judicial attachment to the law of evidence. As it turned out, the judge also had a strong neck. Having refused to tell Wilson's Raiders the location of a gold watch he had buried on his plantation, he was hanged during the war. Revived, however, by the heat and smoke of fires set by his would-be executioners, the judge staggered back to his manor and exclaimed: "Those rascals hanged me and they got my watch."[66] Judges like Hiram Warner were not dainty, but they nonetheless appreciated the comfort provided by settled law.

Unlike Hiram Warner, Alabama's judges found less comfort in the legal grounds for their opinions. Three judges presided over the Supreme Court of Alabama, established by the legislature in 1832. Previously, in 1819, the state's constitution had provided for a conference of judges from the five circuit courts to hear appeals arising from each other's trial courts. But after being relieved in 1832 of the interpersonal friction possible within the conference system, Alabama's supreme court judges faced a discomfort based on the lack of precedents for their opinions on slavery.

Distant historical precedents and strained analogies between British and American common law bothered Alabama's judges after the court reform of 1832. Harry I. Thornton, for example, expressed considerable discomfort with the lack of precedent in *Cawthorn v. Deas,* a case where the trial court had assessed a master for property damages caused by his slave: "It must be conceded that the Common Law upon this particular head, is not framed with reference to any such relation as exists in this country between owner and slave." Rather, Judge Thornton observed, "the resemblance, is much greater, between the condition of slavery with us, and amongst the Romans, than between it, and any condition recognised by the Common Law."[67] In effect, the judge felt sufficient discomfort that he had to search antiquity for an acceptable analogy to the law of slavery in Alabama. Although contemplating the classical origins of humanism would have been satisfying, the judge's search did not ease his struggle to justify his opinion. He relied solely on oratorical form: an analogy.

Judge Thornton's concern was scarcely unique. John J. Ormond toiled on the bench of Alabama's Supreme Court for twelve years after his election in 1837, but never lost an uneasiness about British criminal precedents that he expressed in *State v. Hawkins* near the beginning of his judicial tenure: "It appears to us, that these cases cannot be considered authority in this country. The shadowy, and almost imaginary distinctions upon which they rest, are at war with that precision and certainty which is the boast of the criminal law of England."[68] Unlike its value in other contexts, the common law was unpalatably weak when applied to decisions about domestic bondage in America. This lack of utility bothered Judge Ormond deeply enough that he felt it necessary to derogate "shadowy, and almost imaginary distinctions" in British precedents.

Succeeding Judge Ormond on the bench in 1847, William P. Chilton reviewed *Spence v. State* and summarily distinguished "cases like this, which never did and never could have arisen in England, since slavery as it exists here was unknown to the common law."[69] Like all of his colleagues, Judge Chilton was displeased upon finding no helpful precedent in the common law. Indeed, he shared a commonplace perspective on the positive benefits to be derived from what outsiders might criticize as a devotion to mere formality. "[P]unctilious adherence to the strictest legal technicalities," he declared in *Townsend v. Jeffries' Ex'rs,* "would be far less injurious in its consequences than the uncertainty and confusion which never fail to result from a disregard of established forms and precedents."[70] Noting the "hasty and imperfect" procedures under which trials were sometimes conducted, he ruled against an award of damages in the case. His apologetical discourse is noteworthy because, in uttering it, he degraded the authority of his opinion. Yet such remarks could not entirely be suppressed when a judge felt the humanist urge.

As reflected in the opinions of Judges Thornton, Ormond, and Chilton, Alabama's high court longed for the comfort afforded by settled law. In pragmatic terms, the judges wanted to avoid the charges of "breach of duty and violation of law" brought against Anderson Crenshaw in 1828.[71] Informal but no less damning criticism of their judicial abilities from colleagues was equally troublesome. John M. Taylor, for instance, sarcastically appraised Reuben Saffold as possessing "almost more than human knowledge," one of the state's "prodigies of wisdom and legal learning."[72] Early in 1829 the Alabama Senate acquitted Judges Crenshaw and Saffold of judicial incompetence, but their professional embarrassment lingered.[73]

On a broader scale, the judges felt a tension defined by Henry W. Collier in *Kennedy's Heirs and Ex'rs v. Kennedy's Heirs*. His remarks summarize a major portion of the humanist agenda. Contrasting judicial sensitivity to "the voice of public approbation" with the judges' attention to "the louder and more commanding tones" of their consciences, Judge Collier insisted that "the first duty is correctness of decision; and this is not to be lost sight of, however unpopular it may be." With the memory of Judge Crenshaw's distress still fresh in his mind, Judge Collier also complimented his colleagues on the bench: "We have always supposed that a high moral and official responsibility rested upon us for all our decisions here; but we are not aware, that in any instance our moral courage has faltered; and we are quite sure that we have never stopped to calculate consequences to ourselves personally."[74] Perhaps guilty of protesting too much, Judge Collier's pointed denial that his colleagues ever calculated the personal consequences of their verdicts brings into focus the image of a self-interested judiciary that was at issue. The apologetical message was clear: by following moral dictates—the call of civic duty—a judge necessarily abandoned personal advantage. Elsewhere in the Deep South, notably in Mississippi, judges expressed related sentiments.

Mississippi's 1818 constitution and subsequent legislative acts provided for a conference of the state's four circuit judges as the Supreme Court of law. In addition, two of these judges formed a panel to hear appeals from equitable cases decided by the state's single chancellor. But the constitution of 1832 ended this arrangement—unique in the Old South—by authorizing a High Court of Errors and Appeals.

Several years before he presided over the Nashville Convention—a less than resounding celebration of states' rights—Mississippi's William L. Sharkey reviewed *Brien v. Williamson,* a case of slave trading. In his review, he commented pointedly on the strained relationship he saw between the North and South, specifically between the United States Supreme Court and the high court of Mississippi. Contrary to the federal high court's constitutional analysis, Mississippi's highest bench had three times voided contracts for the sale of slaves imported into its jurisdiction. Judge Sharkey sensed a deterioration in federal respect, and responded in words calculated to demean wrongheaded federal judges and delimit federal authority:

> We regard with great deference the decisions of that exalted tribunal, on questions peculiarly within its province, and in such cases will be always ready to yield to them as authoritative. But state tribunals may justly claim to decide for themselves all questions of state policy, and questions involving the interpretation of state constitutions. Our constitution we are sworn to support, and we cannot therefore yield to any interpretation of it unless we are satisfied of its correctness.

Continuing, the judge adroitly flattered like-minded federal colleagues by noting their dissents from the federal opinion; these members of the court "have established for themselves imperishable monuments of judicial fame."[75] As reflected in Judge Sharkey's words, Alabama's judges preferred the genuinely moral path of service to their state. They valued "correctness" in their endeavors. For William Sharkey, moreover, decisions consistent with states' rights led to "judicial fame." Thus, the judge expressed his humanist belief that, because fulfilling civic duty is moral in itself, the obedient public servant may gain fame for his chivalry.

Stressful professional relationships aside, the judges had to endure weak precedents for their assessments of slave laws. As early as 1820—early indeed in a state still considered legally backward at the time—Joshua G. Clarke denigrated Roman and common law precedents for the crime of slave killing. Judge Clarke maintained a planter's lifestyle at "Claremont," but his attitude toward the status of slaves reflects more of his rearing in Pennsylvania than his planting in the Mississippi territory.[76] Reviewing *State v. Jones*, he cited neither statute nor case law in composing a lengthy opinion that included the sentiments:

> The Roman law has been much relied on by the counsel of the defendant. That law was confined to the Roman empire, giving the power of life and death over captives in war, as slaves, but it no more extended here, than the similar power given to parents over the lives of their children. . . . Villains, in England, were more degraded than our slaves. It is true, that formerly, the murder of a villain was not punished with death, but neither was the murder of a freeman then so punished. The only difference between the freeman and the slave, was in the magnitude of the fine. In England, killing a villain was as much murder, as killing a lord. Yet villains were then the most abject slaves, and could be bought and sold as chattels, but because slaves can be bought and sold, it does not follow that they can be deprived of life.[77]

Judge Clarke recognized in his apologetical discourse the sorry state of precedents being used in Mississippi trials. Omitting references to legal or other authorities, he was forced to compose his own legal history. Compelled to do so, he wanted his potential critics to appreciate his distress.

In 1844 Joseph S. B. Thacher expanded Judge Clarke's analysis of precedent. Judge Thacher had similarly been raised in the North and practiced law in Boston before emigrating to Natchez in 1833. Reviewing

Kelly v. State, he accurately characterized Mississippi laws on slavery as "peculiar" and different from the legal "system in other States of the Union." Moreover, the state's statutory regulation was "unlike the system as it existed among the Jews, the Greeks, the Romans, and differs materially from the villanage of ancient England."[78] Like Judge Clarke, Judge Thacher had to rely on his own authority when recounting legal history. No other authority was cited. Within this type of novel declaration, high court judges of Mississippi expressed discomfort over the lack of precedent for deciding how slaves should be treated under the law—a defensive tactic voiced explicitly in other jurisdictions across the Deep South.

Judicial concerns about professional status and working conditions may be gauged only with considerable speculation where relevant law reports are abbreviated. The high court of Florida lacked substantial tenure within the scope of this present study, but was similar in structure to other courts of the Deep South that fostered judicial apologetics. In each instance, the conference system made it likely that high court judges would be peculiarly sensitive to conferees' feelings. Before the Florida Supreme Court was established in 1846, the judges presiding over superior or district courts had corresponded directly with the territorial governor regarding reviews of their decisions and sentences (i.e., executive clemency). However, the record upon which further review could be based might be scant. Joseph L. Smith, Superior Court Judge of the Eastern District, corresponded with Governor James D. Westcott, Jr., regarding possible clemency for Monday, a slave convicted in Judge Smith's court of raping a white woman and sentenced to death. The following paragraph appears to have contained the trial record: "The Testimony on which Monday was convicted, was clear and uncontradicted, and there appeared nothing, in the opinion of the Court, to mitigate the character of the crime."[79]

Because the brief antebellum tenure of Florida's high court limited judicial need to engage in apologetics, related artifacts from this court are not well represented here. However, the tenure and discourse of Louisiana's high court, in which the conference format was never a factor, offers partial compensation for limited data from Florida.

Richly endowed with Spanish and French legal traditions, the territorial court of New Orleans resisted the introduction of common law as it had been embraced in the formerly British colonies of America. Although Thomas Jefferson had suggested otherwise, and the Code of 1808 had endorsed Jefferson's plan, the 1812 constitutional convention of Louisiana rejected the legal tradition of every other southern state. In effect, Louisiana's high court was insulated against the discomfort of weak common-law precedents in legal decision making.

Pierre A. Rost, for one, felt confident about deciding the ownership of a runaway slave—despite complex and competing claims by the original master, who was a citizen of Louisiana, and the interim master, who worked the slave in Mississippi. In *Oates v. Caffin*, Judge Rost founded his opinion on a legal tradition with which he was thoroughly comfortable: "Our laws regulating the condition of slavery are derived, through those of Spain, from the Roman jurisprudence."[80] No stranger to unsettled conditions, Judge Rost had emigrated from France where he had experienced firsthand the military and political turmoil created by Napoleon. After developing a large plantation in St. Charles parish and serving two terms on the Louisiana Supreme Court, Judge Rost was appointed one of the Confederate emissaries to France and Spain.[81] A person of his experience surely appreciated the advantages of settled law.

The opportunity to rely on settled law made Judge Rost's task and that of his Louisiana colleagues relatively easy. In fact, he alluded to this type of feeling in a later address to the state convention: "What is to come? No one can tell, but we have a great advantage in the contest; we are in the line of safe precedents, and advance into the unknown future with minds tranquil and free from doubt."[82] The judge appreciated conditions, especially in questions about slavery, which enabled judges to arrive at answers tranquilly and confidently.

Unfortunately for some judges, Louisiana often required fluency in alien tongues. Another concern, then, was the languages in which facts and law were expressed. George Mathews was appointed to the Supreme Court upon Louisiana's admission to the Union and retained his seat on the bench until he died.[83] One of his eulogists observed that Judge

Mathews initially knew no French or Spanish,[84] but another eulogist praised him for dutifully acquiring much needed skill in these languages: "Such was his prompt determination on the subject, and, above all, such was his admirable aptitude at learning, that, in a short time, his ear became familiar with French and Spanish to the point of excusing the lawyers, who were not proficient in his own language, from trying to plead in it before him."[85] Judge Mathews, for one, recognized that attention to the case at hand was substantially impaired if the arguments of record were incomprehensible.

Conversational skill in French and Spanish was useful for the judges, but not sufficient. Since English law was irrelevant in the state, the competent judge also had to comprehend the language of the Roman statutes against which pleadings were to be measured. On this count, according to one report, Alexander Porter was the least worthy of Louisiana jurists. A native of Ireland, Judge Porter was more noted for his political accomplishments—such as founding the Whig party in Louisiana—than for his judicial performance.[86] "What he pronounces as law to-day affords no guarantee for to-morrow," a critic ranted. Elaborating further, this detractor explained: "His chief ambition being to appear learned his decisions are weighed down with quotations from various foreign languages, especially the Latin, when everybody knows he is ignorant of the language in which the original text of the civil law is written."[87] Judge Porter was unworthy, according to the report, not only because he lacked languages but also because he attempted clumsily to cover up his linguistic failings. Like George Mathews, Alexander Porter could enjoy the peace of mind afforded judges by settled law only if he overcame language barriers. In this respect, the concerns of several Louisiana judges were unique.

Unique in many other respects, Louisiana's judiciary nonetheless expressed concerns over professional reputations and working conditions that echoed similar complaints elsewhere in the Old South. Francis-Xavier Martin led the way in articulating these concerns. On December 8, 1845, for example, he adjourned the Supreme Court in protest when Rice Garland arrived to take his seat on the bench. Judge Garland had engaged in questionable financial dealings and Judge Martin wanted this potentially scandalous affair investigated.[88] In regard to working conditions, the judge prefaced the first volume of his law reports with an apologetical discourse:

> From the smallness of the number of the judges of the Superior Court, the remoteness of the places where it sits, and the multiplicity of business, it has become indispensable to allow a quorum to consist of a single judge, who often finds himself compelled, alone and un-aided, to determine the most intricate and important questions, both of law and fact.[89]

Judge Martin, a native of France who had received his earliest education in a Jesuit academy, did not suffer the linguistic disability of several colleagues.[90] However, as revealed in his prefatory remarks, he appreciated the concern about case loads and legal resources typically expressed by many of his colleagues across the Deep South.

Court systems and reputations varied from place to place in the Old South. In the Upper South, both institutional and personal credentials generally drew favorable notice. Frontier regions in the Deep South lacked the prestige of other jurisdictions, though high court benches in these regions were frequently populated with judges who had served their apprenticeships in states such as Virginia, North Carolina, and Tennessee. Louisiana's George Mathews, for example, was born in Virginia, moved to Georgia where his father became governor, and completed his preprofessional studies in Lexington, Tennessee.[91]

The conference or committee system of organizing an appellate judiciary was popular with antebellum southern legislatures. Within this system, though, judges routinely felt the need to assuage a colleague's ire over having one of his decisions criticized if not reversed. Under these circumstances it would scarcely be surprising if a judge favored political rhetoric over legal logic. Moreover, the lack of settled law and precedent in slavery cases made criticisms if not reversals likely when a particularly knotty problem arose at trial. On a more personal level, the judges predictably socialized with each other as members of the same class in antebellum society. Indeed, family ties bound many judges together whether in one jurisdiction or across state lines. The judges also shared with each other their complaints, profound and petty, about working conditions.

Judicial apologetics arising from experiences with irate colleagues, shadowy precedent, and tedious working conditions were pervasive. Not only the sheer bulk of this discourse but also the distinctive manner in which judicial concerns were addressed illustrate a felt need to explain lapses in progress toward humanist goals. Feelings of discomfort over accommodating both humanity and interest in reviewing the laws of slavery aroused proportionately intense disclaimers. But even if these apologetics were less than genuine expressions of regret, even if they were petty complaints, they may still be assessed as reliable guides to judicial advocacy— itself a hallmark of the humanist program. Self-conscious of the professional dynamics imposed in many instances by the conference system, the judges resorted to apologetics as a classically approved device for anticipating and deflecting potential criticism. Thus, in either form or substance, judicial apologetics sustained the humanist tradition.

CONCLUSION

The judges did not effortlessly advocate their humanist perspective on slavery. Despite the stability and security they enjoyed socially and professionally, their justification of slave laws was labored. It was also risky. Regardless of how eloquently they spoke and wrote, the judges were violating professional decorum by taking on the roles of advocates. If their eloquence did not conserve both morality and policy, they failed to reach their humanist goal. Moreover, they remain liable for losing sight of substantive issues while indulging themselves in oratorical form—involuntarily becoming creatures of their own advocacy.

By analogy, judges who aspired to humanist advocacy in the Old South assumed the risk of acquiring military fame. Breaking ranks while engaged with the enemy was both unseemly and insubordinate, but warriors who executed this maneuver could gain fame. If unconventional tactics failed, warriors could anticipate defeat and dishonor. Additionally, warriors could suffer severe harm when surrendering themselves to martial frenzy. The judges broke ranks within their professional culture and exhibited a humanist urge, if not a frenzy. They risked a peculiar harm. Defeat and dishonor were not at issue in legal battles because, for members of high courts, victory was assured. In the wider battle, however, the judges risked losing not only their slave property but also their southern traditions.

CREATORS OF ADVOCACY

By using oratorical form in their opinions, the judges risked the displeasure of colleagues: "Polite learning should never be displayed too much or unnecessarily upon the bench," a mid-nineteenth-century biographer warned. "The point ruled in a legal decision should never be covered under figures of speech or flourishes of rhetoric." Yet, "to reach the highest standards of professional excellence and juridical style," critics recognized a need for "something more besides bare, bald professional knowledge." In the end, members of this professional culture were exhorted to revere classical lore and "act upon the maxim of Tully, that an 'orator' should know everything."[1] This conceptual link between expressive skill and wide knowledge—truly a Ciceronian ideal—was attractive to judges who faced a lack of precedent and statutory authority. By skillfully appealing to tradition and custom, the judges could persuasively make their case.

Oratory was a politician's tool, but high courts were not political rostra. In 1832 William Harper referred to a "decorum" that barred judges from speaking out as political partisans. Yet, believing that a great deal was at stake, he struggled with how to serve the "interests of the whole state to which my services are due."[2] Thirty years later, Thomas J. Withers declined an invitation from secessionists to express his related opinions:

> While employed in the Judiciary department of their government, I am dedicated to a very exacting and delicate service, best performed by a careful abstinence from the heat of partizan bias, and thus giving earnest that I seek to maintain the equanimity which warrants a confidence, on all hands, that I am to do right to every litigant before me. . . . My notion is, that a true sense of propriety (though it reinforces a long cherished disposition) admonishes me to shun any temptation that might draw me into the vortex of popular commotion."[3]

Shunning the "vortex" of rough-and-tumble public debate but coping with life on the circuit, some judges did not resist personal and professional impulses to play the role of advocates. In this role, they used oratorical form to justify slavery as both righteous and wise. By design these justifications transcended politics—as Hiram Warner explained in his polite lecture "The Battle of Life." For public debaters he endorsed "a mild, polished, well tempered Damascus blade" instead of a *"butcher's cleaver."* Attentive to the keenness of his arguments and appeals, the ideal debater was "an enlightened, practical statesman, and not a *mere politician.*"[4] Thus, for Judge Warner, the form of advocacy elevated the content of ideas.

The tension between obeying protocol and executing a duty to speak for "the ruling minds" of their era nagged at the judges. Given the culture in which they were born or transplanted, the judges' regard for oratory was predictable. Classical and neoclassical regimens for speaking and writing were staples in educating the gentry. Being compared to Cicero was the highest honor an antebellum declaimer could achieve. Thomas Ruffin made clear to his listeners the incentives for "an almost incessant devotion in the study of oratory."[5] William H. Cabell lectured his son repeatedly about the benefits of oratorical training: "A man who can speak & write well, may do what he pleases, in a government constituted like ours."[6] Some judges won accolades for their eloquence, but most delivered less memorable addresses for the sole purpose of satisfying civic and professional duties. Members of Mississippi's highest bench, for example, took turns delivering commencement addresses at the university's law school. Along with military service, conservative eloquence was an accepted path to civic distinction. This eloquence featured vivid narratives, clever equations of humanity and interest, and crisp apologetics.

The complexity and novelty of slave laws forced judges to rely on the liberal arts as much as professional resources. An engaging recitation of facts was a valuable skill in both venues. By norm and custom the judges were disposed to evaluate the facts asserted by advocates. But the judges crafted their own narratives, not only to resolve disputes over the legal treatment of slaves but also to justify the type of resolution being used. In so doing, they vividly described a South in which slaves were valuable assets deserving of careful supervision and yet so flawed by nature as to challenge the most skillful master. Moreover, judicial credibility was high because, as slaveholders themselves, their stories were based on firsthand experience. The judges' narratives were scarcely innovative. They told and told again an archetypal fable in which enlightened masters improved the lot of Africans by removing them from a savage existence, satisfying their basic needs, and introducing them to Christianity.

Narrative consistency wavered when judges from the Upper South explicitly demeaned the treatment of slaves in portions of the Deep South. When judges narrated the costs of food, clothing, and health care for their slaves, or when they advertised rewards for capturing runaways, tales of life in the Upper South and Deep South were comparable. In this respect, the discourse of Virginia's Briscoe G. Baldwin matched that of Louisiana's Francis-Xavier Martin. Comparable too were judicial narratives of how their slaves were used as collateral, gifts, or other forms of currency. The method for evaluating these assets—a constant source of legal dispute—prompted judicial narratives. David Johnson's answer to this question, sustained by "cases arising out of real life," contained his exemplary story of "the ties . . . by which the master and slave are united." He asked rhetorically: "Is there any thing in a barren sand hill that could attach a purchaser to it, and give it a peculiar and special value that may not be found in an able, honest, and faithful slave?" And then answering his own question, he proposed: "If you put their intrinsic value in competition, it will be found to be as a thousand to one in favor of the slave."[7] Selectively confirming a paternalism toward slaves, the judges insisted that the sensibilities of the master were to be trusted.

Despite their consensus on an idealized relationship between master and slave, the judges were hard-pressed to develop legal formulas that were applicable across a variety of cases. Their narratives expressed agreement only on the general nature of Africans. "The servile race," claimed Judge Baldwin, "carry with them indefinitely the marks of inferiority and degradation."[8] Inherent flaws in slaves made it difficult to apply general rules of law. As Abraham Nott complained: "The character of a slave depends so much upon the treatment he receives, the opportunities he has to commit crimes, and the temptation to which he is exposed, that we can form but a very imperfect opinion of it."[9] In the end, judges declared that planters must exercise foresight in the matter of slavery or vagaries of the institution would overcome the South. The most poignant expression of this caution—attributed to many sources, including Thomas Jefferson—compared the southern experience of slavery with holding a wolf by its ears: your position was undesirable but you were afraid to let go.

Using classically approved technique, the judges founded their argument on narrative premises that were immediately familiar and acceptable to an audience of fellow planters. More provocative was the dual use of these factual assertions as both premise and evidence. Their circular reasoning attests to the judges' confidence in the essential truth of their intuitions. Thus they did not find a fallacious expression of these intuitions troubling.

Despite its value as a liberal art and a professional tool, narrative technique was merely preliminary to substantive equations of humanity and interest. Articulating this humanist ideal satisfied judicial duties to uphold moral and political traditions. Judges dutifully asserted the morality of keeping Africans in bondage. At the same time, they ritualistically invoked peace and prosperity as motives underlying all slave laws. Indeed, many judges insisted that humane provisions and safeguards were imbedded within the politics of slavery. Indistinct boundaries among their roles of legal, political, and moral guides sustained these shallow but indispensable appeals to humanity and interest.

Joint protestations of humanity and interest were merely convenient. The judges could not fail to recognize how irrelevant these claims were to their appellate reviews. John W. Green disclaimed altogether "moral and political considerations" in his opinions.[10] William A. G. Dade, a colleague, expressed contempt for "what may be expedient, or morally, or politically right" in reviewing appeals.[11] Less uniform among opinions authored in the Deep South, these blended appeals to morality and policy reflected judicial pursuit of a humanist ideal that taxed personal and professional resources.

The most sensible method for justifying attention to humanity was locating moral principle in the policies and legislation that expressed the property interest of masters. Francis T. Brooke and other pragmatically inclined judges entertained appeals "to the humanity of the Court" so long as "the right of property" was not invaded.[12] But the prestigious judiciaries were not the only ones capable of arguing this point. For example, in denying the constitutionality of punishing slaves more severely than free whites for the same crimes, Thomas Johnson of Arkansas argued that a provision for equal punishment "was doubtless inserted in the constitution from a feeling of humanity towards the unfortunate African race."[13] Edward Cross similarly affirmed the constitutionality of an Arkansas statute requiring free negroes to post a bond if they wished to remain in the state. Judge Cross declared that the "constitution was the work of the white race" but blacks nonetheless were beneficiaries because "protection of their persons and the right to property is provided for to a humane and just degree."[14] In effect, these judges and their brethren tried to suppress a choice between humanity and interest.

Implausible out of context, judicial claims to moral justification—much less divine authority—for the politics of slavery made sense in the humanist tradition. Classical authorities such as Isocrates and Cicero defined humanism in civic terms as a set of conservative beliefs and values. Within this context, it was reasonable for judges to link goodness with reverence for tradition as well as a defense of tradition in affairs of state. In turn, they applied related appeals to justifying the laws of slavery. They recognized that slavery was a peculiar institution but, as a southern tradition, it merited conservation.

Whether the judges were ineluctably bound to a line of argument equating humanity and interest is yet another question. Part of the answer may be found in the conference system of appellate procedure. The legal presumption afforded trial verdicts—then and now—initially causes appellate courts to question whether a duly recorded decision should be disturbed. But the conference system also put judges in the position of hesitating to review a lower court's verdict—much less reverse it—for less than pristinely professional reasons. In this system, conferees might reasonably question whether they should overrule a colleague who himself was serving on the appellate bench and could return the favor. As Frederick Nash remarked about his experience with conferees, he avoided sitting in judgment "upon their correctness."[15] He regretted "that in the performance of what they considered right any thing should have been done calculated to hurt the feelings of an old friend & associate."[16] Under these conditions, adopting an elevated line of argument made sense.

The unsettled condition of slave laws also made professional life difficult for the judges. Few could claim, as did Pierre A. Rost, that "we are in the line of safe precedents, and advance into the unknown future with minds tranquil and free from doubt."[17] More commonplace was Joshua G.

Clarke's disclaimer in a neighboring jurisdiction that, despite the Roman, British, and other precedents relied on by one advocate, "because slaves can be bought and sold, it does not follow that they can be deprived of life."[18] Onerous under the best of conditions, reviewing the laws of slavery evoked apologetical discourse from the reviewers as they tried to deflect criticism of their efforts.

Added to these revelations of their discomfort, the judges also addressed their working conditions. Across all jurisdictions they bemoaned the travel, the hours, and the pay. The father of Henry St. George Tucker had poetically summarized the problem before he resigned from the bench:

> There was a sorry judge who lived at the Swan by himself,
> He got but little honor, and he got but little pelf,
> He drudged and judged from morn to night, no ass drudged
> more than he,
> And the more he drudged, and the more he judged, the
> sorrier judge was he.[19]

Related self-references by disgruntled judges in all jurisdictions reveal another aspect of the struggle to fashion a humanist jurisprudence on slavery. Whether focussed on professional dynamics or working conditions, judicial apologetics identify the worrisome setting in which slave laws were reviewed. For hard-pressed judges, the humanist defense of slavery was attractive because it was well defined and grounded in traditional principles. By extension, invoking these principles makes it difficult now to classify the judges' advocacy as either relentless logic or legal realism.

CREATURES OF ADVOCACY

Their individual reputations and achievements varied but, as a group including celebrated founders of court systems and persons who survive in name only, the judges aspired to conservative eloquence. Creators of discourse in texts as diverse as law reports and limericks, the judges demonstrated a relationship with the ancient art of advocacy that flourished within their own culture and sustained a centuries-old arrangement in Western civilization. Yet the judges were also creatures of their own art and they adjusted their discourse to its end in ways that invite criticism.

This criticism was expressed in timely fashion at the beginning of the period under scrutiny here. In December 1819, Edward T. Channing, Boylston Professor of Rhetoric and Oratory at Harvard, began a series of lectures that included pointed criticisms of the art of advocacy. In his inaugural lecture, Channing observed that "the orator is the creature of the circumstances in which he is placed." By this he meant that each orator "is formed by the same influences that form his neighbors; he must fall in with their taste, accommodate himself to their wants, and consult their prejudices and general tone and habits of thinking." As a result, students were discouraged from aspiring to "an overwhelming greatness and sway."[20] Judicial orators were subject to this same cautionary advice. Rather than being lionized for expressing a hegemonic viewpoint on the laws of slavery, judicial narratives may be criticized for restating only those facts of life that were plausible and palatable to fellow planters. Moreover, judicial apologetics reflect more of a petty distaste for criticism than an elevated focus on truth, goodness, and beauty.

Professor Channing disowned an oratorical training founded strictly on the classical tradition. Therefore, in one of his lectures on judicial oratory, he discouraged the advocate from appealing "to private feelings of interest . . . or suppose that eloquent declamation about right and wrong will give any force of sanctity to his claim."[21] From Channing's perspective, the humanist ideal of equating policy and morality was outdated and irrelevant to American legal proceedings. Advocates who voiced humanist appeals were ignoring reality, wallowing in oratorical display rather than ascending to serious deliberation. Flattering themselves, these advocates mistook pretentiousness for nobility.

According to the critical standards expressed by Channing, the oratorical portions of judicial opinions are self-serving and deceptive. Illustrative is Richard E. Parker's almost fawning remark that he would trust his opinion, "maturely formed or carefully examined," except that "so large a majority" of his brethren in Virginia had ruled differently. And in the Deep South, Henry W. Collier grossly defended himself and his Alabama colleagues by uttering a sweeping denial that "our moral courage has faltered" or that the judges had stooped "to calculate consequences to ourselves personally." These judges' facility with language seemed to lure them into arguing that form was substance, that assuaging the feelings of colleagues was pertinent to the issues presented for review.

The same criticism may be levelled at judicial narratives wherein the facts of slavery are homogenized and validated. In the Upper South, Briscoe G. Baldwin wondered why slaves craved freedom, since in their bondage "they are exempt from the cares and anxieties of a precarious subsistence, and the wretchedness of actual want."[22] The same judicial intuition was narrated in the Deep South. "Though subordinate servants of white men," remarked John S. Richardson, members of the African race were "contented menials." Judicial choices in composing their narratives sustain charges of paternalism and chauvinism.

More devastating yet are criticisms related to the judicial method of equating humanity and interest. Blended appeals to these values are pervasive in judicial discourse of the Upper South, varying little from law report to memoir to campaign speech. Dabney Carr illustrated how this line of argument could flourish in a variety of contexts. His *Old Bachelor* essays linked "the *political* condition" of people with their "*moral*" character, and in his mature opinions he likewise discovered care for the "scruples of conscience" behind "the legislative will."[23] In asserting the inherent morality of statutes and other expressions of state interest, Judge Carr and his colleagues transcended the already considerable authority enjoyed by common-law judges. Arrogating to themselves the authority to assess moral as well as legal results, the judges celebrated a fundamental tenet in the creed of civic humanists: virtue was the conservation of tradition.

By contrast, in the Deep South, most judges paid mere lip service to humanity in addressing slavery. Pierre Derbigny, for example, considered exclusively the "interest" of Louisiana masters and the community at large when absolving an overseer of civil liability in the death of slave.[24] Pierre A. Rost, speaking at a state convention in Baton Rouge, likewise proclaimed the "advantages of Slavery as a political institution in a Democratic republic."[25] In both instances, these judicial advocates were inclined by training and habit to argue solely in political terms (i.e., peace and prosperity) when confronted with an issue like slavery. Attention solely to a political creed, the good of the dominant class, disabled Judge Derbigny from entertaining thoughts of inhumanity in the killing of a slave. Sectional politics consumed Judge Rost to the extent that he too ignored moral complications when endorsing the peculiar institution. Disabled in this sense, the judges found justifications for their opinions that did not survive the moment because their culture—along with its reverence for classical and oratorical values—was fading.

In the prevailing interpretation, judges deferred to interest and the rule of law rather than humanity and a sense of moral duty. For example, Robert Cover scored the legal formalism by which judges escaped their moral qualms.[26] Mark V. Tushnet has argued that courts did not reach a coherent resolution of the conflict between law and morality.[27] More specifically, Michael S. Hindus has addressed the legal mechanisms for preserving white dominance in selected trial courts.[28] Answering calls for an extension of research outside the bounds of criminal law, scholars have addressed the "fellow servant" rule, sales warranties, the force of the *caveat emptor* caution, and the philosophy underlying business law.[29] Regardless of scholarly focus, an unresolved clash of legal and moral premises has remained prominent.[30]

The judges have been portrayed variously as benign or ruthless, concerned or dispassionate, but have not fared well in the majority of scholarly assessments. Exceptional assessments that attribute professional skill as well as personal dedication to selected judges include treatments by Mark V. Tushnet and Arthur F. Howington, but especially the earlier assessments made by A. E. Kier Nash and Daniel L. Flanigan.[31] In a comparative analysis, Nash concluded that "the goals toward which the appellate courts were working appear manifestly more consonant with decency than could be anticipated by extrapolating backward from the twentieth-century Southern jurisprudence."[32] Detecting "genuine feeling" in the judicial opinions but recognizing practical limits in appellate procedure and statutory direction, Nash investigated the means by which selected judges fashioned liberal protection for victims of the peculiar institution.[33] His analysis of competing interpretations ultimately convinced Nash that, "[a]bsent firm historiographical rules of evidence, we just do not know about the correctness of the verdicts that emerge about the law of slavery."[34] At least in terms of appellate procedure, Flanigan concurred about the fair-minded treatment of slaves by selected judges.[35]

In assessing appellate affirmation of the laws of slavery in the Old South, critics should resist devaluing the judges because few of them possessed charisma. At the time, all of them were credible. Although few of them would fare well in tests of nobility, all of them were dutiful. Only from a romantic perspective were the judges villainous. From a tragic perspective, critics may appreciate the judges' aspirations to heroism. From this perspective, neither villain nor hero prospers.

From this tragic perspective, I dispute several recent assertions by Andrew Fede. Although Fede accurately characterizes judicial appeals to humanity as "rhetorical devices" and the judges themselves as "pro-slavery," this same scholar errs when dismissing the significance of *dicta* in related opinions, and errs again when dismissing "humanity" as a reified notion used to hide the reality of slave laws.[36] Oratorical passages in several law reports figure prominently in Fede's data, and the persuasive force of appeals to "humanity" was more profoundly based on self-references by judicial members of the planter class than on assessments of the nature of slaves.[37] Thus, the extralegal or collateral assertions in law reports that endorse slavery retain significance in deciphering judicial stances, and the humane ideals they perceived in their own characters dictated how judges justified their opinions.

By analogy, recent observations by Alan Watson affirm an alternative basis for adopting a tragic perspective on the judicial advocacy of slavery. Watson finds that the natural law, as interpreted abstractly by seventeenth-century European jurists, accommodated slavery as "consistent with reason, consented in by nations, and fair and good."[38] Ultimately derived from the Roman legal tradition—the proving ground for the rhetorical theory expounded by forensic orators like Cicero—this defense of slavery rested on the same civic humanism from which antebellum southern judges drew strength for their vexing equation of humanity and interest.[39] Unlike seventeenth-century European jurists, members of high courts in the Old South had personal experience of slaves. The only remaining issue is which group of jurists addressed slavery more tragically, those who were experientially naive or those who testified expertly about the place of slaves in antebellum society.

Tragically the judges did not tell the truth about slavery, whatever that is. Instead they narrated their intuitions and their idealized lifestyles. Their advocacy did not diminish the authority they enjoyed on the bench: at worst, they lost the respect of a few knowledgeable colleagues. Neither did the judges' idealism make them incredible: their constituents wanted to believe the judicial narratives. Moreover, the judicial disclosures of hopes and dreams do not render them liars now.

Appealing exclusively to interest or wedding morality to the political establishment was a conceit, but it restrained peers from quickly dismissing judicial decisions about slavery. Since their credibility had been established in their ritualistic ascent to the bench—a process little changed now—the judges' oratorical form merely enhanced popular awe of their lawyerly skills. Judicial apologetics scarcely enhanced their heroic image— then or now—but judicial use of the orator's tools for deflecting criticism was entirely consistent with the humanist agenda.

Rather, the discursive artifacts created by judicial advocates of slavery attest historically to the limits of law. The clash between human rights and property rights occurs regularly in the legal record from its Graeco-Roman origins. This clash continues to vex judges of varied ranks and jurisdictions. In a sheerly pragmatic interpretation, appellate judges of the Old South may be seen as resorting to an accommodation of humanity and interest that was commonplace in the English-speaking world. Well into the nineteenth century, for instance, British orators used a blend of these appeals to criticize the arrangement whereby convicts were transported to a painful exile in Australia.[40] But appellate judges in the Old South may also be seen from a competing and principled perspective. Their disclosures of personal intuition, their labored melding of appeals to morality and politics, and their apologetics may be interpreted as a dutiful but peculiar pursuit of a humanist ideal.

NOTES

ABBREVIATIONS

LIBRARIES/ARCHIVES

ADAH   Alabama Department of Archives and History: Montgomery.

AHC   Arkansas History Commission: Little Rock.

AL   Alderman Library: University of Virgina.

FSA   Florida State Archives: Tallahassee.

HL   Hargrett Library: University of Georgia.

HLCL   Hebert Law Center Library: Louisiana State University.

LC   Library of Congress: Washington, D.C.

LL   Long Library: University of New Orleans.

LSL   Louisiana State Library: Baton Rouge.

MDAH   Mississippi Department of Archives and History: Jackson.

NCC   North Carolina Collection (Wilson Library): University of North Carolina

NCDAH   North Carolina Department of Cultural Resources, Division of Archives and History: Raleigh.

PL   Perkins Library: Duke University.

SCDAH   South Carolina Department of Archives and History: Columbia.

SCL   South Caroliniana Library: University of South Carolina.

SHC	Southern Historical Collection (Wilson Library): University of North Carolina.
TSLA	Tennessee State Library and Archives: Nashville.
UGL	Law Library: University of Georgia.
VHS	Virginia Historical Society: Richmond.
Appleton's Cyclopedia	Appleton's *Cyclopedia of American Biography*. Ed. James Grant Wilson and John Fiske. New York: D. Appleton & Co., 1888–89. Supp. 7th Vol., 1901.
BDAC	*Biographical Dictionary of the American Congress, 1774–1927*. Washington DC: U.S. Government Printing Office, 1928.
DAB	*Dictonary of American Biography*. New York: Charles Scribner's Sons, 1934–61.
Lanman's Annals	Lanman, Charles. *Biographical Annals of the Civil Government of the United States in Its First Century*. Washington DC: James Anglim, 1876.
NCAB	*National Cyclopedia of American Biography*. New York: James T. White, 1906.

INTRODUCTION

1. Robert Ferguson, *Law and Letters in American Culture* (Cambridge, MA: Harvard UP, 1984) 5.

2. See, for example, Waldo W. Braden's introduction to his edition of *Oratory in the Old South 1828–1860* (Baton Rouge: Louisiana State UP, 1970).

3. Gregory Clark and S. Michael Halloran, Introduction, *Oratorical Culture in Nineteenth-Century America: Transformations in the Theory and Practice of Rhetoric*, ed. Gregory Clark and S. Michael Halloran (Carbondale: Southern Illinois UP, 1993); Clement Eaton, *The Mind of the Old South* (Baton Rouge: Louisiana State UP, 1967) 231; the same author's *The Freedom-of-Thought Struggle in the Old South* (New York: Harper & Row, 1964) 50–51; and Braden 3.

4. Nan Johnson, *Nineteenth-Century Rhetoric in North America* (Carbondale: Southern Illinois UP, 1991) 3.

5. See, for example, Dabney Carr's complaint about the compromise in his letter to Senator James Barbour, 11 Feb. 1820, David John Mays Papers, *VHS*.

6. Paul Finkelman, *An Imperfect Union: Slavery, Federalism, and Comity* (Chapel Hill: U of North Carolina P, 1981) 183.

7. William M. Wiecek, *The Sources of Antislavery Constitutionalism in America, 1760–1848* (Ithaca: Cornell UP, 1977) 7–8.

8. Mark V. Tushnet, *The American Law of Slavery 1810–1860: Considerations of Humanity and Interest* (Princeton: Princeton UP, 1981) 230.

9. John B. O'Neall, *Biographical Sketches of the Bench and Bar of South Carolina* (Charleston: S. G. Courtenay & Co., 1859) 198.

10. Daniel L. Flanigan, *The Criminal Law of Slavery and Freedom, 1800–1868* (New York: Garland Publishing, 1987) 105; Mark V. Tushnet, "The American Law of Slavery, 1810–1860: A Study in the Persistence of Legal Autonomy," *Law and Society Review* 10 (Fall 1975): 131.

11. Anthony Grafton and Lisa Jardine, *From Humanism to the Humanities* (Cambridge, MA: Harvard UP, 1986) 210–20.

12. See Carl J. Richard, *The Founders and the Classics: Greece, Rome, and the American Enlightenment* (Cambridge, MA: Harvard UP, 1994); cf. the analogous treatment of the relationship between humanism and science in Anthony Grafton, *Defenders of the Text: The Traditions of Scholarship in an Age of Science, 1450–1800* (Cambridge, MA: Harvard UP, 1991).

13. William W. Fisher III, "Ideology and Imagery in the Law of Slavery," *Chicago-Kent Law Review* 68 (1993): 1080.

14. *A Lecture Delivered before the Georgia Historical Society in the Unitarian Church, Savannah, on Wednesday, 29th March, 1843* (Savannah: W. T. Williams, 1843) 8.

15. *Address by Hon. Nathan Green, Judge of the Supreme Court of Tennessee, Delivered February 28th, 1849, on Entering on the Duties of Professor of Law in Cumberland University, at Lebanon, Tennessee* (Lebanon: J. T. Figures, 1849) 7 and 9 (emphasis is original).

16. Cf. Eaton, *The Freedom-of-Thought Struggle* 37–40; Paul I. Wellman, *The House Divides: The Age of Jackson and Lincoln, from the War of 1812 to the Civil War* (Garden City, NY: Doubleday & Co., 1966) 28; and Robert Lacour-Gayet, *Everyday Life in the United States before the Civil War*, trans. Mary Ilford (New York: Frederick Ungar Publishing Co., 1969) 17–76.

17. Dean E. Ryman, comp., *Joseph Henry Lumpkin: An Unintentional Autobiography* (Atlanta: Atlanta Bar Association, 1913) 15.

18. Chaim Perelman and Lucie Olbrechts-Tyteca, *The New Rhetoric: A Treatise on Argumentation*, trans. John Wilkinson and Purcell Weaver (Notre Dame, IN: U of Notre Dame P, 1969) 65ff.

19. Green v. Robinson, 5 Howard 80 (Miss. 1840).

20. 5 Howard 80, at 102.

21. Ross v. Vertner, 5 Howard 305 (Miss. 1840) (a treatment of testamentary manumission with more than $500,000 at stake that lived on in the appellate courts for years, became precedential authority for a line of Mississippi cases, and attracted the attention of legal scholars in several American law reviews).

"In considering this case, I have not deemed it necessary or proper to follow the counsel into the wide field of discussion upon which some of them have entered, nor to examine the elementary questions which have been raised and very ably argued. The doctrines which have been insisted on, as the foundation in part of the title of the appellants, have formed the topics of fruitful controversy with philosophers and jurists, and are not yet settled in the judgment of mankind. Perhaps they never will be, so far at least, as to command a universal assent. In view of these considerations, it is quite unimportant that this court should express an opinion, and more especially so, since the question has been settled by the paramount authority of the legislative will" (5 Howard 305, at 356–57).

22. 5 Howard 305, at 358.

23. For example, compare John Haywood's attention to the inhumanity of frustrating a father's intent to convey slaves to his daughter ("Mankind must be allowed, notwithstanding the greediness of creditors, to perform the most natural of all duties, and the most grateful to the feelings of a good heart, without incurring the loss of their property appropriated, to a child's support."), in *Allison v. Armstrong*, 2 Yerger 74, at 81 (Tenn. 1820).

24. Letter to L. A. Marshall, 25 Dec. 1837, Governors' Records, RG 27, Microfilm #21, *MDAH*.

25. For example, the length and density of opinions composed by judges Carr, Green, and Coalter, in *Gregory v. Baugh*, 4 Randolph 611 (Va. 1827), illustrates that freedom itself could be gained or lost depending on sufficient evidence of Indian ancestry. Simply put, Indian slavery—where permitted by statute in the early part of the century—was a categorically different status than black slavery.

26. Quite differently, however, the judge's feelings about black slaves appeared to influence his oratory after the Civil War. In his 1866 charge to a grand jury, he

emphasized that as "a *peace offering* upon the altar of the union" the South "made a sacrifice of upwards of 400000 slaves" [in a different hand and ink, the figure has been changed to "4,000,000"]. *Address to the Grand Jury of DeSoto County* (1866) 2, *MDAH*.

27. A. P. Aldrich, *Memoir of Judge A. P. Butler* (Charleston: Walker, Evans & Cogswell, 1878) 8.

28. Robert M. Cover, *Justice Accused: Antislavery and the Judicial Process* (New Haven: Yale UP, 1975) 224.

29. Robert A. Ferguson, "The Judicial Opinion as Literary Genre," *Yale Journal of Law and the Humanities* 2 (1990): 216.

30. Robert Gordon discusses the parameters for strictly legal analysis of an issue—as distinct from "external" legal analysis—in "J. Willard Hurst and the Common Law Tradition in American Historiography," *Law and Society Review* 10 (1975): 10. The actual use of "external" legal analysis in criminal cases is specifically discussed by Andrew Fede, "Legitimized Violent Slave Abuse in the American South, 1619–1865: A Case Study of Law and Social Change in Six Southern States," *American Journal of Legal History* 29 (1985): 97–98. Another relevant distinction is commonly made between holding and dictum. See, for example, Meredith Lang, *Defender of the Faith: The High Court of Mississippi 1817–1875* (Jackson: UP of Mississippi, 1977), in which the author identifies different types of issues as addressed in "holdings" versus "dicta" within antebellum Mississippi case law (4–5).

See the review of this dichotomy in H. L. A. Hart, *Essays in Jurisprudence and Philosophy* (Oxford: Clarendon P, 1983) 98–109. Often classified within legal positivism, Hart's perspective nonetheless accommodates this view of judicial oratory as readily as those perspectives often classified within legal realism, moralism, and other schools of thought. See, for example, David Kairys, ed., *The Politics of Law: A Progressive Criticism* (New York: Pantheon Books, 1982); Ronald Dworkin, *Law's Empire* (Cambridge, MA: Harvard UP, 1988); and Mark V. Tushnet, "Critical Legal Studies: A Political History," *Yale Law Journal* 100 (1991): 1515–44.

31. Ruth Wedgewood, "The South Condemning Itself: Humanity and Property in American Slavery—A Review of Andrew Fede, *People without Rights* (Garland Press 1992)," *Chicago-Kent Law Review* 68 (1993): 1397.

32. Daniel A. Farber and Philip P. Frickey, "Practical Reason and the First Amendment," *UCLA Law Review* 34 (1987): 1646.

33. I have read all appellate cases published in Alabama, Arkansas, Florida, Georgia, Louisiana, Mississippi, North Carolina, South Carolina, Tennessee, Texas,

and Virginia between 1820 and 1850 that address issues related to race and slavery. I have also inspected various and related manuscripts, but have certainly missed reports such as that analyzed in Judith K. Schafer, "Sexual Cruelty to Slaves: The Unreported Case of *Humphreys v. Utz*," *Chicago-Kent Law Review* 68 (1993); 1313–40. After this reading project, I was impressed by the scope and accuracy of Helen Tunnicliff Catterall's edition of *Judicial Cases Concerning American Slavery and the Negro*, 5 vols. (Washington, DC: Carnegie Institution, 1926–1937). As claimed, Catterall "with great care and exactness made her own condensed summary of the law pronounced by the court, using when practicable its own words but studying brevity" (vi). Catterall's edition lacks only a few relevant cases, although valuable discourse is missing in more quoted excerpts than was desirable for my analytical purposes. Whether the issues of race and slavery were major or minor in the case at bar, I made note of judicial discourse that did not rely on statutory or case law, did not flow from leading British, French, Spanish, or American commentaries, and in general did not obey the traditional form of legal reasoning that was normative at the time, and which has continued to direct the composition of opinions. Rather, I noted discourse that followed the antique art of rhetoric first classified by early Greeks and Romans. Surveys of this art are more numerous now than even a few years ago. Among the best, see Patricia Bizzell and Bruce Herzberg, eds., *The Rhetorical Tradition: Readings from Classical Times to the Present* (Boston: Bedford Books–St. Martin's Press, 1990); Thomas M. Conley, *Rhetoric in the European Tradition* (New York: Longman, 1990); and George A. Kennedy, *Classical Rhetoric and Its Christian and Secular Tradition from Ancient to Modern Times* (Chapel Hill: U of North Carolina P, 1980). Also see Professor Kennedy's earlier works, *The Art of Persuasion in Greece* (Princeton: Princeton UP, 1963) and *The Art of Rhetoric in the Roman World 300 B.C.–A.D. 300* (Princeton: Princeton UP, 1972), and his later work, *Greek Rhetoric under Christian Emperors* (Princeton: Princeton UP, 1983). For a recent address to the profound relationship between rhetoric and law, see Gerald B. Wetlaufer, "Rhetoric and Its Denial in Legal Discourse," *Virginia Law Review* 76 (1990): 1545–97.

34. See Richard Leo Enos, *Greek Rhetoric before Aristotle* (Prospect Heights, IL: Waveland, 1993) 65–72.

35. Perry Miller, *The Life of the Mind in America: From the Revolution to the Civil War* (New York: Harcourt, Brace & World, Inc., 1965) 139.

36. State v. Ben, 1 Hawks 434, 435 (N.C. 1821).

37. "The state of our market is dreadful. There is a perfect stagnation of everything but the importation & sale of new negroes, which continues in full ac-

tivity." Letter to Ezekiel Pickens, 10 September 1805, Henry William DeSaussure Papers, *SCL*.

38. Petition for pardon to William L. Sharkey (applying for pardon under the federal Amnesty Proclamation), 22 June 1865, Governors Papers, *MDAH*.

39. John Livingston, ed., *Biographical Sketches of Eminent American Lawyers* (New York: n.p., 1852) Part 4: 555. Nonetheless, the author continued: "[W]e nevertheless believe, that to reach the highest standards of professional excellence and juridical style, something more besides bare, bald, professional knowledge, is requisite. In the United States, particularly, lawyers should lay broad and deep the foundations of their professional knowledge, and act upon the maxim of Tully, that an 'orator' should know everything."

40. *The Encyclopedia of the New West*, ed. William S. Speer and Hon. John Henry Brown (Marshall, TX: U.S. Biographical Pub. Co., 1881) 75. Although entitled an encyclopedia, this work blatantly promoted commercial growth in the region. Other evidence attests to popular respect for Justice Cross. For example, in his 1838 congressional campaign Cross—a Democrat—won twenty-five counties while his Whig opponent took merely twelve, despite substantial Whig support "not merely from slaveholders, but from substantial holders of land, money, and other goods" (Gene W. Boyett, "Quantitative Differences between the Arkansas Whig and Democratic Parties, 1836–1850," *Arkansas Historical Quarterly* 34 [1975]: 217–21).

1. HUMANISTS AND ADVOCATES

1. Richard, *The Founders and the Classics*, passim.

2. "Humanism" resists a universally acceptable definition. Note the range of opinions, from an early commentary in Jacob Burckhardt, *The Civilization of the Renaissance in Italy*, trans. S. G. C. Middlemore (New York: Harper, 1929), through a restatement in Hans Baron, *The Crisis of the Early Italian Renaissance* (Princeton: Princeton UP, 1995), to the summary definition in Paul Oskar Kristeller, *Renaissance Thought and Its Sources*, ed. Michael Mooney (New York: Columbia UP, 1979). One judgement about humanism is secure: the word did not acquire the sense in which it is used here until the Renaissance.

3. Martin Bernal, *Black Athena: The Afroasiatic Roots of Classical Civilization* (New Brunswick: Rutgers UP, 1987) 320.

4. Morton J. Horwitz, *The Transformation of American Law, 1780–1860* (New York: Oxford UP, 1992).

5. Frequent mention of classical authorities is aptly explained in James A. Berlin, *Writing Instruction in Nineteenth-Century American Colleges* (Carbondale: Southern Illinois UP, 1984), and in Mary Rosner, "Reflections on Cicero in Nineteenth-Century England and America," *Rhetorica* 4 (1986): 153–82.

6. Rosamond Kent Sprague, ed., *The Older Sophists* (Columbia: U of South Carolina P, 1972) 18.

7. *Antidosis* 285, trans. George Norlin, Loeb Classical Library (Cambridge, MA: Harvard UP, 1929). See the commentaries in Henri I. Marrou, *A History of Education in Antiquity*, trans. George Lamb (New York: Sheed and Ward, 1956), and in Werner R. Jaeger, *Paideia: The Ideals of Greek Culture*, trans. Gilbert Highet (New York: Oxford UP, 1944).

8. Albert W. Levi, *Humanism and Politics: Studies in the Relationship of Power and Value in the Western Tradition* (Bloomington: Indiana UP, 1969) 8.

9. Cf. Corliss Lamont, *The Philosophy of Humanism* (New York: Philosophical Library, 1957) 14–15, 189.

10. Aristotle, *Art of Rhetoric* 1. 2. 1358a 21ff., trans. John H. Freese, Loeb Classical Library (Cambridge, MA: Harvard UP, 1982). For a clear summary, see Edward P. J. Corbett, *Classical Rhetoric for the Modern Student*, 3d ed. (New York: Oxford UP, 1990) 97–132; and for a brief discussion of the original motive for the system of topics, see John Herman Randall, *Aristotle* (New York: Columbia UP, 1960) 38.

11. See the specific claim about John Calhoun's use of Aristotle as authority in Eaton, *The Freedom-of-Thought Struggle* 144. More generally, see W. S. Jenkins, *Pro-Slavery Thought in the Old South* (Chapel Hill: U of North Carolina P, 1935) 64–65.

12. Harry M. Hubbell, *The Influence of Isocrates on Cicero, Dionysius, and Aristides* (New Haven: Yale UP, 1914) 39.

13. Kennedy, *Art of Rhetoric in the Roman World* 195–97.

14. Guy Achard, "Pourquoi Ciceron a-t-il-ecrit le *De Oratore*? (Why did Cicero write the *De Oratore*?)," *Latomus* 46 (1987): 324.

15. *Institutio Oratoria* (On the Education of an Orator), trans. H. E. Butler, Loeb Classical Library (Cambridge, MA: Harvard UP, 1921).

16. Alan Brinton, "Quintilian, Plato, and the *Vir Bonus*," *Philosophy and Rhetoric* 16 (1983): 167–84.

17. See Walter Ullmann, *Medieval Foundations of Renaissance Humanism* (Ithaca: Cornell UP, 1977).

18. Margaret L. King, *Venetian Humanism in an Age of Patrician Dominance* (Princeton: Princeton UP, 1986) 4.

19. Hanna H. Gray, "Renaissance Humanism: The Pursuit of Eloquence," *Journal of the History of Ideas* 24 (1963): 497–514.

20. Linton C. Stevens, "Machiavelli's *Virtù* and the Voluntarism of Montaigne," *Renaissance Papers* (1967): 123. Also see my "Machiavelli's 'Heroic' Political Oratory," *Southern Speech Communication Journal* 47 (1981): 10–22.

21. Jerrold E. Seigel, *Rhetoric and Philosophy in Renaissance Humanism* (Princeton: Princeton UP, 1968); Ernesto Grassi, *Rhetoric as Philosophy: The Humanist Tradition* (University Park: Pennsylvania State UP, 1980). But note an inquiry into the relationship between action and meditation in Lauro Martines, *The Social World of the Florentine Humanists 1390–1460* (Princeton: Princeton UP, 1968).

22. See the assessment of an educated humanist's ideals in William Hunt, "Civic Chivalry and the English Civil War," *The Transmission of Culture in Early Modern Europe*, ed. Anthony Grafton and Ann Blair (Philadelphia: U of Pennsylvania P, 1990) 206–7.

23. R. R. Bolgar, Introduction, *Classical Influences on European Culture A.D. 1500–1700*, ed. R. R. Bolgar (Cambridge, England: Cambridge UP, 1976) 27.

24. Lisa Jardine, "Humanism and Dialectic in Sixteenth-Century Cambridge: A Preliminary Investigation," in Bolgar 145.

25. Robert Mandrou, *From Humanism to Science 1480–1700*, trans. Brian Pearce (Atlantic Highlands, NJ: Humanities Press, 1979) 125–27.

26. See several essays by Richard J. Schoeck, including "Humanism and Jurisprudence," *Renaissance Humanism: Foundations, Forms, and Legacy*, 3 vols., ed. Albert Rabil, Jr. (Philadelphia: U of Pennsylvania P, 1988) 3:310–26; "Lawyers and Rhetoric in Sixteenth-Century England," *Renaissance Eloquence: Studies in the Theory and Practice of Renaissance Rhetoric*, ed. James J. Murphy (Berkeley: U of California P, 1983) 331–55; and "Rhetoric and Law in Sixteenth-Century England," *Studies in Philology* 50 (1953): 110–27. Also see my "Common Law Reflections of a Forensic 'Urge' in the Art of Letter Writing," *Southern Communication Journal* 56 (1991): 268–78.

27. Ernesto Grassi, Renaissance Humanism: *Studies in Philosophy and Poetics*, Medieval and Renaissance Texts and Studies, 51 (Binghamton, NY: Center for Medieval and Early Renaissance Studies, 1988) 53.

28. Donald R. Kelley, "'Second Nature': The Idea of Custom in European Law, Society, and Culture," in Grafton and Blair 132–33.

29. Michael Lobban, *Common Law and English Jurisprudence 1760–1850* (New York: Oxford UP, 1991).

30. John G. A. Pocock, "Cambridge Paradigms and Scotch Philosophers: A Study of the Relations between the Civic Humanist and the Civil Jurisprudential Interpretations of Eighteenth-Century Social Thought," *Wealth and Virtue: The Shaping of Political Economy in the Scottish Enlightenment*, ed. Istvan Hont and Michael Ignatieff (Cambridge, England: Cambridge UP, 1983) 235–52.

31. Thomas P. Miller, "John Witherspoon and Scottish Rhetoric and Moral Philosophy in America," *Rhetorica* 10 (1992): 382.

32. Clark and Halloran 6–7.

33. See, for example, the recent study by William P. LaPiana, *Logic and Experience: The Origin of Modern American Legal Education* (New York: Oxford UP, 1993). Also note Anton-Hermann Chroust, *The Rise of the Legal Profession in America*, 2 vols. (Norman: U of Oklahoma P, 1965), especially the chapter entitled "Training for the Practice of Law" (2:173–223).

34. Bruce A. Kimball, "Legal Education, Liberal Education, and the Trivial Artes," *Journal of General Education* 38 (1986): 182–210; also see *Orators and Philosophers: A History of the Idea of Liberal Education* (New York: Teachers College Press, 1986).

35. S. C. Humphreys, "The Discourse of Law in Archaic and Classical Greece," *Law and History Review* 6 (1988): 465–93; also see Robert J. Bonner, *Lawyers and Litigants in Ancient Athens: The Genesis of the Legal Profession* (Chicago: U of Chicago P, 1927) 135–74.

36. Anthony M. Honore, *Tribonian* (London: Duckworth, 1978) 31; also see Kimball, "Legal Eduction" 189–90.

37. See an estimate of rhetoric's "pervasive" influence in Vincent M. Bevilacqua, "Rhetoric and the Circle of Moral Studies: An Historiographic View," *Quarterly Journal of Speech* 55 (1969): 343–44.

38. William Charvat, *The Origins of American Critical Thought, 1810–1835* (New York: Russell and Russell, 1968) 44. Blair "provided the theoretical model" for popular nineteenth-century rhetorics (Johnson 128). Along with the other Scottish rhetoricians, George Campbell and Alexander Jamieson, Blair's lectures themselves "became widely popular as textbooks" (Clark and Halloran 15).

39. Cf. Quintilian, *Institutio Oratoria* 1. proem. 9–20.

40. Qtd. in Chroust 2:181.

41. *Lectures on Rhetoric and Belles Lettres*, ed. Harold F. Harding, 2 vols. (Carbondale: Southern Illinois UP, 1965) lec. 1, pp. 9–10.

42. *Lectures on Rhetoric and Belles Lettres* lec. 1, p. 13. The more observant judges would have shuddered at Blair's ranking of forensic speechmaking below "high Eloquence" (lec. 25, p. 6).

43. *Lectures on Rhetoric and Belles Lettres* lec. 32, p. 179.

44. *Lectures on Rhetoric and Belles Lettres* lec. 32, p. 180.

45. General Rule, 6 Martin (O.S.) 280 (La. 1819).

46. F. B. Fogg, "Obituary," 11 Humphrey 425 (Tenn. 1858). Martin & Yerger 5, at 21–22 (Tenn. 1827).

47. *Commencement Address Delivered before the Law Students of the University of Mississippi, July 5, 1859* (Oxford: n.p., 1859).

48. *Commencement Address Read before the Law Students of the University of Mississippi, June 26, 1860* (Oxford: n.p., 1860).

49. Josiah H. Shinn, *Pioneers and Makers of Arkansas* (n.p.: Genealogical and Historical Publishing Co., 1908) 161: "On this occasion. . . . Townshend Dickinson, a young lawyer from Yonkers, New York, afterwards supreme judge of the state, made a speech which 'set the boys wild.'"

50. Clayton Rand, "Derbigny Helped Design Law Education Units of the State," (New Orleans) *Times Picayune* 15 Mar. 1942: 1.

51. William Harper, *Memoir of the Life, Character, and Public Services of the Late Hon. Henry Wm. De Saussure* (Charleston: W. Riley, 1841) 12.

52. Letter to Ezekiel Pickens, 1 Dec. 1805, and Letter to John E. Colhoun, 20 Jan. 1808, Henry William DeSaussure Papers, *SCL*.

53. *An Oration Prepared to be Delivered in St. Phillip's Church, Before the Inhabitants of Charleston, South Carolina, on the Fourth of July, 1798* (Charleston: W. P. Young, 1798) 1–2.

54. O'Neall, *Biographical Sketches* 197.

55. *Anniversary Oration: The South Carolina Society for the Advancement of Learning, Dec. 9, 1835* (Washington, DC: Duff Green, 1836) 21.

56. *Speech Delivered in the Senate of the United States* [12 June 1856] (Washington, DC: Globe Printing Office, 1856) 11, 5.

57. John Smyth Richardson Papers, *SCL*.

58. *An Oration Delivered at Newberry Court House on the Fourth of July, 1827* (Columbia: Sweeny & Sims, 1827) 4.

59. O'Neall, *Biographical Sketches* xv–xvi.

60. John Livingston, "Memoir of Joseph Henry Lumpkin," *United States Law Magazine* July & August 1851: 34–41.

61. *Address Delivered before the Societies of Oglethorpe University* [16 Nov. 1842] (Milledgeville: Georgia Journal Office, 1842) 6.

62. *Thoughts on the Beautiful: An Address Delivered at the Commencement of the Griffin Synodical Female College in June 1857* (Griffin, GA: "Empire State" Job Office Printers, 1857) 6.

63. Livingston, *Biographical Sketches* 4:554.

64. Eulogy, 43 Ga. 658, at 662 (1871).

65. *Lecture Delivered before the Georgia Historical Society* 10–11.

66. "Inaugural as President of the Whig Society," 27 Aug. 1804, rpt. in *Papers of Thomas Ruffin*, ed. J. G. de Roulhac Hamilton, 4 vols. (Raleigh: Edwards & Broughton, 1918) 4:248.

67. Letter to his son William, 5 Nov. 1827, rpt. in Hamilton, *Ruffin Papers* 1:415.

68. James Iredell Jr. and Sr. Papers, *PL*; Letter of 14 Apr. 1822 and brochure, Richmond Mumford Pearson Collection #584, *SHC*.

69. Letter of 29 Oct. 1824, rpt. in Hamilton, *Ruffin Papers* 4:318: "You have a turn of thought, fancy and expression, which if duly cultivated will form a pretty epistolary style. Do not spoil it in the attempt to mend it. The art of letter writing consists in being easy, polite, candid and affectionate and treating a subject as a well bred person would in a familiar unrestrained and good humour conversation." Letter of 22 Aug. 1820, William Gaston Papers #272, Folder 28, *SHC*.

70. *Speech in Support of the Proposition of Mr. Stanford to Expunge from the Rules of the House of Representatives the "Previous Question"* (Georgetown, DC: James B. Carter, 1816).

71. Diary of Samuel H. Perkins, 24 Apr. 1818, Historical Society of Pennsylvania (Perkins was a tutor visiting New Bern, North Carolina).

72. For example, letter to John Bryan (assessing his borther's political speech-making as "excellent for its matter & admirable for its manner"), 29 June 1835, William Shepard Bryan Papers #3481, *SHC*.

73. *Address Delivered before the Philanthropic and Dialectic Societies at Chapel-Hill June 20, 1832* (Raleigh: Jos. Gales & Son, 1832) 5. See Barbara Warnick, "Charles Rollin's *Traite* and the Rhetorical Theories of Smith, Campbell, and Blair," *Rhetorica* 3 (1985): 45–66.

74. Cf. the accounts of training received by Judges Baldwin (67–72), Lomax (359–66), and Tucker (601–13) in W. Hamilton Bryson, *Legal Education in Virginia 1779–1979: A Biographical Approach* (Charlottesville: UP of Virginia, 1982).

75. *A Narrative of My Life for My Family* (Richmond: n.p., 1849).

76. Daniel Call attended to Judge Roane among the introductory biographical sketches in 4 Call 627 (Va. 1803–4).

77. Letter to the editor, *Richmond Enquirer* 11 June 1819.

78. 4 Call 627.

79. *Introductory lecture delivered by the professor of law in the University of Virginia at the opening of the Law School in September, 1841* (Charlottesville: Magruder & Noel, 1841) 23.

80. Copy of undated letter, David John Mays Papers, *VHS.*

81. Letter of 17 Apr. 1787, Palmer F. Carr Papers, *VHS.*

82. *The Old Bachelor* (Richmond: *Richmond Enquirer* Press, for Thomas Ritchie & Fielding Lucas, 1814) 31:199–201.

83. *The Old Bachelor* 32:218.

84. *The Old Bachelor* 31:210.

85. *The Old Bachelor* 6.

86. *The Old Bachelor* 16 (emphasis in original).

87. Letter of 25 July 1837, Cabell Family Papers, *VHS.*

88. Letter of 13 Sept. 1837, Cabell Family Papers, *VHS.*

89. Letter of 8 Sept. 1837, Cabell Family Papers, *VHS.*

90. Letter of 13 Sept. 1837, Cabell Family Papers, *VHS.*

91. Randolph 194 (Va. 1828).

92. Aristotle 1. 2. 1357a 12–13.

93. *De Inventione* (On Rhetorical Invention) 1. 17. 24, trans. Harry M. Hubbell, Loeb Classical Library (Cambridge, MA: Harvard UP, 1959). This device was also discussed by the anonymous author of *De Ratione Dicendi* (Rhetoric to Herennius) 1. 6. 9, trans. Harry Caplan, Loeb Classical Library (Cambridge, MA: Harvard UP, 1981). For a full explanation and illustration, see Paul Prill, "Cicero in Theory and Practice: The Securing of Good Will in the *Exordia* of Five Forensic Speeches," *Rhetorica* 4 (1986): 93–110.

94. Herman Cohen, "Hugh Blair's Theory of Taste," *Quarterly Journal of Speech* 44 (1958): 265–74.

95. *De Ratione Dicendi* 3. 8. 15.

96. Cf. *De Ratione Dicendi* 3. 6. 10ff.

97. 4 Leigh 163 (Va. 1833).

98. Aristotle 1. 14. 1375a 7.

99. *The Old Bachelor* 17.

100. *The Old Bachelor* 31:212–13, 220. Well known for his law lectures and "fond of belles lettres" (4 Call 629 [Va. 1803–4]), St. George Tucker also composed an evaluation of Patrick Henry's courtroom eloquence—paying attention to appearance, clothing, voice, and facial expressions (extract of a letter to William Wirt, undated, Henry Family Papers, *VHS*). One scholar has speculated that the judge authored Patrick Henry's "liberty or death" speech, a composition more often attributed to William Wirt (Stephen T. Olsen, "Patrick Henry's 'Liberty or Death' Speech: A Study in Disputed Authorship," *American Rhetoric: Context and Criticism*, ed. Thomas W. Benson [Carbondale: Southern Illinois UP, 1989] 19–65).

101. Letter of 12 Feb. 1824, in Hamilton, *Ruffin Papers* 1:292.

102. Letter to William Gaston, 1 Nov. 1829, William Gaston Papers #272, Folder 44, *SHC*.

103. James B. White, *When Words Lose Their Meaning: Constitutions and Reconstitutions of Language, Character, and Community* (Chicago: U of Chicago P, 1984) 266.

104. James B. White, *Justice as Translation: An Essay in Cultural and Legal Criticism* (Chicago: U of Chicago P, 1990) xiv. In the second part of this volume, White illustrates his principles of criticism with reference to United States Supreme Court opinions. Also see the same author's "Rhetoric and Law: The Arts of Cultural and Communal Life," *The Rhetoric of the Human Sciences: Language and Argument in Scholarship and Public Affairs*, ed. John S. Nelson, Allan Megill, and Donald N. McCloskey (Madison: U of Wisconsin P, 1987) 298–318.

105. For example, in an informal sense, David J. Grindle assessed reflections of the "inner societal turmoil that the institution of slavery created" in the "rationale and rhetoric judges used" ("Manumission: The Weak Link in Georgia's Law of Slavery," *Mercer Law Review* 41 [1990]: 721). Also see Mark V. Tushnet's reference to the formal system of legal argument propounded by Max Weber ("The American Law of Slavery" [1975] 629).

106. Perelman and Olbrechts-Tyteca 44. Perelman's thesis garnered mixed reviews in the international community of legal scholars. See my "Critical Perspectives on Perelman's Philosophy of Legal Argument," *Journal of the American Forensic Association* 22 (1985): 88–95.

107. Chaim Perelman, *Justice, Law, and Argument: Essays on Moral and Legal Reasoning*, trans. William Kluback (Dordbrecht, Netherlands: D. Reidel Publish-

ing Co., 1980) 131. Cf. the treatment of arguments as justifying claims rather than inferring these claims, in Stephen Toulmin, Richard Rieke, and Allan Janik, *An Introduction to Reasoning* (New York: Macmillan, 1979) 9; and see the underlying theory in Stephen Toulmin, *The Uses of Argument* (Cambridge, England: Cambridge UP, 1958) 94–107.

108. Mark V. Tushnet contends that the judges primarily addressed Southern audiences with secondary attention to Northern and abolitionist audiences (*The American Law of Slavery* 23). Also see the same author's earlier characterization of judicial opinions as "documents designed to persuade" ("The American Law of Slavery" 626). As noted below, I agree that the judges directly addressed internal or Southern audiences, most closely addressing audiences in the North when appealing to citizens of border states in the Upper South.

109. Letter to his brother, 2 Apr. 1818, Crenshaw Family Papers (Microfilm #15), *ADAH*.

110. Letter to Governor Lynch, 17 July 1837, Governors' Records, RG 27 (Microfilm #22), *MDAH*.

111. *Oration Delivered before the Agricultural and Mechanics' Association of Louisiana on the 12th Day of May, 1845* (Philadelphia: J. Van Court, 1845).

112. *Cannibals All! or Slaves without Masters* (Cambridge, MA: Harvard UP, 1960) 60–61.

2. INTUITION IN JUDICIAL ADVOCACY OF THE UPPER SOUTH

1. Kim Lane Scheppele, "Facing Facts in Legal Interpretation," *representations* (Spring 1990): 60.

2. A survey of contemporary literature on narrative lies outside my scope. Recent and well-received readings include W. J. T. Mitchel, ed., *On Narrative* (Chicago: U of Chicago P, 1980); Paul Ricoeur, *Time and Narrative* (Chicago: U of Chicago P, 1984); and Walter R. Fisher, *Human Communication as Narration: Toward a Philosophy of Reason, Value, and Action* (Columbia: U of South Carolina P, 1987. Also see the illustrative applications of narrative theory to legal texts in David Ray Papke, ed., *Narrative and the Legal Discourse: A Reader in Storytelling and the Law* (Liverpool, England: Deborah Charles Publications, 1991).

3. Maria v. Surbaugh, 2 Randolph 228, at 236–41 (Va. 1824).

4. State v. Tom, 2 Devereaux 569, at 571–72 (N.C. 1830).

5. 4 Leigh 163, at 185 (Va. 1833).

6. Pleasants v. Pleasants, 2 Call 319, at 270 (Va. 1799).

7. St. George Tucker, *A Dissertation on Slavery* (Philadelphia: Printed for Mathew Carey, 1796) 91–94.

8. Letters of 2 Dec. 1804, 11 Dec. 1804, 31 Dec. 1800, and 14 Dec. 1802, Cabell-Reid-Hare Papers #3810, *AL*.

9. Indenture Agreement of 20 June 1815, Tayloe Family Papers, *VHS*.

10. 9 Oct. 1834 entry, James B. McCaw ledger, Acc. no. 38–54, *AL*.

11. 1 Leigh 588, at 592 (Va. 1829).

12. 5 Randolph 577, at 582 and 593 (Va. 1827).

13. 6 Randolph 194, at 197 and 199 (Va. 1828).

14. *A Narrative of My Life for My Family*.

15. Letter from H. H. Stuart, 4 Feb. 1842, Stuart-Baldwin Papers #10378, *AL*.

16. 5 Grattan 12, at 19 (Va. 1848).

17. 5 Grattan 12, at 22 (Va. 1848).

18. Tax list for 1843, rpt. in Hamilton, *Ruffin Papers* 2:213.

19. Letter to Sterling Ruffin, 14 July 1833, rpt. in Hamilton, *Ruffin Papers* 2:82.

20. Letter to Joseph B. G. Roulhac, 13 May 1837, and Letter to Catherine Ruffin, 21 Jan. 1831, rpt. in Hamilton, *Ruffin Papers* 2:169 and 2:24.

21. Letter to Joseph B. G. Roulhac, 3 Oct. 1846, rpt. in Hamilton, *Ruffin Papers* 2:246.

22. William A. Graham, *Life and Character of the Hon. Thomas Ruffin: A Memorial Oration* (Raleigh: Nichols & Gorman, 1871) 25.

23. Address Delivered before the State Agricultural Society of North Carolina, October 18th, 1855, rpt. in Hamilton, *Ruffin Papers* 4:332.

24. 11 Iredell 640, at 643 (N.C. 1850).

25. 3 Iredell 455, at 458 (N.C. 1843).

26. 3 Iredell Eq. 562, at 564–65 (N.C. 1845).

27. See Tushnet, *The American Law of Slavery* 54–65; Patrick S. Brady, "Slavery, Race, and the Criminal Law in Antebellum North Carolina: A Reconsideration of the Thomas Ruffin Court," *North Carolina Central Law Journal* 10 (1979): 249, n. 1.

28. 9 Iredell 391, at 423 (N.C. 1849).

29. See letters of 12 Sept. 1841 and 11 Jan. 1842, Francis Nash Papers #539, *SHC*.

30. Letter of 7 July 1852, Francis Nash Papers #539, *SHC*.

31. 9 Iredell 391, at 408–9 (emphasis is original).

32. 8 Iredell 256, at 257 (N.C. 1848).

33. Application to President Johnson, 16 Aug. 1865, R. M. Pearson Papers #584, *SHC*; Receipt from Daniel K. Fowler, 1 Sept. 1856, R. M. Pearson Papers #584, *SHC*.

34. 9 Iredell 391, at 406.

35. 10 Iredell 402, at 408 (N.C. 1849).

36. 1 Iredell 76, at 86 (N.C. 1840).

37. *An Address Delivered before the American Whig and Cliosophic Societies of the College of New Jersey, September 29, 1835* (Princeton: John Bogart, 1835) 31.

38. 1 Iredell 76, at 86.

39. Address: To the Freemen of the Counties of Johnston, Wayne, Greene, Lenoir, Jones, Carteret and Craven (Newbern, June 20th 1810), *NCC*.

40. 10 Yerger 29, at 39 (Tenn. 1836).

41. 7 Humphreys 50, at 53 (Tenn. 1846).

42. 8 Humphreys 707, at 709–10 (Tenn. 1848).

43. Flanigan, *The Criminal Law of Slavery and Freedom* 208.

44. 7 Humphreys 91, at 95–96 (Tenn. 1846). Cf. the rhetorical analysis in Arthur F. Howington, "'Not in the Condition of a Horse or Ox': *Ford v. Ford*, the Law of Testamentary Manumission and the Tennessee Court's Recognition of Slave Humanity," *Tennessee Historical Quarterly* 34 (1975): 257–58.

45. "A Tribute to the Memories of Hon. Nathan Green and Hon. A. W. O. Totten," 44 Tenn. 535, at 537–39 (1867).

46. 7 Yerger 367, at 380 (Tenn. 1835).

47. 10 Humphreys 518, at 529 (Tenn. 1850).

48. Will of 1862, recorded 29 June 1965, Davidson County Courthouse, John Catron Papers, IV-D-5, *TSLA*.

49. 6 Yerger 120, at 139 (Tenn. 1834).

50. 6 Yerger 120, at 139 (Tenn. 1834).

51. Letter of 24 Sept. (1845?), James Knox Polk Papers, Box 1, Folder 4 (Microfilm #805, Reel 1), *TSLA*.

52. Thomas Fletcher, "Memorial Resolution for Pulaski County Chancery Court," *Daily Arkansas Gazette* 22 May 1878, Small Manuscript Collection, *AHC*; *Prominent Members of the Early Arkansas Bar*, comp. Clio Harper, typescript dated Oct. 1940, WPA #6715-3, *AHC*.

53. Charles F. M. Noland, "Early Times in Arkansas," *State Gazette and Democrat* 26 Nov. 1857, Small Manuscript Collection, *AHC*.

54. 4 Ark. 563, at 564 (1842) (emphasis added).

55. Letter to Major R. B. Hyde, 24 Jan. 1841, Small Manuscript Collection, *AHC.* Also see earlier and related correspondence from 22 Oct. 1837 through 26 Dec. 1840.

56. 6 Ark. 509, at 512 (1844).

57. Thomas D. Morris, "Slaves and the Rules of Evidence in Criminal Trials," *Chicago-Kent Law Review* 68 (1993): 1239.

3. INTUITION IN JUDICIAL ADVOCACY
OF THE DEEP SOUTH

1. Fable v. Brown, 2 Hill Eq. 378, at 393–94 (S.C. 1835).

2. Spalding v. Taylor, 1 La. Ann. 195, at 197 (1846).

3. Henderson v. Vaulx, 10 Yerger 29, at 39 (Tenn. 1836).

4. O'Neall, *Biographical Sketches,* 123; *DAB* 7. 1. 579.

5. 1 McCord 220, at 223 (S.C. 1821).

6. Letter to Ezekiel Pickens, 10 Sept. 1805, Henry William DeSaussure Papers, *SCL.* The judge made several related observations in his other correspondence with Pickens during the period.

7. *A Series of Numbers Addressed to the Public on the Subject of the Slaves and Free People of Colour* (Columbia: State Gazette Office, 1822) 5.

8. *A Series of Numbers Addressed to the Public on the Subject of the Slaves* 16.

9. O'Neall, *Biographical Sketches* 127.

10. Harper 495, at 499 (S.C. 1826).

11. Harper 495, at 498.

12. Harper 495, at 500.

13. Autobiography, in O'Neall, *Biographical Sketches* 278–84.

14. Letter of 3 May 1830; letters of 5 Feb. 1831 and 1 Aug. 1850; letter of 23 Feb. 1843. These documents, along with a "Rules of the Plantation" (January 1850) and Will (26 Nov. 1853) naming ten slaves, are collected in the David Johnson Papers, *SCL.*

15. 1 Hill 401, at 402 (S.C. 1833).

16. 1 Hill 150, at 151–52 (S.C. 1833).

17. Rice Eq. 343, at 370 (S.C. 1839).

18. McMullan Eq. 255, at 262–64 (S.C. 1841).

19. Virginia G. Meynard, *The Venturers: The Hampton, Harrison, and Earle Families of Virginia, South Carolina, and Texas* (Easley, SC: Southern Historical Press, 1981) 637.

20. O'Neall, *Biographical Sketches* 196.

21. Lacy K. Ford, Jr., *Origins of Southern Radicalism: The South Carolina Up-country, 1800–1860* (New York: Oxford UP, 1988) 267.

22. Rice 229, at 231 (S.C. 1839).

23. O'Neall, *Biographical Sketches* 190.

24. *Cyclopedia of Eminent and Representative Men of the Carolinas of the Nineteenth Century* (Madison, WI: Brant & Fuller, 1892) 1:212.

25. Letter to Col. C. W. Dudley, 5 Nov. 1840, Kirkland-Withers-Snowden-Trotter Family Papers, *SCL.*

26. *The Massachusetts Resolutions on the Sumner Assault and the Slavery Issue: The Speech of Hon. Josiah J. Evans* (23 June 1856) (Washington, DC: Globe Printing Office, 1856) 15.

27. The railway project fell victim to the Civil War (*Cyclopedia of Eminent and Representative Men* 1:144); several 1861 letters, *SCL,* attest to his administrative duties as Treasury Secretary.

28. "The Life of Thomas Jefferson Withers," undated typescript, 2–4, Kirkland-Withers-Snowden-Trotter Papers, SCL.

29. 5 Strobhart 21, at 25–26 (S.C. 1850).

30. "My estate has not yet been rifled and destroyed by the Yankees, but I have only a fixed income, not a whit more, in Conf. currency, than it was, in Coin, of 5 yrs ago; & you know, therefore, that my means of support are reduced 9/10th." Letter to General G. T. Beauregard, 10 Nov. 1863, Kirkland-Withers-Snowden-Trotter Papers, *SCL.* Also see the judge's inventory of no mules and three horses, one twenty-five years old and another nearly blind, in a letter to Capt. Coles, 28 Dec. 1863, Kirkland-Withers-Snowden-Trotter Papers, *SCL.*

31. *Cyclopedia of Representative and Eminent Men* 232.

32. 2 Richardson 106, at 107–8 (S.C. 1845).

33. 2 Strobhart 266, at 269 (S.C. 1848).

34. 2 Strobhart 536, at 545–46 (S.C. 1845).

35. 4 Strobhart 445, at 451 (S.C. 1848).

36. 4 Strobhart 445, at 451. Edward Frost dissented on procedural grounds, pointing out that Judge Richardson's distinction between Indians and blacks rested legally on "dictum" that was ultimately recanted by its judicial author (4 Strobhart 445, at 458).

37. Setting aside a jury's award of damages to one planter who lost his corn harvest due to the negligence of another planter's slaves, the court unanimously

declared its perception that slaves "were in general a headstrong, stubborn race of people, who had a volition of their own, and the physical power of doing great injuries to neighbours and others." Moreover, the court observed from experience "how little they adhered to advice and direction when left alone" (Snee v. Trice, 2 Bay 345, at 351 [S.C. 1802]). Judge Bay had presided over the trial and doubtlessly felt affirmed by appellate support for his original opposition to the verdict. More significantly, his intuition of slaves' nature carried the day on appeal though it apparently had been incongruous with the jury's perceptions. For the judge, slaves were fickle and naturally presented a menace unless constantly supervised—a legally unreasonable demand on masters for the appellate court.

38. *Anniversary Oration, The South Carolina Society for the Advancement of Learning, Dec. 9, 1835* (Washington, DC: Duff Green, 1836) 14–15.

39. *Memoir on Slavery, Read before the Society for the Advancement of Learning of South Carolina 1837* (Charleston: James S. Burges, 1838) 36.

40. 2 Hill 459, at 465, 463 (S.C. 1834).

41. 2 Hill Eq. 121, at 135 (S.C. 1835).

42. See his descriptions of planting routines in Percival v. Herbemont, Adm'r, 1 McMullan 59, at 65 (S.C. 1840).

43. *Speech on the Bill Providing for the Surrender of Fugitive Slaves (Jan. 24, 1850)* (Washington, DC: Globe Printing Office, 1850) 11.

44. *Speech on the Compromise Bill (July 9, 1850)* (Washington, DC: Globe Printing Office, 1850) 9.

45. *Speech on the Kansas/Nebraska Act (Feb. 24 and 25, 1854)* (Washington, DC: Globe Printing Office, 1854) 3. Judge Butler continued in a particularly biting tone with another rhetorical question about the likely response of a "romantic young man" who finds his betrothed to be black: "He sees her white teeth; but lo! she has a black skin and kinky hair. Now, what do you suppose that youth would say?"

46. *Speech on the Difficulty of Messrs. Brooks & Sumner, and the Causes thereof (June 12–13, 1856)* (Washington, DC: Globe Printing Office, 1856) 11.

47. 2 McMullan 403, at 407 (S.C. 1842).

48. A. E. Kier Nash, "Negro Rights, Unionism, and Greatness on the South Carolina Court of Appeals: The Extraordinary Chief Justice John Belton O'Neall," *South Carolina Law Review* 21 (1969): 189; Eugene Genovese, *Roll, Jordan, Roll: The World the Slaves Made* (New York: Pantheon Books, 1974) 52.

49. O'Neall, *Biographical Sketches* xxv.

50. "An Agricultural Address Delivered before the State Agricultural Society, 29th Dec. 1842," *Proceedings of the Agricultural Convention and of the State Agricultural Society of South Carolina from 1839 to 1845—Inclusive* (Columbia: Summer & Carroll Publishers, 1846) 199–200 (emphasis is original).

51. George White, *Historical Collections of Georgia: Containing the Most Interesting Facts, Traditions, Biographical Sketches, Anecdotes, etc. Relating to Its History and Antiquities, from Its First Settlement to the Present Time*, 3d ed. (New York: Pudney & Russell, 1855) 559.

52. Eulogy, 68 Ga. 845, at 847 (1881).

53. 6 Ga. 205, at 206 (1849).

54. Mason W. Stephenson and D. Grier Stephenson, Jr., "'To Protect and Defend': Joseph Henry Lumpkin, the Supreme Court of Georgia, and Slavery," *Emory Law Journal* 25 (Summer 1976): 582.

55. Robert J. Cottrol, "Liberalism and Paternalism: Ideology, Economic Interest and the Business Law of Slavery," *American Journal of Legal History* 31 (1987): 367. Also see the more specific claim that Judge Lumpkin was given "willing obedience" by his slaves, partly because he seldom if ever addressed them harshly (Livingston, "Memoir of Joseph Henry Lumpkin" 36–37).

56. Letter of 24 Apr. 1856, Joseph Henry Lumpkin Papers, *UGL*. Two years later, the judge embellished *Martin v. State* with a related observation of slave discipline: "The manner of punishing slaves, is different with different persons. The *unusual* modes of punishing slaves resorted to by some owners, are not necessarily, nor always the most cruel or severe. It is frequently so in the *seeming* only" (25 Ga. 494, at 511 [1858] [emphasis is original]). Although the judge wanted to be seen by his slaves as Daddy Lumpkin, he also claimed a stern father's right to punish them—however "unusual" that punishment might be. Statutory and precedential citations were secondary to this judge's personal interpretation of sanctions that were extreme "in the *seeming* only."

57. 1 Ga. 195, at 199–200 (1846) (emphasis is original).

58. See Paul Finkelman, "Slaves as Fellow Servants: Ideology, Law, and Industrialization," *American Journal of Legal History* 31 (1987): 269–305.

59. 6 Ga. 213, at 218–20 (1849).

60. Letter of 12 Jan. 1815, Crenshaw Family Papers (Microfilm #15), *ADAH*; Agreement with G. W. Colman, 9 Jan. 1826, Crenshaw Family Papers (Microfilm #16), *ADAH*.

61. 1 Stewart 320, at 343 (Ala. 1828).

62. 8 Porter 511, at 520 (Ala. 1839).

63. Letter to John W. Walker, 8 Dec. 1819, Walker Family Papers, Box 3, LPR 52, *ADAH*.

64. 4 Stewart & Porter 282, at 285 (Ala. 1833).

65. Letter to his daughter (addressing worms, likely production, and prices), 1 Oct. 1846, Reuben Saffold Papers, Box 216, *ADAH*.

66. 2 Stewart 170, at 173 (Ala. 1829).

67. 2 Stewart & Porter 361, at 371 (Ala. 1832).

68. Message to the Gentlemen of the Senate and House of Representatives 1853–54, Unprocessed Governors' Records, BS 2–5, *ADAH*.

69. Letter to Matthew P. Blue, 5 Aug. 1854, Matthew P. Blue Papers, Box 5, Folder 4, *ADAH*.

70. 9 Ala. 395, at 396 (1846).

71. Message to the Gentlemen of the Senate and House of Representatives 1853–54, Unprocessed Governors' Records, BS 2–5, *ADAH*. In the case under review, the court addressed the availability of damages for a master when his overseer severely beat a slave in the master's absence. However, Judge Collier was most likely referring to an agreement among masters, not including their employees, when using the phrase "all of us."

72. Thomas McAdory Owen, *History of Alabama and Dictionary of Alabama Biography* (Chicago: S. J. Clarke, 1921) 4:1324.

73. Letter from the Secretary of State, 18 Oct. 1823, Governors' Letter Book #2, SG 5680, Folder 2, *ADAH*.

74. 18 Ala. 276 (1850).

75. 13 Ala. 102, at 105–6 (1848).

76. 15 Ala. 682, at 687 (1849).

77. 17 Ala. 451 (1850).

78. Register of Applications for Amnesty and Pardon 1865, Secretary of State, SG 8037(a), *ADAH*.

79. 3 Ala. 747, at 750, 749 (1842).

80. 5 Ala. 308, at 314, 313 (1843).

81. 7 Ala. 349, at 350 (1845).

82. 10 Ala. 928, at 932 (1847).

83. 5 Ala. 666, at 672 (1843).

84. James D. Lynch, *Bench and Bar of Mississippi* (New York: E. J. Hale and Son, 1881) 89.

85. Deed of sale to Claiborne Steele (identifying 920 acres in Warren County), 21 Apr. 1841, *MDAH*.

86. Lynch, *Bench and Bar of Mississippi* 507; Letter to Jefferson Davis, 3 Sept. 1861, Civil War Collections: Confederate and Federal, Box 8 "Letters" Folder 24, *MDAH*; Petition for pardon to William L. Sharkey, 22 June 1865, *MDAH*.

87. 1 Smedes & Marshall 221, at 233–36 (Miss. 1834).

88. 9 Smedes & Marshall 115, at 120 (Miss. 1847).

89. Glenn R. Conrad, gen. ed., *A Dictionary of Louisiana Biography* (New Orleans: Louisiana Historical Society, 1988) 1:239.

90. Qtd. in Wendell Holmes Stephenson, *Alexander Porter: Whig Planter of Old Louisiana* (New York: Da Capo Press, 1969) 126.

91. Speech in the United States Senate, 7 Jan. 1836, qtd. in Stephenson, *Alexander Porter* 77.

92. *The History of Louisiana from the Earliest Period* (New Orleans: Lyman & Beardslee, 1827) 1:210.

93. Recollection of William W. Howe, qtd. in Francis-Xavier Martin, *History of Louisiana from the Earliest Period, with a Memoir of the Author by Judge W. W. Howe, to which is Appended Annals of Louisiana by John F. Condon* (New Orleans: James A. Gresham, 1882) xxix.

94. 16 La. 15, at 18 (1840).

95. Andry v. Foy, 6 Martin (O.S.) 689, at 697 (La. 1819), affirmed on rehearing, 7 Martin (O.S.) 33.

96. Henry Bullard, "A Discourse on the Life, Character, and Writings of the Hon. Francois Xavier Martin, LL.D.," *Historical Collections of Louisiana*, ed. Benjamin J. French (Philadelphia: Daniels and Smith, 1850) 17–40. Judge Martin personally cited Pothier regularly in his opinions.

97. See my "The Logic and Rhetoric of Slavery in Early Louisiana Civil Law Reports," *Legal Studies Forum* 12 (1988): 453.

98. 7 Martin (O.S.) 371, at 373 (La. 1820) (emphasis added).

99. 12 La. 267, at 270 (1838).

100. 5 Martin (N.S.) 635, at 636 (La. 1827).

101. 5 La. 1, at 5 (1832).

102. 8 Martin (N.S.) 478, at 480 (La. 1830).

103. Conrad, A Dictionary of Louisiana Biography 2:697.

104. 1 La. Ann. 195, at 197 (1846).

105. 3 La. Ann. 497, at 500 (1848).

106. State v. Belmont, 4 Strobhart 445, at 451 (S.C. 1848).

4. EQUATIONS OF HUMANITY AND INTEREST
IN THE UPPER SOUTH

1. Paul Finkelman, *An Imperfect Union: Slavery, Federalism, and Comity* (Chapel Hill: U of North Carolina P, 1981) 334, 285.

2. Finkelman, *An Imperfect Union* 183.

3. 3 Grattan 655, at 756 (Va. 1846).

4. 2 Randolph 228, at 229 (Va. 1824).

5. 5 Randolph 678 (Va. 1827).

6. *A Charge Delivered to the Grand Jury of Rockingham County at the Opening of the Superior Court September Term, 1813* (Harrisonburg: Davidson & Bourne, 1813).

7. See, e.g., his letters to William B. Hare, of 11 Jan. 1800, 16 Dec. 1800, 24 Dec. 1800, and 14 Dec. 1802, Cabell-Reid-Hare Papers #3810, *AL*, in which state and federal politics are discussed prominently; 6 Randolph 194, at 202 (Va. 1828).

8. Letter of 17 June 1850, Stuart Family Papers, *VHS*.

9. *Preamble and Resolutions Offered to the House of Delegates on the Missouri Question* (Richmond: Thomas Ritchie, 1819).

10. 3 Randolph 170, at 178 (Va. 1825).

11. 11 Leigh 616, at 624 (Va. 1841).

12. 5 Randolph 66, at 665 (Va. 1827).

13. 5 Randolph at 690 (Va. 1827).

14. Cf. the statutory basis for the court's denial of an appeal from a master convicted of murdering his slave, in Souther v. Commonwealth, 7 Grattan 673 (Va. 1851).

15. 7 Leigh 689, at 701 (Va. 1836).

16. 3 Randolph 170, at 173 (Va. 1825).

17. 4 Randolph 256, at 261 (Va. 1826).

18. *The Old Bachelor* 26.

19. 2 Grattan 227, at 229 (Va. 1845).

20. 12 Leigh 495, at 501 (Va. 1842).

21. "Preamble and Resolution" (Botecourt County, Dec. 10, 1860), *Southern Historical Society Papers* (Richmond: J. Wm. Jones, 1876) 1:15–16.

22. Letter of 16 Nov. 1859, Lewis Family Papers, *VHS*.

23. Letter of 17 Nov. 1859, Lewis Family Papers, *VHS.*

24. 7 Grattan 602, at 608 (Va. 1850).

25. 7 Leigh 689, at 709 (Va. 1836) (emphasis added).

26. Letter to James Barbour, 11 Feb. 1820, David John Mays papers, *VHS.*

27. *Lectures on Constitutional Law for the Use of the Law Class at the University of Virginia* (Richmond: Shepherd and Colin, 1843) 204.

28. *A Few Lectures on Natural Law* (Charlottesville: James Alexander, 1844) 179.

29. 2 Va. Cas. 394 (1824).

30. 2 Va. Cas. 447 (1824).

31. 8 Leigh 584 (Va. 1837).

32. 10 Leigh 467 (Va. 1839).

33. 8 N.C. 210, at 216 (1820); 9 N.C. 582, at 583 (1823).

34. *A Charge Delivered to the Grand Jury of Edgecombe Superior Court* (Raleigh: J. Gales, 1817) 5.

35. 1 Devereux 189, at 203 (N.C. 1827).

36. 1 Devereux 189, at 207 (1827).

37. In *State v. Boon,* for example, the two judges had debated political and moral aspects of slave killing (1 N.C. 103 [1801]). Judge Taylor remarked that slavery "ought not to be aggravated by an evil, at which reason, religion, humanity and policy equally revolt" (discourse like this has moved scholars to attribute progressive motives and influence to Judge Taylor; see A. E. Kier Nash, "A More Equitable Past? Southern Supreme Courts and the Protection of the Antebellum Negro," *North Carolina Law Review* 48 [1970]: 211). Diverging from his colleague's discussion of morality, Judge Hall discussed the salutary policy behind denying most civil rights to slaves.

38. 9 N.C. 454, at 455–57 (1823) (the judge's similarity, in this respect, to John Louis Taylor has also drawn favorable mention from Professor Nash in his "More Equitable Past?" 211).

39. 1 Devereux 189, at 205 (1827).

40. 1 Devereux Eq. 493, at 496 (N.C. 1830).

41. See, e.g., his letter of 22 Dec. 1824, Bartlett Yancey Papers #805, Folder 5, *SHC.*

42. 5 Iredell 250, at 252 (N.C. 1844).

43. 9 Iredell 391, at 409 (N.C. 1849).

44. *An Address Delivered before the Members of Eagle Lodge No. 71 on the Anniversary of St. John the Evangelist, Dec. 27, 1838* (Hillsborough: Dennis Heartt, 1839).

45. See, e.g., his several letters to John H. Bryan during the 1820s, William Shepard Bryan Papers, *SHC*; Letter of 14 Sept. 1831, William Gaston Papers #272, Folder 52, *SHC*.

46. Letter of 8 May 1833, William Gaston Papers #272, Folder 56, *SHC*.

47. *Address Delivered before the Philanthropic and Dialectic Societies at Chapel-Hill June 20, 1832* (Raleigh: Jos. Gales & Son, 1832) 15–16.

48. "The Old North State," *NCC*.

49. *An Address Delivered before the American Whig and Cliosophic Societies of the College of New Jersey, September 29, 1835* (Princeton: John Bogart, 1835) 21.

50. 1 Iredell 76, at 83 (N.C. 1840).

51. *Speech Delivered in the Recent State Convention of N.C. Assembled for the Purpose of Revising the Constitution* (Baltimore: Fielding Lucas, Jr., 1836).

52. 1 Devereux & Battle 121, at 165, 171 (N.C. 1834).

53. 20 N.C. 144, at 147, 162 (1838).

54. Letter of 29 Oct. 1824, rpt. in Hamilton, *Ruffin Papers*, 1:319.

55. Letter of 5 Mar. 1827, rpt. in Hamilton, *Ruffin Papers*, 1:381.

56. Letter of 17 July 1833, rpt. in Hamilton, *Ruffin Papers*, 2:81.

57. Address Delivered before the State Agricultural Society of North Carolina, October 18th, 1855, rpt. in Hamilton, *Ruffin Papers* 4:332–33.

58. Address Delivered before the State Agricultural Society of North Carolina, October 18th, 1855.

59. 2 Devereux 263 (N.C. 1829).

60. Rpt. in Hamilton, *Ruffin Papers* 1:249–54.

61. 9 Iredell 391 (N.C. 1849).

62. Scroggins v. Scroggins, 3 Devereux 535 (N.C. 1832); Barden v. Barden, 3 Devereux 548 (N.C. 1832); Hansley v. Hansley, 10 Iredell 506 (N.C. 1849).

63. State v. Samuel, 2 Devereux & Battle 177 (N.C. 1836).

64. Mayho v. Sears, 3 Iredell 224 (N.C. 1842).

65. Cox v. Williams, 4 Iredell Eq. 15 (N.C. 1845).

66. State v. Hart, 4 Iredell 246 (N.C. 1844); State v. Newsom, 5 Iredell 250 (N.C. 1844).

67. See, for example, correspondence with Yancey on 2 July 1822, 3 Dec. 1824, and 25 Aug. 1826, Bartlett Yancey Papers #805, Folder 2, *SHC*. Also see correspondence with Iredell on 22 Jan. 1829, James Iredell Jr. and Sr. Papers, *PL*.

68. Letter of 16 July 1857, Welden Nathaniel Edwards Papers #3381, Folder 4, *SHC*.

69. Address Delivered before the State Agricultural Society of North Carolina, October 18th, 1855.

70. Letter of 21 May 1862, rpt. in Hamilton, *Ruffin Papers* 3:239.

71. Letter to E. J. Hale, 11 Aug. 1863, rpt. in Hamilton, *Ruffin Papers* 3:328.

72. Petition of 19 Aug. 1865, rough draft and final application rpt. in Hamilton, *Ruffin Papers* 4:11–21.

73. Letters to David L. Swain of 11 Sept., 18 Sept., and 18 Nov. 1865, Walter Clark Papers, *NCDAH*.

74. Letter to Edward Conigland, 2 July 1866, rpt. in Hamilton, *Ruffin Papers* 4:63.

75. Letter of 8 July 1869, Thomas Ruffin Papers, *PL*.

76. The same may be said of Henry Seawell who, in writing to Judge Ruffin, stylishly indicted Congress and the Supreme Court for destroying states' rights. Judge Seawell remarked: "The Constitution of the United States, appears to be acquiring in the political world what was ascribed to the philosopher's stone in the physical regions. It is gathering by its *own growth*, the capacity of converting every thing, into exclusive Jurisdiction of Congress: . . . I shall soon expect to learn, that our fornication laws are unconstitutional: for the favorite doctrine now is, the sole power of acting upon that subject is transferred to (Congress)" (Letter of 12 Feb. 1824, rpt. in Hamilton, *Ruffin Papers* 1:292).

77. 11 Iredell 555 (N.C. 1850).

78. Application to President Johnson, 16 Aug. 1865, Richmond Mumford Pearson Papers #584, *SHC*.

79. Letter—An Appeal to the Calm Judgment of North Carolinians, 20 July 1868, 3, *NCC*.

80. 4 Yerger 84, at 92–93 (Tenn. 1833).

81. 6 Yerger 120, at 126, 129, and 131 (Tenn. 1834).

82. Letter of 24 Nov. 1820, Governor Joseph McMinn Correspondence, Box 1, Folder 6, *TSLA*.

83. Letter to Andrew J. Donelson, 2 Dec. 1829, Andrew J. Donelson Papers (Microfilm #403), *TSLA*.

84. Letter of 2 Jan. 1833, John Catron Papers, IV-D-5, *TSLA*.

85. Scott v. Sandford, 60 U.S. 393, at 522–23 (1856).

86. Meigs 331, at 339 (Tenn. 1838).

87. Letter of 20 Aug. 1843, Robert Looney Caruthers Papers, *SHC*.

88. 11 Humphreys 172, at 175 (Tenn. 1850).

89. 1 Yerger 156, at 165, 164 (Tenn. 1829).

90. Letter to Gerrit Smith, 30 Nov. 1841, qtd. in Henry L. Swint, "Ezechiel Birdseye and the Free State of Frankland," *Tennessee Historical Quarterly* 3 (1944): 229.

91. See W. A. Henderson, *Life and Character of Judge McKinney: A Paper Read before the Bar Association of Tennessee Thursday, July 3d, 1884* (Nashville: Albert B. Tavel, 1884) 10; and Tribute of Respect to the Memory of Hon. William B. Reese, 39 Tenn. 403, at 406 (1859).

92. 10 Yerger 29, at 37 (Tenn. 1836). The court adopted verbatim Judge Reese's opinion in chancery. See Henderson v. Vaulx (6th Cir. Tenn., 25 Aug. 1831), Box 53A, *TSLA*.

93. 1 Humphreys 102, at 104 (Tenn. 1839).

94. 4 Ark. 563, at 570 (1842).

95. John Hallum, *Biographical and Pictorial History of Arkansas* (Albany: Weed, Parsons and Co., 1887) 153.

96. 11 Ark. 390, at 404–5 (1850).

97. Hallum, *Biographical and Pictorial History of Arkansas* 240.

98. William S. Speer and Hon. John Henry Brown, eds., *The Encyclopedia of the New West* (Marshall, TX: U.S. Biographical Pub. Co., 1881) 75.

99. 6 Ark. 509, at 512 (1844).

100. Perelman and Olbrechts-Tyteca 190.

5. EQUATIONS OF HUMANITY AND INTEREST
IN THE DEEP SOUTH

1. *Cyclopedia of Eminent and Representative Men of the Carolinas of the Nineteenth Century* 1:298.

2. Richardson Eq. 294, at 301 (S.C. 1832).

3. 2 Hill Eq. 378, at 391–92 (S.C. 1835).

4. *An Address to a Public Meeting of the Citizens of Union District* (Columbia: *Times & Gazette* Office, 1831); *Speech before the Charleston State Rights and Free Trade Association, Apr. 1, 1832* (Charleston: E. J. Van Brunt, 1832).

5. *Anniversary Oration, the South Carolina Society for the Advancement of Learning, Dec. 9, 1835* 6, 10, and 15.

6. *Memoir on Slavery, Read before the Society for the Advancement of Learning of South Carolina 1837* 14.

7. O'Neall, *Biographical Sketches* 53.

8. Letter from Abraham Ottolengui, 9 Oct. 1829, *SCL*.

9. 2 Nott & McCord 456, at 463 (S.C. 1820).

10. Harper 508, at 514 (S.C. 1830).

11. O'Neall, *Biographical Sketches* 250.

12. See his *Address to the Citizens of South Carolina on the Approaching Election of President and Vice-President of the United States by a Federal Republican* (Charleston: W. P. Young, 1800); and *An Answer to a Dialogue between a Federalist and a Republican* (Charleston: W. P. Young, 1800).

13. *A Series of Numbers Addressed to the Public on the Subject of the Slaves and Free People of Colour* (Columbia: State Gazette Office, 1822) 20–21.

14. 2 Hill Eq. 304, at 307 (S.C. 1835).

15. A member of the Episcopal Church for thirty years, Judge Colcock was sufficiently devout to help substantially in building St. Peter's Church in Charleston (O'Neall, *Biographical Sketches* 127). Judge Nott counted prominent clergymen among his ancestors and was trained for the ministry at Yale (O'Neall, *Biographical Sketches* 121; *DAB* 7.1.579; Appleton's *Cyclopedia* 4.5.10).

16. 1 McCord 430 (S.C. 1821).

17. 4 McCord 156 (S.C. 1827).

18. Autobiography, in O'Neall, *Biographical Sketches* 278.

19. Letters of 7 May 1835 and 6 May 1850, David Johnson Papers, *SCL*.

20. Decree attributed in a misspelling to "Johnston, Ch." 1 Richardson Eq. 61 (S.C. 1844).

21. O'Neall, *Biographical Sketches* 187.

22. 2 Strobhart 41, at 47 (S.C. 1847).

23. Report of trial verdict, 1 Bailey 275 (S.C. 1829). Judge O'Neall also felt that free negroes "ought, by law, to be compelled to demean themselves as inferiors, from whom submission and respect, to the whites, in all their intercourse in society, is demanded" (State v. Harden, 2 Speers 152, at 155 [S.C. 1832]).

24. Dudley 83, at 85–86 (S.C. 1837).

25. 2 McMullan 454, at 470 (S.C. 1842).

26. 2 McMullan 472, at 492 (S.C. 1842).

27. 2 Strobhart 536, at 548 (S.C. 1845).

28. O'Neall, *Biographical Sketches* 204.

29. Remarks on the Resolution of Mr. Waddy Thompson, Jr., to Amend the Rules Relative to the Reception and Disposal of Abolition Petitions, in the United States House of Representatives, Jan. 21, 1840, *SCL*.

30. *Remarks of Messrs. Clemens, Butler, and Jefferson Davis, on the Vermont Resolutions Relating to Slavery (Jan. 10, 1850)* (Washington, DC: Globe Printing

Office, 1850); *Remarks on the Proposition to Admit California as a State into the Union (Feb. 15, 1850)* Washington, DC: Globe Printing Office, 1850).

31. Speech before the Convention of the Southern Rights Associations [c. 1850], James Lawrence Orr Papers, *SCL.*

32. *Speech on the Kansas/Nebraska Act (Feb. 24 and 25, 1854)* (Washington, DC: Globe Printing Office, 1854) 3.

33. *Repeal of the Fugitive Slave Law: Remarks in Rely to Remarks of Mr. Sumner of Massachusetts (June 25, 1854)* (Washington, DC: Globe Printing Office, 1854) 3. But see Judge Butler's self-deprecating comments two years later in which he admitted to "three peculiarities of manner—impatience, excitability, and perhaps absent-mindedness." *Speech Delivered in the Senate of the United States (June 12, 1856)* (Washington, DC: Globe Printing Office, 1856) 12.

34. Baylis J. Earle, in his only contribution to the genre, invoked social policy about the "indecent and degrading" sexual relations between masters and slaves (Farr v. Thompson, Chaves 37, at 48 [S.C. 1839]).

35. *Speech of Senator Evans in the United States Senate (June 12, 1856)* (Washington, DC: Globe Printing Office, 1856) 15–16.

36. *Charleston Daily Courier* 15 Apr. 1861: 1.

37. Ex Parte Boylston, 2 Strobhart 41, at 43 (S.C. 1847).

38. A nullifier and staunch secessionist, Thomas Withers readily endorsed this argument from necessity; see Richardson v. Broughton, 2 Strobhart 1, at 9 (S.C 1848).

39. 3 Strobhart 573, at 575 (S.C. 1849).

40. *Argument against William Harper on Nullification of the Protective Tariff* (Columbia: *Times & Gazette* Office, 1830); *Speech Delivered at Statesburgh Dinner, in Opposition to Disunion, Convention, and Nullification (Aug. 19, 1830)* (Charleston: Office of the *Irishman and Southern Democrat*, 1830).

41. 2 Strobhart 536, at 545, 548 (S.C. 1845).

42. 2 Strobhart 266, at 268 (S.C. 1848).

43. White, *Historical Collections of Georgia* 394.

44. Notes & Reflections—1827, Joseph Henry Lumpkin Papers, *HL.*

45. Letters of 15 Oct. 1847 and 20 Oct. 1852, Joseph Henry Lumpkin Papers, *HL;* Letter of 18 Sept. 1854, Joseph Henry Lumpkin Papers, *UGL.*

46. Address Delivered before Hopewell Presbytery, the Board of Trustees of Oglethorpe University, and a Large Concourse or Ladies and Gentlemen, at the Methodist Church in the City of Milledgeville, after the Conclusion of the Cere-

mony of Laying the Cornerstone of Oglethorpe University, 31 March 1837, Joseph Henry Lumpkin Papers, *HL.*

47. 4 Ga. 445, at 459 (1848).

48. Notes & Reflections–1827, Joseph Henry Lumpkin Papers, *HL.*

49. Livingston, ed., *Biographical Sketches* 557.

50. Letter of 21 Oct. 1831, Eugenius A. Nisbet Papers, *HL.*

51. Letter of 16 Oct. 1856, Joseph Henry Lumpkin Papers, *HL.*

52. Letter of 25 Oct. 1830, Eugenius A. Nisbet Papers, *HL*; *A Lecture Delivered before the Georgia Historical Society in the Unitarian Church, Savannah, on Wednesday, 29th March, 1843* (Savannah: W. T. Williams, 1843) 12 and 22.

53. 4 Ga. 75, at 94 (1848).

54. Address to Constituents, May 27, 1840, Eugenius A. Nisbet Papers, *HL.*

55. Letter of 23 July 1841, Eugenius A. Nisbet Papers, *HL.*

56. 7 Ga. 157, at 159 (1850).

57. 7 Ga. 453, at 455 (1850).

58. *The Battle of Life: An Address Delivered before the Thalian and Phi-Delta Societies of Oglethorpe University* (Macon: *Georgia Telegraph* Steam Printing House, 1858) 16.

59. *Slavery in the Territories: Speech Delivered in the House of Representatives, April 1, 1856* (Washington, DC: Globe Printing Office, 1856) 1, 6, and 7.

60. 4 Ga. 68 (1848).

61. 2 Ga. 240, at 243 (1847).

62. Edmund S. Dargan may be cited as an exception because of his sheerly instrumental perception of slaves. In *Wragg v. State* (14 Ala. 492 [1848]), for example, he reviewed the procedures for sampling cotton—that is, assessing the quality of an entire bale by testing a sample taken from the bale—and found it statutorily permissible for slaves or free blacks to perform the physical act of sampling as long as an overseer was present: "The slave in such a case, cannot be said to be the sampler of the cotton, but the white man samples it; he exercises the power and control over the cotton, the act of sampling gives; and the physical strength of the slave, is the means by which he takes the sample from the bale" (495).

63. *Tuskaloosa Gazette* 29 Dec. 1887, qtd. in *Alabama Historical Quarterly* (Winter 1942): 567.

64. Message to the Gentlemen of the Senate and House of Representatives 1853–54, Unprocessed Governors' Records, BS 2–5, *ADAH.*

65. 9 Ala. 534, at 540 (1846).

66. Letter to Alabama's Congressional delegation, 22 Dec. 1849, Unprocessed Governors' Records, AAC-2, Drawer 61, *ADAH.*

67. 4 Porter 449, at 459 (Ala. 1837).

68. 6 Porter 269, at 291 (Ala. 1838).

69. 6 Ala. 664, at 665 (1844).

70. 1 Stewart 320, at 341 (1828).

71. 1 Ala. 449, at 451 (1840).

72. Gibson v. Andrews, 4 Ala. 66 (1842); Rasco & Brantley v. Willis, 5 Ala. 38 (1843).

73. Secretary of State, Register of Applications for Amnesty and Pardon 1865, SG 8037(b), *ADAH*; Claudius Lysias Chilton, *Centenary Sketch of William P. Chilton* (Montgomery: Paragon Press, 1910) 3.

74. 14 Ala. 437, at 445 (1848).

75. Walker 83 (Miss. 1820).

76. 6 Howard 35, at 42 (Miss. 1841).

77. 2 Howard 837, at 843 (Miss. 1838).

78. (Vicksburg) *Daily Sentinel,* 5 Oct. 1850, qtd. in Thelma Jennings, *The Nashville Convention: Southern Movement for Unity, 1848–1851* (Memphis: Memphis State UP, 1980) 115.

79. 5 Howard 80, at 102 (Miss. 1840).

80. 5 Howard 305, at 358, 360 (Miss. 1840).

81. Address to the Grand Jury of DeSoto County (1866), *MDAH.*

82. Letter to William L. Sharkey, 22 June 1865, Governors' Papers, *MDAH.*

83. 6 Smedes & Marshall 93 (Miss. 1846).

84. 8 Smedes & Marshall 145 (Miss. 1847).

85. *Centennial Address on the History of Marshall County (August 12, 1876)* (Washington, DC: R.O. Polkinhorn, 1880) 23, 30.

86. 2 Fla. 533, at 562 (1849).

87. Report of the Committee on the Judiciary (1845), Florida Legislative Council (Bi-cameral) Session Documents, RG 910, Series 877, Box 6, Folder 5, *FSA.*

88. 2 Fla. 520, at 527 (1849).

89. The judge had taken the time and trouble to write to Florida's acting governor to point out a flaw in new legislation: "In the printed copy of the law prohibiting trading with the Indiana I perceive that a mistake is made in that part of it respecting the infliction of the punishment in the first section of the act. As copied in the Pensacola Gazette the punishment is that the party liable be indicted & *fined in a sum not exceeding thirty nine stripes.* If this is in the original

there must have been a mistake which should be corrected" (Letter of 24 Mar. 1832, Correspondence of the Territorial Governors, RG 101, Series 177, Folder 5, *FSA*).

90. 11 Martin (O.S.) 4, at 8 (La. 1822).

91. Speech in the United States Senate, 21 Dec. 1835, qtd. Stephenson, *Alexander Porter* 76.

92. 3 La. 581 (1831).

93. 3 La. Ann. 618 (1848).

94. 4 La. Ann. 430, at 431 (1849).

95. 3 La. Ann. 339, at 344 (1848).

96. 9 Martin (O.S.) 643, at 646 (La. 1821).

97. Manuscript opinion, *LL*.

98. 4 La. 175 (1832).

99. 6 Robinson 454 (La. 1844).

100. 8 Martin (O.S.) 699, at 701 (La. 1820).

101. Letter to Henry Clay, 11 Oct. 1831, and A Plan of the Standing Army of 200,00 Men, 26 May 1840; both cited in Mark Fernandez, "From Chaos to Continuity: Early Reforms of the Supreme Court of Louisiana, 1845–1852," *Louisiana History* 25 (1984): 26.

102. *Speech of the Hon. P. A. Rost, June 19, 1855* (Baton Rouge: Office of the *Louisiana Courier*, n.d.) 3, 6, 7.

103. Finkelman, "Slaves as Fellow Servants" 305.

6. JUDICIAL APOLOGETICS

1. A full account of court systems falls outside my scope, but interested persons may find the official record in constitutions, statutes, and law reports of the several states. In addition, surveys like that of Helen Tunnicliff Catter-all, ed., *Judicial Cases Concerning American Slavery and the Negro*, provide accurate sketches of several court systems. I have also consulted specialized sources such as James W. Paulsen, "A Short History of the Supreme Court of the Republic of Texas," *Texas Law Review* 65 (Dec. 1986): 237–303; Joseph A. Boyd, Jr., "A History of the Florida Supreme Court," *University of Miami Law Review* 35 (Sept. 1981): 1019–66; and Randall O. Reder, "The Antebellum Supreme Court of Florida," *Florida Bar Journal* 58 (Dec. 1984): 664–69.

2. *DAB* 7. 2. 235–36.

3. 2 Va. Cases 447, at 454–55 (1824).

4. 5 Randolph 678 (Va. 1827).

5. 4 Leigh 163, at 176 (Va. 1833).

6. *DAB* 2. 1. 390. The judge may have penned a brief autobiography, "Mem. of Certain Periods in the Life of W. H. Cabell," in which he recounts his education at Hampden-Sydney College and at William and Mary, the completion of his legal preparation at Richmond, his political career, and judicial experience until April, 1811. Cabell Family Papers, *VHS*; 4 Leigh 163, at 180 (Va. 1833).

7. *DAB* 1. 1. 199.

8. Letter of 25 Aug. 1844, Stuart-Baldwin Papers #10378, *AL*.

9. Letter of 9 Oct. 1844, Stuart-Baldwin Papers #10378, *AL*.

10. Letter of 7 Feb. 1831, rpt. in Hamilton, *Ruffin Papers* 2:27–30.

11. Leter of 4 Jan. 1835, rpt. in Hamilton, *Ruffin Papers* 2:139.

12. Letter of 26 Nov. 1824, William Green Papers, *VHS*.

13. Letter of 25 July 1837, Cabell Family Papers, *VHS*.

14. Cabell Family Papers, *VHS*.

15. Undated letter to James Iredell, Sr., James Iredell Jr. and Sr. Papers, *PL*.

16. 9 Iredell 391, at 410 (N.C. 1849).

17. Letter of 15 Feb. 1854, Francis Nash Papers #539, *SHC*.

18. Letter of 11 Oct. 1823, William Gaston Papers #272, Folder 34, *SHC*.

19. Letter of 7 Dec. 1827, James Iredell Jr. and Sr. Papers, *PL*; Letter of 28 Sept. 1828, William Gaston Papers #272, Folder 41, *SHC*.

20. Letter of 5 Feb. 1829, Thomas Ruffin Papers #641, *SHC*.

21. Judges Pearson and Nash also maintained cordial correspondence with Judge Ruffin during the early 1850s. See Hamilton, *Ruffin Papers* 2:352–53, 370–71, and 380–82.

22. "Address: To the Freemen of the Counties of Johnston, Wayne, Greene, Lenoir, Jones, Carteret and Craven (Newbern, June 20th 1810)," *NCC*.

23. *An Address Delivered before the American Whig and Cliosophic Societies of the College of New Jersey, September 29, 1835* (Princeton: John Bogart, 1835) 27.

24. Letter of 22 Jan. 1829, James Iredell Jr. and Sr. Papers, *PL*.

25. Letter of 31 July 1833, rpt. in Hamilton, *Ruffin Papers* 2:85.

26. 20 N.C. 144, at 151 (1838).

27. See Joseph H. Schauinger, *William Gaston, Carolinian* (Milwaukee: Bruce Publishing Co., 1949).

28. *DAB* 4. 2. 529; Lanman's *Annals* 198.

29. 9 N.C. 454, at 456 (1823).

30. Letter of 18 Nov. 1852. rpt. in Hamilton, *Ruffin Papers* 2:352. And note Thomas Ruffin's earnest request for personal news from Leonard Henderson in a letter of 31 July 1833, rpt. in Hamilton, *Ruffin Papers* 2:85.

31. *DAB* 7. 2. 360–61.

32. Letter of 5 Mar. 1827, rpt. in Hamilton, *Ruffin Papers* 1:380.

33. Letter to his wife, 27 Jan. 1829, Thomas Ruffin Papers #641, *SHC.*

34. Letter to David L. Swain, 19 Mar. 1859, rpt. in Hamilton, *Ruffin Papers* 3:25–26.

35. Joshua Caldwell, *Sketches of the Bench and Bar of Tennessee* (Knoxville: Ogden Brothers & Co., 1898) 62–63.

36. 4 Yerger 120, at 166 (Tenn. 1834).

37. Letter of 12 Mar. 1829, Governor's Papers 1827–29 (Microfilm), *TSLA.*

38. Caldwell, *Sketches* 33ff.

39. John Haywood Papers, THS, I-A-3, Box 1, *TSLA.*

40. Caldwell, *Sketches* 40–41.

41. Letter to John S. Claybrooke, 4 Nov. 1855, Claybrooke Collection, Claybrooke and Overton Papers, THS, Box 18, Folder 12, *TSLA.*

42. Caldwell, *Sketches* 85–91.

43. Letter of 23 Sept. 1831, John Catron Papers, *TSLA.*

44. 6 Yerger 120, at 157.

45. Letter to James Kent (co-authored by Thomas Lacy), 23 Aug. 1842, James Kent Papers, *LC.*

46. Speer and Brown, *Encyclopedia of the New West* 74.

47. O'Neall, *Biographical Sketches* 246–47.

48. O'Neall, *Biographical Sketches* 202.

49. *Anniversary Oration: The South Carolina Society for the Advancement of Learning, Dec. 9, 1835* (Washington, DC: Duff Green, 1836) 10.

50. 2 Hill Eq. 378, at 394 (S.C. 1835).

51. Letter of 8 Dec. 1829, Waddy Thompson Papers, *SCL.*

52. 3 McCord 400 (S.C. 1835).

53. Speech before the Convention of Southern Rights Associations [c. 1850], James Lawrence Orr Papers, *SCL.* But note the later assertion: "This is an age more of utilitarian sagacity than romantic honor."

54. *Proceedings of the House of Representatives of South Carolina against Judge J. S. Richardson on the Charge of "Bodily and Mental Infirmity"* (Charleston: Walker & Burke, 1848) 21.

55. Reply to request from Charles Lanman, 26 April 1858, Josiah James Evans Papers, *SCL*.

56. Letter to Col. C. W. Dudley, 5 Nov. 1840, Kirkland-Withers-Snowden-Trotter Family Papers, *SCL*.

57. O'Neall, *Biographical Sketches* 1:271–73.

58. O'Neall, *Biographical Sketches* 1:xix.

59. *Cyclopedia of Eminent and Representative Men* 1:668–71.

60. Letter of 30 Mar. 1856, Joseph Henry Lumpkin Papers, *UGL*.

61. White, *Historical Collections of Georgia* 559.

62. Letter of 24 June 1846, Eugenius A. Nisbet Papers, *HL*.

63. T.U.P.C. 247, at 252 (Superior Courts of the Eastern District, Ga. 1809).

64. R.M.C. 178, at 179 (Superior Courts of the Eastern District, Ga. 1822).

65. 6 Ga. 139 (1849).

66. As recalled by Hiram Warner's grandson, Judge Hiram Warner Hill, and reported in the *Atlanta Journal* 23 Nov. 1930: 6.

67. 2 Porter 276, at 279 (Ala.. 1835).

68. 8 Porter 461, at 465 (Ala. 1839).

69. 17 Ala. 192, at 196 (1850).

70. 17 Ala. 276, at 279 (1850).

71. Letter of William Kelly to Nicholas Davis (President of the Alabama Senate), 13 Jan. 1829, Crenshaw Papers, Microfilm #16, *ADAH*.

72. Letter to John W. Walker, 20 Jan. 1820, Walker Family Papers, Box 3, LPR 52, *ADAH*.

73. See Henderson M. Somerville, "The Trial of the Alabama Supreme Court Judges in 1829; And Its Lessons to Posterity—An Address Delivered before the Alabama State Bar Association on June 16, 1899, at Montgomery, Alabama," *LC*.

74. 2 Ala. 624, at 630 (1841).

75. Howard 14, at 16 (Miss. 1843).

76. Lynch, *Bench and Bar of Mississippi* 89.

77. Walker 83, at 84–85 (Miss. 1820).

78. 3 Smedes & Marshall 518, at 525 (Miss. 1844).

79. Letter of 2 Jan. 1830, Correspondence of the Territorial Governors, RG 101, Series 177 (Box 1: 1825–1836, Folder 10), *FSA*.

80. 3 La. Ann. 339, at 341 (1848).

81. Conrad, *Dictionary of Louisiana Biography* 2:697.

82. *Speech of the Hon. P. A. Rost, Baton Rouge, June 19, 1855* 8.

83. Conrad, *Dictionary of Louisiana Biography* 1:557.

84. Charles Watts, "Discourse on the Life and Character of the Hon. George Mathews," 10 La. iii (1837).

85. "Panegyric Delivered January, 1837, by Etienne Mazureau, Attorney General, and Dean of the Bar, by Virtue of a Resolution Adopted at New Orleans by His Fellow Bar Members Assembled Nov. 16, 1836," trans. Mrs. H. H. Cruzat, in *Louisiana Historical Quarterly* 4 (April 1921): 162.

86. Conrad, *Dictionary of Louisiana Biography* 2:658; *DAB* 8. 1. 81; Appleton's *Cyclopedia* 5. 71.

87. *New Orleans Bee* 7 Dec. 1833, qtd. in Stephenson, *Alexander Porter* 30.

88. New Orleans *Daily Picayune*, 11 Dec. 1845. And see Fernandez, "From Chaos to Continuity" 26–28.

89. 1 Martin (O. S.) iii (La. 1810).

90. Among other biographical sources, old and new, I have consulted Martin's *History of Louisiana from the Earliest Period, with a Memoir of the Author by Judge W. W. Howe, to Which is Appended Annals of Louisiana by John F. Condon* (New Orleans: James A. Gresham, 1882); Bullard, "A Discourse on the Life, Character, and Writings of the Hon. Francois Xavier Martin, LL.D."; and Edward Larocque Tinker, "Jurist and Japer—François Xavier Martin and Jean Leclerc," *Bulletin of the New York Public Library* 39 (1935): 675–97.

91. Conrad, *Dictionary of Louisiana Biography* 2:557.

CONCLUSION

1. Livingston, *Biographical Sketches of Eminent American Lawyers* Part 4: 555.

2. *The Remedy by State Interposition or Nullification*, Political Tract No. 5 (Charleston: E. J. Van Brunt, 1832) 1.

3. Letter of 6 Aug. [1851], Southern Rights and Cooperation Documents, *CL*.

4. An Address Delivered before the Thalian and Phi-Delta Societies of Oglethorpe University 13.

5. "Inaugural as President of the Whig Society" 4.

6. Letter of 13 Sept. 1837, Cabell Family Papers, *VHS*.

7. Young v. Burton, McMullan Eq. 255, at 264 (S.C. 1841).

8. Peter v. Hargrave, 5 Grattan 12, at 22 (Va. 1848).

9. Smith v. McCall, 1 McCord 220, at 223 (S.C. 1821)

10. Maria v. Surbaugh, 2 Randolph 228, at 229 (Va. 1824).

11. Commonwealth v. Turner, 5 Randolph 678 (Va. 1827).

12. Allen v. Freeland, 3 Randolph 170, at 178 (Va. 1825).

13. Charles v. State, 11 Ark. 390, at 405 (1850).

14. Pendleton v. State, 6 Ark. 509, at 512 (1844).

15. State v. Caesar, 9 Iredell 391, at 410 (N.C. 1849).

16. Undated letter to James Iredell, Sr., James Iredell Jr. and Sr. Papers, *PL*.

17. *Speech of the Hon. P. A. Rost, Baton Rouge, June 19, 1855* 8.

18. State v. Jones, Walker 83, at 85 (Miss. 1820).

19. Rpt. in William S. Prince, "St. George Tucker, Bard on the Bench," *Virginia Magazine of History and Biography* 84 (1976): 273.

20. *Lectures Read to the Seniors in Harvard College*, ed. Dorothy I. Anderson and Waldo W. Braden (Carbondale: Southern Illinois UP, 1968) 13–14.

21. *Lectures Read to the Seniors in Harvard College* 97.

22. Peter v. Hargrave, 5 Grattan 12, at 22 (Va. 1848).

23. *The Old Bachelor* 26; Manns v. Givens, 7 Leigh 689, at 701 (Va. 1836).

24. Martineau v. Hooper, 8 Martin (O.S.) 699, at 701 (La. 1820).

25. *Speech of the Hon. P. A. Rost, June 19, 1855* 3.

26. *Justice Accused: Antislavery and the Judicial Process* (New Haven: Yale UP, 1975).

27. "The American Law of Slavery, 1810–1860: A Study in the Persistence of Legal Autonomy," *Law and Society Review* 10 (Fall 1975): 119–86.

28. *Prison and Plantation: Crime, Justice, and Authority in Massachusetts and South Carolina, 1767–1878* (Chapel Hill: U of North Carolina P, 1980).

29. For example, the study reported in Daniel L. Flanigan, *The Criminal Law of Slavery and Freedom, 1800–1868* (New York: Garland, 1987). See Finklelman, "Slaves as Fellow Servants"; Judith K. Schafer, "'Guaranteed Against the Vices and Maladies Prescribed by Law': Consumer Protection, the Law of Slave Sales, and the Supreme Court in Antebellum Louisiana," *American Journal of Legal History* 31 (1987): 306–21; Andrew Fede, "Legal Protection for Slave Buyers in the U.S. South: A Caveat Concerning *Caveat Emptor*," *American Journal of Legal History* 31 (1987): 322–58; and Robert J. Cottrol, "Liberalism and Paternalism: Ideology, Economic Interest and the Business Law of Slavery," *American Journal of Legal History* 31 (1987): 359–73.

30. See, for example, William Nelson, "The Impact of the Antislavery Movement upon Styles of Judicial Reasoning in Nineteenth-Century America," *Harvard Law Review* 87 (1974): 513–66; Peter J. Riga, "The American Crisis over Slavery: An Example of the Relationship between Legality and Morality," *American Journal of Jurisprudence* 26 (1981): 80–111; Aviam Soifer, "Status, Contract,

and Promises Unkept," *Yale Law Journal* 96 (1987): 1916–59 [stressing the Reconstruction period]; and Leon A. Higginbotham, Jr., and Barbara K. Kopytoff, "Property First, Humanity Second: The Recognition of the Slave's Human Nature in Virginia Civil Law," *Ohio State Law Journal* 50 (1989): 511–40.

31. Tushnet, *The American Law of Slavery*; Arthur F. Howington, *What Sayeth the Law: The Treatment of Slaves and Free Blacks in the State and Local Courts of Tennessee* (New York: Garland, 1986).

32. "A More Equitable Past? Southern Supreme Courts and the Protection of the Antebellum Negro," *North Carolina Law Review* 48 (1970); 234–35.

33. "Fairness and Formalism in the Trials of Blacks in the State Supreme Courts of the Old South," *Virginia Law Review* 56 (Feb. 1970): 64–100 [focus on the disposition of violent crimes].

34. "Reason of Slavery: Understanding the Judicial Role in the Peculiar Institution," *Vanderbilt Law Review* 32 (1979): 93.

35. "Criminal Procedure in Slave Trials in the Antebellum South," *Journal of Southern History* 40 (1974): 564.

36. *People without Rights: An Interpretation of the Fundamentals of the Law of Slavery in the U. S. South* (New York: Garland, 1992) x, 53; 61 n.1; 244.

37. See Fede, *People without Rights* 133, 161, etc.

38. "Seventeenth-Century Jurists, Roman Law, and the Law of Slavery," *Chicago-Kent Law Review* 68 (1993): 1349–50.

39. Cf. Watson's survey of the translation of ancient concepts to the Americas in *Slave Law in the Americas* (Athens: U of Georgia P, 1989).

40. Sir Jerome Fitzpatrick argued in 1801 for improved treatment of convicts while they awaited transportation "in justice to the cause of humanity or to the profit of the Colony"; he also argued that better treatment during the voyage to Australia was required "in the Political as the human sense" (Letter to Rev. Charles Lindsay, Pelham Papers, Add. Ms. 33107, British Library, qtd. in Robert Hughes, *The Fatal Shore* [New York: Alfred A. Knopf, 1987] 149). In a protest uttered later that same year, Fitzpatrick asserted that he "seldom could discover a rational system in respect either to a profit arising from [convict] labor, or the exercise of reason & humanity in its application" (Letter to Lord Pelham, Pelham Papers, Add. Ms. 33107, British Library, qtd. in Hughes 149).

WORKS CONSULTED

JUDICIAL PAPERS

ALABAMA

Chilton, William P. Petition for Amnesty, Register of Applications for Pardon 1865, Secretary of State. SG8037(b), *ADAH*.

Collier, Henry W. Letter of 22 Dec. 1849. Unprocessed Governors' Records, AAC-2, Drawer 61, *ADAH*.

———. Message to the Gentlemen of the Senate and House of Representatives, 22 Dec. 1849 (typescript from Journal of the Senate, Annual Session of 1849–50). Unprocessed Governors' Records, BS 2–5, *ADAH*.

———. Message to the Gentlemen of the Senate and House of Representatives 1853–54. Unprocessed Governors' Records, BS 2–5, *ADAH*.

———. Letter to Matthew P. Blue, 5 Aug. 1854. Matthew P. Blue Papers, Box 5, Folder 4, *ADAH*.

Crenshaw, Anderson. Letter of 12 Jan. 1815. Crenshaw Family Papers (Microfilm #15), *ADAH*.

———. Letter of 2 Apr. 1818. Crenshaw Family Papers (Microfilm #15), *ADAH*.

———. Agreement with G. W. Colman, 9 Jan. 1826. Crenshaw Family Papers (Microfilm #16), *ADAH*.

———. Letter to John Sergeant, 1 June 1840. Crenshaw Family Papers (Microfilm #16), *ADAH*.

———. Letter to John Sergeant, 17 Aug. 1840. Crenshaw Family Papers (Microfilm #16), *ADAH*.

———. Letter of 21 Nov. 1840. Crenshaw Family Papers (Microfilm #16), *ADAH*.

Dargan, Edmund S. *Speech [on the Oregon Question] in the House of Representatives (February 5, 1846)*. Washington, DC: Blair & Rives, 1846.

———. Letter of 17 June 1846. William P. Browne Papers, Box 15, Folder 19, *ADAH*.

———. An Ordinance to Dissolve the Union between the State of Alabama and Other States United under the Compact Styled the Constitution of the United States, 11 Jan. 1861. Vault-7n, *ADAH*.

———. Letter of 30 Sept. 1878. Amos Reeder Manning Papers, Box 123, Folder 5, *ADAH*.

Goldthwaite, Henry B. Letter of 15 June 1845. William P. Browne Papers, Box 15, Folder 17 (Microfilm #M154), *ADAH.*

——. Letter of 23 Dec. 1845. William P. Browne Papers, Box 15, Folder 17 (Microfilm #M154), *ADAH.*

——. Letter of 25 Dec. 1845. William P. Browne Papers, Box 15, Folder 17 (Microfilm #M154), *ADAH.*

Ormond, John J. Register of Applications for Amnesty and Pardon 1865. Secretary of State, SG 8037(a), *ADAH.*

Parsons, Silas. Letter of 18 Oct. 1823. Governors' Letter Book #2, SG 5680, Folder 2, *ADAH.*

Saffold, Reuben. Letter of 15 Sept. 1818. Reuben Saffold Papers, Box 216, *ADAH.*

——. Letter of 1 Oct. 1846. Reuben Saffold Papers, Box 216, *ADAH.*

Taylor, John M. Letter to John W. Walker, 8 Dec. 1819. Walker Family Papers, *ADAH.*

——. Letter to John W. Walker, 20 Jan. 1820. Walker Family Papers, Box 3, LPR 52, *ADAH.*

——. Letter of 20 Dec. 1821. Alabama Governors' Records, ALAV 87-A783, Container SG5680, Folder 1, *ADAH.*

——. Letter of 1 Mar. 1825. Alabama Governors' Correspondence 1821–1847, ALAV 87-A783, Container SG5680, Folder 3, *ADAH.*

ARKANSAS

Cross, Edward. Letter of 25 July 1839. Small Manuscript Collection, Box 3, No. 14, *AHC.*

——. Letter of 22 May 1840. Small Manuscript Collection, Box 3, No. 14, *AHC.*

——. Letter of 26 Dec. 1840. Small Manuscript Collection, Box 3, No. 14, *AHC.*

——. Letter of 24 Jan. 1841. Small Manuscript Collection, Box 3, No. 14, *AHC.*

Dickinson, Townshend. Letter of 3 Sept. 1827. Letter Books of Governors George Izard and John Pope 1827–1829, Small Manuscript Collection, Box 65, No. 3, *AHC.*

——. Letter to James Kent (co-authored by Thomas Lacy), 23 Aug. 1842. James Kent Papers, *LC.*

FLORIDA

Baltzell, Thomas. Letter of 24 Mar. 1832. Correspondence of the Territorial Governors, RG 101, Series 177, Folder 5, *FSA.*

———. Memorial of the People of the Territory of Florida, For Admission into the Union. Florida Legislative Council (Unicameral) Session Documents, RG 910, Series 876, Box 6: 1838, Folder 3, *FSA*.

———. Report of the Committee on the Judiciary. Florida Legislative Council (Bicameral) Session Documents, RG 910, Series 877, Box 6: 1845, Folder 5, *FSA*.

GEORGIA

Lumpkin, Joseph H. Notes & Reflections—1827. Joseph Henry Lumpkin Papers, *HL*.

———. Letter of 4 Mar. 1833. Joseph Henry Lumpkin Papers, *HL*.

———. Address Delivered before Hopewell Presbytery, the Board of Trustees of Oglethorpe University and a Large Concourse of Ladies and Gentlemen, at the Methodist Church in the City of Milledgeville, after the Conclusion of the Ceremony of Laying the Cornerstone of Oglethorpe University, 31 Mar. 1837. Joseph Henry Lumpkin Papers, *HL*.

———. Letter of 15 Oct. 1847. Joseph Henry Lumpkin Papers, *HL*.

———. Letter of 13 Dec. 1851. Joseph Henry Lumpkin Papers, *HL*.

———. Letter of 20 Oct. 1852. Joseph Henry Lumpkin Papers, *HL*.

———. Letter of 18 Sept. 1854. Joseph Henry Lumpkin Papers, *UGL*.

———. Letter of 2 Feb. 1856. Joseph Henry Lumpkin Papers, *UGL*.

———. Letter of 14 Feb. 1856. Joseph Henry Lumpkin Papers, *UGL*.

———. Letter of 18 Mar. 1856. Joseph Henry Lumpkin Papers, *UGL*.

———. Letter of 30 Mar. 1856. Joseph Henry Lumpkin Papers, *UGL*.

———. Letter of 24 Apr. 1856. Joseph Henry Lumpkin Papers, *UGL*.

———. Letter of 9 Sept. 1856. Joseph Henry Lumpkin Papers, *UGL*.

———. Letter of 18 Sept. 1856. Joseph Henry Lumpkin Papers, *UGL*.

Nisbet, Eugenius A. Letter of 29 Nov. 1829. Eugenius A. Nisbet Papers, *HL*.

———. Letter of 25 Oct. 1830. Eugenius A. Nisbet Papers, *HL*.

———. Letter of 21 Oct. 1831. Eugenius A. Nisbet Papers, *HL*.

———. Address of J. C. Alford, William C. Dawson, Richard W. Habersham, Thos. Butler King, E. A. Nisbet, and Lott Warren, Representatives from the State of Georgia in the Twenty-Sixth Congress of the United States, to Their Constituents, May 27, 1840. *HL*.

———. Letter of 23 July 1841. Eugenius A. Nisbet Papers, *HL*.

———. *A Lecture Delivered before the Georgia Historical Society in the Unitarian Church, Savannah, on Wednesday, 29th March, 1843.* Savannah: W. T. Williams, 1843.

———. Letter of 1 Nov. 1847. Eugenius A. Nisbet Papers, *HL*.

———. An Essay on the Ends of Government (April 1849). Nisbet Family Papers #548, *SHC*.

———. Letter of 16 Oct. 1856. Joseph Henry Lumpkin Papers, *HL*.

———. *Thoughts on the Beautiful: An Address Delivered at the Commencement of the Griffin Synodical Female College in June 1857*. Griffin, GA: "Empire State" Job Office Printers, 1857.

———. The Address. Presented by Judge Nisbet, Chairman of the Committee of 17 Appointed to Draft Ordinance of Secession (1861). *HL*.

Warner, Hiram. Letter to Eugenius A. Nisbet, 24 June 1846. Nisbet Letters, MS 987, *HL*.

———. *Slavery in the Territories: Speech Delivered in the House of Representatives, April 1, 1856*. Washington, DC: Globe Printing Office, 1856.

———. *The Battle of Life: An Address Delivered before the Thalian and Phi-Delta Societies of Oglethorpe University*. Macon: *Georgia Telegraph* Steam Printing House, 1858.

LOUISIANA

Derbigny, Pierre A. C. B. *Additions and Amendments to the Civil Code of the State of Louisiana Proposed in Obedience to the Resolution of the Legislature of the 14th of March, 1822, by the Jurists Commissioned for That Purpose*. New Orleans: Benj. Levy & Co., 1823.

———. *Civil Code of the State of Louisiana*. New Orleans: J. C. de St. Romes, 1825.

Garland, Rice. Letter to Henry Clay, 11 Oct. 1831. Qtd. in Fernandez, "From Chaos to Continuity."

———. Plan of the Standing Army of 200,000 Men, 26 May 1840. Qtd. in Fernandez, "From Chaos to Continuity."

Martin, Francis-Xavier. 1 Martin (O.S.) iii (La. 1810).

———. *The History of Louisiana from the Earliest Period*. 2 vols. New Orleans: Lyman & Beardslee, 1827.

———. *History of Louisiana from the Earliest Period, with a Memoir of the Author by Judge W. W. Howe, to which is Appended Annals of Louisiana by John F. Condon*. New Orleans: James A. Gresham, 1882.

Porter, Alexander. Speech in the United States Senate, 21 Dec. 1835. Qtd. in Stephenson, *Alexander Porter*.

Rost, Pierre A. *Oration Delivered before the Agricultural and Mechanics' Association of Louisiana on the 12th Day of May, 1845*. Philadelphia: J. Van Court, 1845.

——. *Speech of the Hon. P. A. Rost, Baton Rouge, June 19, 1855.* Baton Rouge: Office of the *Louisiana Courier*, n.d.

MISSISSIPPI

Clayton, Alexander M. *Commencement Address Read before the Law Students of the University of Mississippi, June 26, 1860.* Oxford: n.p., 1860.

——. Letter to Jefferson Davis, 3 Sept. 1861, Civil War Collections: Confederate and Federal, Box 8 "Letters" Folder 24, *MDAH*.

——. Petition for pardon in letter to William L. Sharkey, 22 June 1865. Governors Papers, *MDAH*.

——. *Centennial Address on the History of Marshall County (August 12, 1876).* Washington, DC: R. O. Polkinhorn, 1880.

Sharkey, William L. Letter of 13 Sept. 1831. RG 27 (Microfilm #14), *MDAH*.

——. Deed of Sale, 21 Apr. 1841. *MDAH*.

——. Letter to the editor. *Southron* 21 June 1850.

——. *Commencement Address Delivered before the Law Students of the University of Mississippi, July 5, 1859.* Oxford: n.p., 1859.

——. Authorizations of rations (1865). RG 27, No. 63B, *MDAH*.

——. Oath of Allegiance, 14 June 1865. *MDAH*.

Trotter, James F. Letter of 20 May 1835. RG 27 (Microfilm #20), *MDAH*.

——. Letter to L. A. Marshall, 25 Dec. 1837. Governors' Records, RG 27 (Microfilm #21), *MDAH*.

——. Speech in the Senate of the United States, July 3, 1838. Qtd. *Columbus Democrat* 4 Aug. 1838: 1.

——. Address to the Grand Jury of DeSoto County, 1866, *MDAH*.

NORTH CAROLINA

Gaston, William. Address: To the Freemen of the Counties of Johnston, Wayne, Greene, Lenoir, Jones, Carteret and Craven (Newbern, June 20th 1810). *NCC*.

——. *Speech in Support of the Proposition of Mr. Stanford to Expunge from the Rules of the House of Representatives the "Previous Question."* Georgetown, DC: James B. Carter, 1816.

——. Letter of 22 Aug. 1820. William Gaston Papers #272, Folder 28, *SHC*.

——. Letter of 1 June 1823. William Gaston Papers #272, Folder 33, *SHC*.

——. Letters to John H. Bryan, various dates 1820s. William Shepard Bryan Papers #3481, *SHC*.

——. Letter to Thomas Ruffin, 5 Feb. 1829. Thomas Ruffin Papers #641, *SHC*.

——. Letter of 14 Sept. 1831. William Gaston Papers #272, Folder 52, *SHC*.

——. *Address Delivered before the Philanthropic and Dialectic Societies at Chapel-Hill June 20, 1832.* Raleigh: Jos. Gales & Son, 1832.

——. Letter of 8 May 1833. William Gaston Papers #272, Folder 56, *SHC*.

——. Letter to John Bryan, 29 June 1835. William Shepard Bryan Papers #3481, *SHC*.

——. *An Address Delivered before the American Whig and Cliosophic Societies of the College of New Jersey, September 29, 1835.* Princeton: John Bogart, 1835.

——. *Speech Delivered in the Recent State Convention of N.C. Assembled for the Purpose of Revising the Constitution.* Baltimore: Fielding Lucas, Jr., 1836.

——. "The Old North State." *NCC*.

Nash, Frederic. Letter of 22 Dec. 1824. Bartlett Yancey Papers #805, Folder 5, *SHC*.

——. *An Address Delivered before the Members of the Eagle Lodge No. 71 on the Anniversary of St. John the Evangelist, Dec. 27, 1838.* Hillsborough: Dennis Heartt, 1839.

——. Letter of 12 Sept. 1841. Francis Nash Papers #539, *SHC*.

——. Letter of 11 Jan. 1842. Francis Nash Papers #539, *SHC*.

——. Letter of 7 July 1852, Francis Nash Papers #539, *SHC*.

——. Letter to Thomas Ruffin, 27 Dec. 1852. Rpt. in Hamilton, *Ruffin Papers*.

——. Letter to Thomas Ruffin, 30 Jan. 1853. Rpt. in Hamilton, *Ruffin Papers*.

——. Letter to James Iredell, Sr. (n.d.). James Iredell Jr. and Sr. Papers, *PL*.

Pearson, Richmond M. Letter of 14 Apr. 1822. Richmond Mumford Pearson Papers #584, *SHC*.

——. Letter to Thomas Ruffin, 18 Nov. 1852. Rpt. in Hamilton, *Ruffin Papers*.

——. Receipt, 1 Sept. 1856. Richmond Mumford Pearson Papers #584, *SHC*.

——. Application to President Johnson, 16 Aug. 1865. Richmond Mumford Pearson Papers #584, *SHC*.

——. 1867 Brochure of the Oxford Classical and Mathematical School. Richmond Mumford Pearson Papers #584, *SHC*.

——. Letter–An Appeal to the Calm Judgment of North Carolinians, 20 July 1868. *NCC*.

Ruffin, Thomas. Inaugural as President of the Whig Society, 27 Aug. 1804. Rpt. in Hamilton, *Ruffin Papers*.

——. Letter of 2 July 1822. Bartlett Yancey Papers #805, Folder 2, *SHC*.

——. Letter of 29 Oct. 1824. Rpt. in Hamilton, *Ruffin Papers*.

——. Letter of 3 Dec. 1824. Bartlett Yancey Papers #805, Folder 2, *SHC.*

——. Letter of 25 Aug. 1826. Bartlett Yancey Papers #805, Folder 2, *SHC.*

——. Letter of 5 Mar. 1827. Rpt. in Hamilton, *Ruffin Papers.*

——. Letter of 5 Nov. 1827. Rpt. in Hamilton, *Ruffin Papers.*

——. Letter to James Iredell, Sr., 22 Jan. 1829. James Iredell Jr. and Sr. Papers, *PL.*

——. Letter of 27 Jan. 1829. Thomas Ruffin Papers #641, *SHC.*

——. Letter to Catherine Ruffin, 21 Jan. 1831. Rpt. in Hamilton, *Ruffin Papers.*

——. Letter to Sterling Ruffin, 14 July 1833. Rpt. in Hamilton, *Ruffin Papers.*

——. Letter to Leonard Henderson, 31 July 1833. Rpt. in Hamilton, *Ruffin Papers.*

——. Letter to Joseph B. G. Roulhac, 13 May 1837. Rpt. in Hamilton, *Ruffin Papers.*

——. Entry in tax list, 1843. Rpt. in Hamilton, *Ruffin Papers.*

——. Letter to Joseph B. G. Roulhac, 3 Oct. 1846. Rpt. in Hamilton, *Ruffin Papers.*

——. Address Delivered before the State Agricultural Society of North Carolina, 18 Oct. 1855. Rpt. in Hamilton, *Ruffin Papers.*

——. Letter of 16 July 1857. Welden Nathaniel Edwards Papers #3381, Folder 4, *SHC.*

——. Letter to David L. Swain, 19 Mar. 1859. Rpt. in Hamilton, *Ruffin Papers.*

——. Letter of 21 May 1862. Rpt. in Hamilton, *Ruffin Papers.*

——. Letter to E. J. Hale, 11 Aug. 1863. Rpt. in Hamilton, *Ruffin Papers.*

——. Preliminary and Final Drafts of Petition of 19 Aug. 1865. Rpt. in Hamilton, *Ruffin Papers.*

——. Letter to Walter Clark, 31 Aug. 1865. Walter Clark Manuscripts, P.C.8.4., *NCDAH.*

——. Letter to David L. Swain, 11 Sept. 1865. Walter Clark Papers, *NCDAH.*

——. Letter to David L. Swain, 18 Sept. 1865. Walter Clark Papers, *NCDAH.*

——. Letter to David L. Swain, 18 Nov. 1865. Walter Clark Papers, *NCDAH.*

——. Letter to Edward Conigland, 2 July 1866. Rpt. in Hamilton, *Ruffin Papers.*

——. Letter of 8 July 1869. Thomas Ruffin Papers, *PL.*

Taylor, John Louis. *Address Delivered to the Grand Lodge of North Carolina at Their Annual–Communication at Raleigh.* Raleigh: Wm. Boylan, 1804.

——. *A Charge Delivered to the Grand Jury of Edgecombe Superior Court.* Raleigh: J. Gales, 1817.

——. Letter to William Gaston, 11 Oct. 1823. William Gaston Papers #272, Folder 34, *SHC.*

——. Letter to James Iredell, Sr., 7 Dec. 1827. James Iredell Jr. and Sr. Papers, *PL*.

——. Letter to William Gaston, 28 Sept. 1828. William Gaston Papers #272, Folder 41, *SHC*.

SOUTH CAROLINA

Bay, Elihu H. Letter of 9 Oct. 1829. Abraham Ottolengui Papers, *SCL*.

Butler, Andrew P. Remarks on the Resolution of Mr. Waddy Thompson, Jr., to Amend the Rules Relative to the Reception and Disposal of Abolition Petitions, in the United States House of Representatives, 21 Jan. 1840. *SCL*.

——. *Remarks of Messrs. Clemens, Butler, and Jefferson Davis, on the Vermont Resolutions Relating to Slavery (Jan. 10, 1850)*. Washington, DC: Globe Printing Office, 1850.

——. *Speech on the Bill Providing for the Surrender of Fugitive Slaves (Jan. 24, 1850)*. Washington, DC: Globe Printing Office, 1850.

——. *Remarks on the Proposition to Admit California as a State into the Union (Feb. 15, 1850)*. Washington, DC: Globe Printing Office, 1850.

——. *Speech on the Compromise Bill (July 9, 1850)*. Washington, DC: Globe Printing Office, 1850.

——. Speech before the Convention of Southern Rights Associations [c. 1850]. James Lawrence Orr Papers, *SCL*.

——. *Speech on the Kansas/Nebraska Act (Feb. 24 and 25, 1854)*. Washington, DC: Globe Printing Office, 1854.

——. *Repeal of the Fugitive Slave Law: Remarks in Reply to Remarks of Mr. Sumner of Massachusetts (June 25, 1854)*. Washington, DC: Globe Printing Office, 1854.

——. *Speech Delivered in the Senate of the United States (June 12, 1856)*. Washington, DC: Globe Printing Office, 1856.

——. *Speech on the Difficulty of Messrs. Brooks & Sumner, and the Causes thereof (June 12–13, 1856)*. Washington, DC: Globe Printing Office, 1856.

DeSaussure, Henry W. *Address to the Citizens of South Carolina on the Approaching Election of President and Vice-President of the United States by a Federal Republican*. Charleston: W. P. Young, 1800.

——. *An Answer to a Dialogue between a Federalist and a Republican*. Charleston: W. P. Young, 1800.

——. Letter to Ezekiel Pickens, 1 Dec. 1805. Henry William DeSaussure Papers, *SCL*.

——. Letter to John E. Colhoun, 20 Jan. 1808. Henry William DeSaussure Papers, *SCL*.

——. *A Series of Numbers Addressed to the Public on the Subject of the Slaves and Free People of Colour*. Columbia: State Gazette Office, 1822.

——. *Anniversary Oration: The South Carolina Society for the Advancement of Learning, Dec. 9, 1835*. Washington, DC: Duff Green, 1836.

Evans, Josiah J. Letter to Col. C. W. Dudley, 5 Nov. 1840. Kirkland-Withers-Snowden-Trotter Family Papers, *SCL*.

——. *Speech of Senator Evans in the United States Senate (June 12, 1856)*. Washington, DC: Globe Printing Office, 1856.

——. *The Massachusetts Resolutions on the Sumner Assault and the Slavery Issue: The Speech of Hon. Josiah J. Evans (23 June 1856)*. Washington, DC: Globe Printing Office, 1856.

——. Letter of 26 April 1858. Josiah James Evans Papers, *SCL*.

Frost, Edward. Correspondence of the Acting Secretary of the Treasury (1861). Edward Frost Papers, *SCL*.

Harper, William. *An Address to a Public Meeting of the Citizens of Union District*. Columbia: *Times & Gazette* Office, 1831.

——. *Speech before the Charleston State Rights and Free Trade Association Apr. 1, 1832*. Charleston: E. J. Van Brunt, 1832.

——. *The Remedy by State Interposition or Nullification*, Political Tract No. 5. Charleston: E. J. Van Brunt, 1832.

——. *Anniversary Oration, the South Carolina Society for the Advancement of Learning, Dec. 9, 1835*. Washington, DC: Duff Green, 1836.

——. *Memoir on Slavery, Read before the Society for the Advancement of Learning of South Carolina 1837*. Charleston: James S. Burges, 1838.

Johnson, David. Letter of 3 May 1830. David Johnson Papers, *SCL*.

——. Letter of 5 Feb. 1831. David Johnson Papers, *SCL*.

——. Letter of 7 May 1835. David Johnson Papers, *SCL*.

——. Letter of 23 Feb. 1843. David Johnson Papers, *SCL*.

——. Rules of the Plantation (January 1850). David Johnson Papers, *SCL*.

——. Letter of 6 May 1850. David Johnson Papers, *SCL*.

——. Letter of 1 Aug. 1850. David Johnson Papers, *SCL*.

——. Letter of 12 Oct. 1851. David Johnson Papers, *SCL*.

——. Letter of 3 Oct. 1852. David Johnson Papers, *SCL*.

——. Will of 26 Nov. 1853. David Johnson Papers, *SCL*.

——. Autobiography. Rpt. in O'Neall, *Biographical Sketches.*

Nott, Abraham. Letter of 8 Dec. 1829. Waddy Thompson Papers, *SCL.*

O'Neall, John B. *An Oration Delivered before the Clariosophic Society Incorporate, and the Inhabitants of Columbia, on the Anniversary of the Society, Dec. 5th, 1826.* Charleston: A. E. Miller, 1827.

——. *An Oration Delivered at Newberry Court House on the Fourth of July, 1827.* Columbia: Sweeny & Sims, 1827.

——. "An Agricultural Address Delivered before the State Agricultual Society, 29th Dec. 1842." *Proceedings of the Agricultural Convention and of the State Agricultural Society of South Carolina from 1839 to 1845–Inclusive.* Columbia: Summer & Carroll Publishers, 1846.

——. *The Negro Law of South Carolina.* Columbia: John G. Bowman, 1848.

——. *Biographical Sketches of the Bench and Bar of South Carolina.* Charleston: S. G. Courtenay & Co., 1859.

Richardson, John S. Notebook [1809]. John Smyth Richardson Papers, *SCL.*

——. *An Oration Delivered in St. Michael's Church before the Inhabitants of Charleston (July 5, 1813) (the 4th Being Sunday).* Charleston: W. P. Young, 1813.

——. *Argument against William Harper on Nullification of the Protective Tariff.* Columbia: *Times & Gazette* Office, 1830.

——. *To the People: An Address in Five Numbers Originally Published in the* Camden Journal *by "Jefferson."* Charleston: Office of the *Irishman and Southern Democrat,* 1830.

——. *Speech Delivered at Statesburgh Dinner, in Opposition to Disunion, Convention, and Nullification (Aug. 19, 1830).* Charleston: Office of the *Irishman and Southern Democrat,* 1830.

——. Speech of Defense. *Proceedings of the House of Representatives of South-Carolina against Judge J. S. Richardson on the Charge of "Bodily and Mental Infirmity."* Charleston: Walker & Burke, 1848.

Withers, Thomas J. Letter Addressed to the Committee of Invitation of the Co-operation Meeting, Held at Yorkville, S.C., on the 6th Aug. (1851). Southern Rights and Cooperation Documents, *SCL.*

——. Letter to General G. T. Beauregard, 10 Nov. 1863. Kirkland-Withers-Snowden-Trotter Papers, *SCL.*

——. Letter to Capt. Coles, 28 Dec. 1863. Kirkland-Withers-Snowden-Trotter Papers, *SCL.*

——. "The Life of Thomas Jefferson Withers," undated typescript. Kirkland-Withers-Snowden-Trotter Papers, *SCL.*

TENNESSEE

Catron, John. Letter to Joseph McMinn, 24 Nov. 1820. Governor Joseph McMinn Correspondence, Box 1, Folder 6, *TSLA*.

———. Letter to Andrew J. Donelson, 2 Dec. 1829. Andrew J. Donelson Papers, Microfilm #403, *TSLA*.

———. Letter of 23 Sept. 1831. John Catron Papers, IV-D-5, *TSLA*.

———. Letter of 2 Jan. 1833. John Catron Papers, IV-D-5, *TSLA*.

———. Letter to Andrew Jackson, 5 Feb. 1838. John Catron Papers, IV-D-5, *TSLA*.

———. Letter of 24 Sept. [1845]. James Knox Polk Papers, Box 1, Folder 4 (Microfilm #805), *TSLA*.

———. Will of 1862, recorded 29 June 1865, Davidson County Courthouse. John Catron Papers, IV-D-5, *TSLA*.

Green, Nathan. Letter of 5 Jan. 1826. Claybrooke & Overton Papers, THS, I-B-2, 3, 4, 5, Box 5, Folder 8 (Microfilm #812), *TSLA*.

———. Letter of 20 Aug. 1843. Robert Looney Caruthers Papers, *SHC*.

———. Letter of 27 Sept. 1847. Robert Looney Caruthers Papers, *SHC*.

———. Letter of 11 Nov. 1848. Robert Looney Caruthers Papers, *SHC*.

———. *Address by Hon. Nathan Green, Judge of the Supreme Court of Tennessee, Delivered February 28th, 1849, on Entering on the Duties of Professor of Law in Cumberland University, at Lebanon, Tennessee.* Lebanon: J. T. Figures, 1849.

McKinney, Robert J. Letter to Sam Houston, 19 June 1828. Governors' Papers 1827–1829 (Microfilm), *TSLA*.

Peck, Jacob. Letter to Sam Houston, 12 March 1829. Governors' Papers 1827–29 (Microfilm), *TSLA*.

———. Undated letter to William Carroll. Governors' Papers 1829–1835 (Microfilm), *TSLA*.

———. Letter of 21 May 1858. THS Misc. Collection, I-A-1-3, Box 12, Folder P-20, *TSLA*.

Reese, William B. Letter of 4 Feb. 1845. Cooper Family Papers, V-1-1-3, Box 3, Folder 4 (Microfilm #810), *TSLA*.

———. Letter of 28 Dec. 1848. Yeatman-Polk Collection, VIII-B-E, Box 11, Folder 16 (Microfilm #1073), *TSLA*.

———. "Growth and Development of Nashville from 1780 to 1796" and "Nashville from 1796 to 1843" and "Bench and Bar." *History of Nashville, Tennessee.* Ed. John Wooldridge. Nashville: Barbie & Smith, 1890. 73–91; 92–109; 506–19.

Totten, Archibald W. O. Letter to John S. Claybrooke, 4 Nov. 1855. Claybrooke Collection, Claybrooke and Overton Papers, THS, Box 18, Folder 12 (Microfilm #812), *TSLA*.

——. Entry 22082, Provost Marshal File. Union Provost Marshals' File of Papers Relating to Individual Citizens, Acc. No. 1047 (Microfilm #345), *TSLA*.

VIRGINIA

Allen, John J. Letter to Briscoe G. Baldwin, 19 Aug. 1844. Stuart-Baldwin Papers #10378, *AL*.

——. Letter to Briscoe G. Baldwin, 25 Aug. 1844. Stuart-Baldwin Papers #10378, *AL*.

——. Letter to Briscoe G. Baldwin, 9 Oct. 1844. Stuart-Baldwin Papers #10378, *AL*.

——. Letter of 20 Apr. 1851. John James Allen Papers, *VHS*.

——. "Preamble and Resolution" (Offered in a large mass meeting of the people of Botecourt County, 10 Dec. 1860). *Southern Historical Society Papers*. Richmond: J. Wm. Jones, 1876. 1:1–16.

Baldwin, Briscoe G. *Preamble and Resolutions Offered to the House of Delegates on the Missouri Question*. Richmond: Thomas Ritchie, 1819.

——. Letter of 26 Oct. 1829. Stuart Family Papers, *VHS*.

——. Letter of 4 Feb. 1842. Stuart-Baldwin Papers #10378, *AL*.

——. Letter of 17 June 1850. Stuart Family Papers, *VHS*.

Brockenbrough, William. Letter to Thomas Ruffin, 7 Feb. 1831. Rpt. in Hamilton, *Ruffin Papers*.

——. Letter to Thomas Ruffin, 4 Jan. 1835. Rpt. in Hamilton, *Ruffin Papers*.

Brooke, Francis T. *A Narrative of My Life for My Family*. Richmond: n.p., 1849.

——. Letter of 11 June 1850. Henry Clay Papers #6273, *AL*.

Cabell, William H. Letter to William B. Hare, 11 Jan. 1800. Cabell-Reid-Hare Papers #3810, *AL*.

——. Letter to William B. Hare, 16 Dec. 1800. Cabell-Reid-Hare Papers #3810, *AL*.

——. Letter to William B. Hare, 24 Dec. 1800. Cabell-Reid-Hare Papers #3810, *AL*.

——. Letter to William B. Hare, 31 Dec. 1800. Cabell-Reid-Hare Papers #3810, *AL*.

——. Letter to William B. Hare, 14 Dec. 1802. Cabell-Reid-Hare Papers #3810, *AL*.

———. Letter to William B. Hare, 8 Feb. 1803. Cabell-Reid-Hare Papers, *AL*.

———. Letter of 2 Dec. 1804. Cabell-Reid-Hare Papers #3810, *AL*.

———. Letter of 11 Dec. 1804. Cabell-Reid-Hare Papers #3810, *AL*.

———. *Circular respecting insurrections of negroes*. Richmond: Samuel Pleasants, Jr., 21 Dec. 1808.

———. Letter of 25 July 1837. Cabell Family Papers, *VHS*.

———. Letter of 8 Sept. 1837. Cabell Family Papers, *VHS*.

———. Letter of 13 Sept. 1837. Cabell Family Papers, *VHS*.

———. Memorandum Book. Cabell Family Papers, *VHS*.

———. Mem. of Certain Periods in the Life of W. H. Cabell (n.d.). Cabell Family Papers, *VHS*.

Carr, Dabney. Letter to Thomas Jefferson, 17 April 1787. Palmer F. Carr Papers, *VHS*.

———. Essays in *The Old Bachelor*. Ed. William Wirt. Richmond: *Richmond Enquirer* Press, for Thomas Ritchie & Fielding Lucas, 1814.

———. Letter of 26 Nov. 1824. William Green Papers, *VHS*.

Dade, William A. G. *A Charge Delivered to the Grand Jury of Rockingham County at the Opening of the Superior Court September Term, 1813*. Harrisonburg: Davidson & Bourne, 1813.

Green, John W. Report Card (for descendant) from William and Mary College, 4 July 1856. William Green Papers, *VHS*.

Lomax, John T. Indenture Agreement of 20 June 1815, Tayloe Family Papers, *VHS*.

———. Letter of 28 Mar. 1829. Hunter-Garnett Papers #38-45, *AL*.

———. *Treatise on Executors and Administrators*. 2 vols. Philadelphia: John L. Littell, 1841; 2d ed. Richmond: Adolphus Morris, 1857.

———. *Digest of the Laws Respecting Real Property*. Richmond: Adolphus Morris, 1855.

———. Letter of 16 Nov. 1859. Lewis Family Papers, *VHS*.

———. Letter of 17 Nov. 1859. Lewis Family Papers, *VHS*.

Parker, Richard E. Letters (January–July, 1829). James H. Rochelle Papers, *PL*.

Tucker, Henry St. George. Letter to James Barbour, 11 Feb. 1820. David John Mays Papers, *VHS*.

———. Letter to Briscoe G. Baldwin, 5 May 1831. Stuart-Baldwin Papers, *VHS*.

———. *Introductory lecture delivered by the professor of law in the University of Virginia at the opening of the Law School in September, 1841*. Charlottesville: Magruder & Noel, 1841.

——. Letter to Wm. Cocke, 26 May 1842. Cocke Family Papers #640, Box 104, *AL.*

——. *Lectures on Constitutional Law for the Use of the Law Class at the University of Virginia.* Richmond: Shepherd and Colin, 1843.

——. *A Few Lectures on Natural Law.* Charlottesville: James Alexander, 1844.

——. Letter (n.d.). David John Mays Papers, *VHS.*

JUDICIAL OPINIONS

Aldridge v. Commonwealth, 2 Va. Cas. 447 (1824).

Allen v. Freeland, 3 Randolph 170 (Va. 1825).

Allison v. Armstrong, 2 Yerger 74 (Tenn. 1820).

Anderson's Ex'ors v. Anderson, 11 Leigh 616 (Va. 1841).

Baalam v. State, 17 Ala. 451 (1850).

Bacon v. Commonwealth, 7 Grattan 602 (Va. 1850).

Baker v. Rowan, 2 Stewart & Porter 361 (Ala. 1832).

Barden v. Barden, 3 Devereux 548 (N.C. 1832).

Barrett v. Bullard, 16 La. 281 (1841).

Belew v. Clark, 5 Humphrey 506 (Tenn. 1844).

Bertrand v. Arcueil, 4 La. Ann. 430 (1849).

Bethea v. McColl, 5 Ala. 308 (1843).

Black & Manning v. Oliver, 1 Ala. 449 (1840).

Bowers v. Newman, 2 McMullan 472 (S.C. 1842).

Brandon v. Planters' & Merchants' Bank, 1 Stewart 320 (Ala. 1828).

Brien v. Williamson, 7 Howard 14 (Miss. 1843).

Bruce v. Stone, 5 La. 1 (1832).

Caldwell v. Wallace, 4 Stewart & Porter 282 (Ala. 1833).

Carmille v. Carmille's Adm'r, 2 McMullan 454 (S.C. 1842).

Carroll v. Brumby, 13 Ala. 102 (1848).

Cawthorn v. Deas, 2 Porter 276 (Ala. 1835).

Charles v. State, 11 Ark. 390 (1850).

Chartran v. Schmidt, Rice 229 (S.C. 1839).

Commonwealth v. Boone, 2 Va. Cas. 394 (1824).

Commonwealth v. Carver, 5 Randolph 66 (Va. 1827).

Commonwealth v. Garner, 3 Grattan 655 (Va. 1846).

Commonwealth v. Turner, 5 Randolph 678 (Va. 1827).

Cooper v. Mayor of Savannah, 4 Ga. 68 (1848).

Cox v. Williams, 4 Iredell Eq. 15 (N.C. 1845).

Dabney v. Taliaferro, 4 Randolph 256 (Va. 1826).

Davenport v. Commonwealth, 1 Leigh 588 (Va. 1829).

Delery v. Mornet, 11 Martin (O.S.) 4 (La. 1822).

Elijah v. State, 1 Humphreys 102 (Tenn. 1839).

Ex Parte Boylston, 2 Strobhart 41 (S.C. 1847).

Fable v. Brown, 2 Hill Eq. 378 (S.C. 1835).

Farr v. Thompson, Cheves 37 (S.C. 1839).

Felder v. Louisville, Cincinnati and Charleston Railroad Co., 2 McMullan 403 (S.C. 1842).

Fields v. State, 1 Yerger 156 (Tenn. 1829).

Fisher's Negroes v. Dabbs, 4 Yerger 120 (Tenn. 1834).

Ford v. Ford, 7 Humphreys 91 (Tenn. 1846).

Frazier v. Ex'rs of Frazier, 2 Hill Eq. 304 (S.C. 1835).

Gardiner v. Cross, 6 Robinson 454 (La. 1844).

Gibson v. Andrews, 4 Ala. 66 (1842).

Gillian v. Senter, 9 Ala. 395 (1846).

Gist v. Cole, 2 Nott & McCord 456 (S.C. 1820).

Gordon v. Blackman, 1 Richardson Eq. 61 (S.C. 1844).

Green v. Robinson, 5 Howard 80 (Miss. 1840).

Gregory v. Baugh, 4 Randolph 611 (Va. 1827).

Hansley v. Hansley, 10 Iredell 506 (N.C. 1849).

Hardcastle's Estate v. Porcher, Harper 495 (S.C. 1826).

Hardeman v. Sims, 3 Ala. 747 (1842).

Heathcock v. Pennington, 11 Iredell 640 (N.C. 1850).

Henderson v. Vaulx (6th Cir. Tenn., 25 Aug. 1831). Box 53 A, *TSLA*.

Henderson v. Vaulx, 10 Yerger 29 (Tenn. 1836).

Hendricks v. Phillips, 3 La. Ann. 618 (1848).

Heno v. Heno, 9 Martin (O.S.) 643 (La. 1821).

Herring v. Wilmington and Raleigh Railroad Co., 10 Iredell 402 (N.C. 1849).

Hicks v. Moore, 2 Ga. 240 (1847).

Hinds v. Brazealle, 2 Howard 837 (Miss. 1838).

Isham v. State, 6 Howard 35 (Miss. 1841).

Johnson v. Field, 5 Martin (N.S.) 635 (La. 1827).

Johnson v. State, 7 Ga. 453 (1850).

Jolly v. State, 8 Smedes & Marshall 145 (Miss. 1847).

Jones v. Mason, 5 Randolph 577 (Va. 1827).

Jung v. Doriocourt, 4 La. 175 (1832).

Kelly v. State, 3 Smedes & Marshall 518 (Miss. 1844).

Kennedy v. Williams, 7 Humphreys 50 (Tenn. 1846).

Kennedy's Heirs and Ex'rs v. Kennedy's Heirs, 2 Ala. 624 (1841).

Kinloch v. Harvey, Harper 508 (S.C. 1830).

Landreaux v. Campbell, 8 Martin (N.S.) 478 (La. 1830).

Leech v. Cooley, 6 Smedes & Marshall 93 (Miss. 1846).

Lewis v. State, 9 Smedes & Marshall 115 (Miss. 1847).

Loftin v. Espy, 4 Yerger 84 (Tenn. 1833).

Macon & Western R.R. Co. v. Holt, 7 Ga. 157 (1850).

McRaeny v. Johnson and Moore, 2 Fla. 520 (1849).

Manns v. Givens, 7 Leigh 689 (Va. 1836).

Maria v. Surbaugh, 2 Randolph 228 (Va. 1824).

Markham v. Close, 3 La. 581 (1831).

Marshall v. Gantt, 15 Ala. 682 (1849).

Martin v. Martin, 12 Leigh 495 (Va. 1842).

Martineau v. Hooper, 8 Martin (O.S.) 699 (La. 1820).

Mayho v. Sears, 3 Iredell 224 (N.C. 1842).

Mayor and Council of Columbus v. Howard, 6 Ga. 213 (1849).

Mayor of Columbus v. Goetchius, 6 Ga. 139 (1849).

Mayor of Memphis v. Winfield, 8 Humphreys 707 (Tenn. 1848).

Moore v. Dudley, 2 Stewart 170 (Ala. 1829).

Murphy v. Clark, 1 Smedes & Marshall 221 (Miss. 1834).

Nelson v. Biggers, 6 Ga. 205 (1849).

Nelson v. State, 10 Humphreys 518 (Tenn. 1850).

Nix v. State, 13 Texas 575 (1855).

Nowell v. O'Hara, 1 Hill 150 (S.C. 1833).

Oates v. Caffin, 3 La. Ann. 339 (1848).

Palfrey v. Rivas, 7 Martin (O.S.) 371 (La. 1820).

Parris v. Jenkins, 2 Richardson 106 (S.C. 1845).

Paup's Adm. v. Mingo, 4 Leigh 163 (Va. 1833).

Pendleton v. State, 6 Ark. 509 (1844).

Percival v. Herbemont, 1 McMullan 59 (S.C. 1840).

Perry v. Dunlap, 1 Hill 401 (S.C. 1833).

Poulard v. Delamare, 12 La. 267 (1838).

Pyeatt v. Spencer, 4 Ark. 563 (1842).

Rainsford v. Rainsford, Rice Eq. 343 (S.C. 1839).

Randolph v. Randolph, 6 Randolph 194 (Va. 1828).

Rasco & Brantley v. Willis, 5 Ala. 38 (1843).

Richardson v. Broughton, 2 Strobhart 1 (S.C. 1848).

Richardson v. Dukes, 4 McCord 156 (S.C. 1827).

Ross v. Vertner, 5 Howard 305 (Miss. 1840).

Ruddle's Ex'r v. Ben, 10 Leigh 467 (Va. 1839).

Sarter v. Gordon, 2 Hill Eq. 121 (S.C. 1835).

Scroggins v. Scroggins, 3 Devereux 535 (N.C. 1832).

Scudder v. Woodbridge, 1 Ga. 195 (1846).

Sibley v. Maria, 2 Fla. 533 (1849).

Smith v. McCall, 1 McCord 220 (S.C. 1821).

Sorrelle v. Craig, 9 Ala. 534 (1846).

Spalding v. Grigg, 4 Ga. 75 (1848).

Spalding v. Taylor, 1 La. Ann. 195 (1846).

Spence v. State, 17 Ala. 192 (1850).

Spencer v. Negroes Amy and Thomas, R.M.C. 178 (Superior Courts of the Eastern District, Ga. 1822).

Spencer v. Pilcher, 8 Leigh 565 (Va. 1837).

State v. Abram, 10 Ala. 928 (1847).

State v. Belmont, 4 Strobhart 445 (S.C. 1848).

State v. Ben, 1 Hawks 434 (N.C. 1821).

State v. Boozer, 5 Strobhart 21 (S.C. 1850).

State v. Bowen, 3 Strobhart 573 (S.C. 1849).

State v. Caesar, 9 Iredell 391 (N.C. 1849).

State v. Chandler, 2 Strobhart 266 (S.C. 1848).

State v. Cheatwood, 2 Hill 459 (S.C. 1834).

State v. Claiborne, Meigs 331 (Tenn. 1838).

State v. Hale, 9 N.C. 582 (1823).

State v. Harden, 2 Speers 152 (S.C. 1832).

State v. Hart, 4 Iredell 246 (N.C. 1844).

State v. Hawkins, 8 Porter 461 (Ala. 1839).

State v. Hayes, 1 Bailey 275 (S.C. 1829).

State v. Hoover, 4 Devereux & Battle 365 (N.C. 1839).

State v. Isaac, Walker 83 (Miss. 1820).

State v. Jarrott, 1 Iredell 76 (N.C. 1840).

State v. Jones, Walker 83 (Miss. 1820).

State v. Jones, 5 Ala. 666 (1843).

State v. Jowers, 11 Iredell 555 (N.C. 1850).

State v. Lane, 8 Iredell 256 (N.C. 1848).

State v. McDonald, 4 Porter 449 (Ala. 1837).

State v. Mann, 2 Devereux 263 (N.C. 1829).

State v. Manuel, 20 N.C. 144 (1838).

State v. Nelson, 3 La. Ann. 497 (1848).

State v. Newsom, 5 Iredell 250 (N.C. 1844).

State v. Reed, 9 N.C. 454 (1823).

State v. Samuel, 2 Devereux & Battle 177 (N.C. 1836).

State v. Tackett, 8 N.C. 210 (1820).

State v. Watters, 3 Iredell 455 (N.C. 1843).

State v. Will, 1 Devereux & Battle 121 (N.C. 1834).

State v. Wisdom, 8 Porter 511 (Ala. 1839).

Stevens v. Ely, 1 Devereux Eq. 493 (N.C. 1830).

Taylor v. Andrus, 16 La. 15 (1840).

Tennent v. Dendy, Dudley 83 (S.C. 1837).

Thurman v. State, 18 Ala. 276 (1850).

Tidyman v. Rose, Richardson Eq. 294 (S.C. 1832).

Townsend v. Jeffries' Ex'rs, 17 Ala. 276 (1850).

Trotter v. Blocker, 6 Porter 269 (Ala. 1838).

Trustees v. Dickenson, 1 Devereux 189 (N.C. 1827).

Turnipseed v. State, 6 Ala. 664 (1844).

Vance v. Crawford, 4 Ga. 445 (1848).

Vaughan v. Phebe, Martin & Yerger 5 (Tenn. 1827).

Vinyard v. Passalaigue, 2 Strobhart 536 (S.C. 1845).

Waddill v. Martin, 3 Iredell Eq. 562 (N.C. 1845).

Werley v. State, 11 Humphreys 172 (Tenn. 1850).

Wheat v. Groom, 7 Ala. 349 (1845).

White v. Helmes, 1 McCord 430 (S.C. 1821).

Wilks's Adm'r v. Greer, 14 Ala. 438 (1848).

Wingis v. Smith, 3 McCord 400 (S.C. 1825).

Wragg v. State, 14 Ala. 492 (1848).

Wright v. Weatherly, 7 Yerger 367 (Tenn. 1835).

Wynn v. Carrell, 2 Grattan 227 (Va. 1845).

Young v. Burton, McMullan Eq. 255 (S.C. 1841).

COLLATERAL CASES, LETTERS, MEMOIRS, AND DESCRIPTIVE SOURCES

Alba, Peter. Letter of 31 Oct. 1831. Correspondence of the Territorial Governors, RG 101, Series 177, Box 1: 1825–1836, Folder 10, *FSA*.

Aldrich, A. P. *Memoir of Judge A. P. Butler*. Charleston: Walker, Evans & Cogswell, 1878.

Andry v. Foy, 6 Martin (O.S.) 689 (La. 1819), aff. 7 Martin (O.S.) 33 (La. 1819).

Bank v. Marchand, T.U.P.C. 247 (Superior Courts of the Eastern District, Ga. 1809).

Bullard Henry. "A Discourse on the Life, Character, and Writings of the Hon. Francois Xavier Martin, LL.D." *Historical Collections of Louisiana*. Ed. Benjamin J. French. Philadelphia: Daniels and Smith, 1850. 17–40.

Caldwell, Joshua. *Sketches of the Bench and Bar of Tennessee*. Knoxville: Ogden Brothers & Co., 1898.

Call, Daniel. Biographical Sketches. 4 Call 627 (Va. 1803–4).

Chandler v. State, 2 Tex. 306 (1847).

Charlton, Robert. *An Address Delivered before the Societies of Oglethorpe University*. Milledgeville, GA: Georgia Journal Office, 1842.

Chilton, Claudius Lysias. *Centenary Sketch of William P. Chilton*. Montgomery: Paragon Press, 1910.

Cyclopedia of Eminent and Representative Men of the Carolinas of the Nineteenth Century. Madison, WI: Brant & Fuller, 1892.

Eulogy [of Hiram Warner], 68 Ga. 845 (1881).

Featherston, W. S. *A Tribute to the Memory of Hon. Alexander M. Clayton by His Friends and Associates of the Holly Spings Bar*. Holly Springs, MS: n.p., 1889.

Fitzhugh, George. *Cannibals All! or Slaves without Masters*. 1857. Cambridge, MA: Harvard UP, 1960.

Fletcher, Thomas. "Memorial Resolution for Pulaski County Chancery Court." *Daily Arkansas Gazette* 22 May 1878. Small Manuscript Collection, *AHC*.

Fogg, F. B. "Obituary [of William B. Turley]." 11 Humphrey 425 (Tenn. 1858).

General Rule. 6 Martin (O.S.) 280 (La. 1819).

Graham, William A. *Life and Character of the Hon. Thomas Ruffin: A Memorial Oration*. Raleigh: Nichols & Gorman, 1871.

Hallum, John. *Biographical and Pictorial History of Arkansas.* Albany: Weed, Parsons and Co., 1887.

Hamilton, J. G. de Roulhac, ed. *Papers of Thomas Ruffin.* 4 vols. Raleigh: Edwards & Broughton, 1918.

Haywood, John. Letter to John Overton (n.d.). John Haywood Papers, THS, I-A-3, Box 1, *TSLA.*

Henderson, W. A. *Life and Character of Judge McKinney: A Paper Read before the Bar Association of Tennessee Thursday, July 3d, 1884.* Nashville: Albert B. Tavel, 1884.

"In Memoriam: Meeting of the Bar Association in Respect to the Death of the Hon. Thomas Johnson." *Daily Arkansas Gazette* 27 Mar. 1878: 4.

Iredell, James. Speech Book, Edenton Academy, 1802. James Iredell Sr. and Jr. Papers, *PL.*

Jarnagin, Milton P. Memoir [of Robert J. McKinney]. Confederate Collection: Diaries and Memoirs, IV-B-5, Box C26, Folder 5 (Microfilm #824), *TSLA.*

Jefferson, Thomas. Letter to William A. G. Dade, 31 May 1825. Jefferson Papers #201, 3185, *AL.*

Kelly, William. Letter to Nicholas Davis, 13 Jan. 1829. Crenshaw Family Papers (Microfilm #16), *ADAH.*

Livingston, John. "Memoir of Joseph Henry Lumpkin." *United States Law Magazine* July & August 1851: 34–41.

——, ed. *Biographical Sketches of Eminent American Lawyers.* New York: n.p., 1852.

Lochrane, O. A. Eulogy [of Eugenius A. Nisbet]. 53 Ga. 658 (1981).

Lynch, James D. *Bench and Bar of Mississippi.* New York: E. J. Hale and Son, 1881.

McCaw, James B. Ledger, entry of 9 Oct. 1834, Acc. no. 38–54, *AL.*

Mazureau, Etienne. "Panegyric Delivered January, 1837, by Etienne Mazureau, Attorney General, and Dean of the Bar, by Virtue of a Resolution Adopted at New Orleans by His Fellow Members Assembled Nov. 16, 1836." Trans. Mrs. H. H. Cruzat. *Louisiana Historical Quarterly* 4 (April 1921): 154–66.

Memoranda [Memorial of John L. Taylor]. 16 N.C. 308 (1829).

Miller, Stephen F. *The Bench and Bar of Georgia: Memoirs and Sketches.* 2 vols. Philadelphia: J. B. Lippincott, 1858.

Neal v. Farmer, 9 Ga. 555 (1851).

Noland, Charles F. M. "Early Times in Arkansas." *State Gazette and Democrat* 26 Nov. 1857. Small Manuscript Collection, *AHC.*

Perkins, Samuel H. Diary: 24 April 1818. Historical Society of Pennsylvania.

Polk, Marshall T. Letter to James K. Polk, 1 Sept. 1830, James K. Polk Papers, Box 5, Folder 22 (Microfilm #805, Reel 1), *TSLA*.

"Resolution" [in memory of Eugenius Nisbet], (Macon) *Telegraph and Messenger* 27 Apr. 1871.

Scott v. Sanford, 60 U.S. 393 (1856).

Scott, Henry W. *Distinguished American Lawyers with Their Struggles and Triumphs in the Forum.* New York: Charles L. Webster, 1891.

Scott, Nancy N., ed. *Memoir of Hugh Lawson White.* Philadelphia: J. B. Lippincott, 1856.

Shinn, Josiah H. *Pioneers and Makers of Arkansas.* N.p.: Genealogical and Historical Publishing Co., 1908.

Smith, Joseph L. Letter of 2 Jan. 1830. Correspondence of the Territorial Governors, RG 101, Series 177, Box 1: 1825–1836, Folder 10, *FSA*.

Snee v. Trice, 2 Bay 345 (S.C. 1802).

Somerville, Henderson M. The Trial of the Alabama Supreme Court Judges in 1829; And Its Lessons to Posterity—An Address Delivered before the Alabama State Bar Association on June 16, 1899, at Montgomery, Alabama. *LC*.

Souther v. Commonwealth, 7 Grattan 673 (Va. 1851).

Speer, William S., and Hon. John Henry Brown, eds. *The Encyclopedia of the New West.* Marshall, TX: U.S. Biographical Pub. Co., 1881.

State v. Boon, 1 N.C. 103 (1801).

Tribute of Respect to the Memory of the Hon. William B. Reese. 39 Tenn. 403 (1859).

Tribute to Hon. David L. Wardlaw, *Charleston Daily Courier*, 15 Apr. 1861: 1.

Tribute to Hon. Henry W. Collier, *Tuscaloosa Gazette* 29 Dec. 1887. Rpt. *Alabama Historical Quarterly* (Winter 1942): 567.

Tribute to the Memories of Hon. Nathan Green and Hon. A. W. O. Totten. 44 Tenn. 535 (1867).

Tucker, St. George. *A Dissertation on Slavery.* Philadelphia: Printed for Matthew Cary, 1796.

Watts, Charles. "Discourse on the Life and Character of the Hon. George Mathews." 10 La. iii (1837).

White, George. *Historical Collections of Georgia: Containing the Most Interesting Facts, Traditions, Biographical Sketches, Anecdotes, etc. Relating to Its History and Antiquities, from Its First Settlement to the Present Time.* 3d ed. New York: Pudney & Russell, 1855.

SELECTED SCHOLARSHIP

BOOKS

Aptheker, Herbert. *American Negro Slave Revolts*. New York: Columbia UP, 1943.

Aristotle. *Art of Rhetoric*. Trans. John H. Freese. Loeb Classical Library. Cambridge, MA: Harvard UP, 1982.

Baron, Hans. *The Crisis of the Early Italian Renaissance*. Princeton: Princeton UP, 1955.

Berlin, James A. *Writing Instruction in Nineteenth-Century American Colleges*. Carbondale: Southern Illinois UP, 1984.

Bernal, Martin. *Black Athena: The Afroasiatic Roots of Classical Civilization*. New Brunswick: Rutgers UP, 1987.

Bizzell, Patricia, and Bruce Herzberg, eds. *The Rhetorical Tradition: Readings from Classical Times to the Present*. Boston: Bedford Books-St. Martin's Press, 1990.

Blair, Hugh. *Lectures on Rhetoric and Belles Lettres*. 2 vols. Ed. Harold F. Harding. Carbondale: Southern Illinois UP, 1965.

Blassingame, John W., ed. *Slave Testimony: Two Centuries of Letters, Speeches, Interviews, and Autobiographies*. Baton Rouge: Louisiana State UP, 1977.

Bolgar, R. R., ed. *Classical Influences on European Culture A.D. 1500–1700*. Cambridge, England: Cambridge UP, 1976.

Bonner, Robert J. *Lawyers and Litigants in Ancient Athens: The Genesis of the Legal Profession*. Chicago: U of Chicago P, 1927.

Braden, Waldo W., ed. *Oratory in the Old South 1828–1860*. Baton Rouge: Louisiana State UP, 1970.

Bryson, W. Hamilton. *Legal Education in Virginia 1779–1979: A Biographical Approach*. Charlottesville: UP of Virginia, 1982.

Burckhardt, Jacob. *The Civilization of the Renaissance in Italy*. Trans. S. G. C. Middlemore. New York: Harper, 1929.

Burton, Steven J. *Judging in Good Faith*. Cambridge, England: Cambridge UP, 1992.

Catterall, Helen Tunnicliff, ed. *Judicial Cases Concerning American Slavery and the Negro*. 5 vols. Washington, DC: Carnegie Institution, 1926–37.

Channing, Edward T. *Lectures Read to the Seniors in Harvard College*. Ed. Dorothy I. Anderson and Waldo W. Braden. Carbondale: Southern Illinois UP, 1968.

Channing, Steven A. *Crisis of Fear: Secession in South Carolina.* New York: Simon and Schuster, 1970.

Charvat, William. *The Origins of American Critical Thought, 1810–1835.* New York: Russell and Russell, 1968.

Choper, Jesse H. *Judicial Review and the National Political Process.* Chicago: U of Chicago P, 1980.

Chroust, Anton-Hermann. *The Rise of the Legal Profession in America.* 2 vols. Norman: U of Oklahoma P, 1965.

Cicero. *De Inventione* (On Rhetorical Invention). Trans. Harry M. Hubbell. Loeb Classical Library. Cambridge, MA: Harvard UP, 1959.

——. *De Ratione Dicendi* (*Rhetorica ad Herennium*) (Rhetoric to Herennius). Trans. Harry Caplan. Loeb Classical Library. Cambridge, MA: Harvard UP, 1981.

Clark, Gregory, and S. Michael Halloran, eds. *Oratorical Culture in Nineteenth-Century America: Transformations in the Theory and Practice of Rhetoric.* Carbondale: Southern Illinois UP, 1993.

Clarke, Martin L. *Classical Education in Britain, 1500–1900.* Cambridge, England: Cambridge UP, 1959.

Conley, Thomas M. *Rhetoric in the European Tradition.* New York: Longman, 1990.

Conrad, Glenn R., gen. ed. *A Dictionary of Louisiana Biography.* 2 vols. New Orleans: Louisiana Historical Society, 1988.

Corbett, Edward P. J. *Classical Rhetoric for the Modern Student.* 3d ed. New York: Oxford UP, 1990.

Cover, Robert M. *Justice Accused: Antislavery and the Judicial Process.* New Haven: Yale UP, 1975.

Cullen, Charles T. *St. George Tucker and Law in Virginia 1772-1804.* New York: Garland Publishing, 1987.

David, Paul A. *Reckoning with Slavery: A Critical Study in the Quantitative History of American Negro Slavery.* New York: Oxford UP, 1976.

Deen, Braswell D., Jr., and William Scott Henwood. *Georgia's Appellate Judiciary: Profiles and History.* Norcross, GA: Harrison, 1987.

Dworkin, Ronald. *Law's Empire.* Cambridge, MA: Harvard UP, 1986.

Eaton, Clement. *The Freedom-of-Thought Struggle in the Old South.* New York: Harper & Row, 1964.

——. *The Growth of Southern Civilization, 1790–1860.* New York: Harper & Row, 1963.

——. *The Mind of the Old South*. Baton Rouge: Louisiana State UP, 1967.

Elkins, Stanley M. *Slavery: A Problem in American Institutional and Intellectual Life*. Chicago: U of Chicago P, 1959.

Ely, James W., and David J. Bodenhamer, eds. *Ambivalent Legacy: A Legal History of the South*. Jackson: UP of Mississippi, 1984.

Enos, Richard Leo. *Greek Rhetoric before Aristotle*. Prospect Heights, IL: Waveland, 1993.

Faust, Drew Gilpin. *The Ideology of Slavery: Proslavery Thought in the Antebellum South, 1830–1860*. Baton Rouge: Louisiana State UP, 1981.

Fede, Andrew. *People without Rights: An Interpretation of the Fundamentals of the Law of Slavery in the U.S. South*. New York: Garland, 1992.

Ferguson, Robert A. *Law and Letters in American Culture*. Cambridge, MA: Harvard UP, 1984.

Finkelman, Paul. *An Imperfect Union: Slavery, Federalism, and Comity*. Chapel Hill: U of North Carolina P, 1981.

——, ed. *Free Blacks, Slaves, and Slaveowners in Civil and Criminal Courts: The Pamphlet Literature*, Series 6, Vols. 1 and 2, in *Slavery, Race, and the American Legal System 1700–1872*. New York: Garland Publishing, 1988.

——, ed. *Slave Rebels, Abolitionists, and Southern Courts*, Series 4, Vol. 1 in *Slavery, Race, and the American Legal System 1700–1872*. New York: Garland Publishing, 1988.

Fisher, Walter R. *Human Communication as Narration: Toward a Philosophy of Reason, Value, and Action*. Columbia: U of South Carolina P, 1987.

Flanigan, Daniel L. *The Criminal Law of Slavery and Freedom, 1800–1868*. New York: Garland, 1987.

Fogel, Robert W., and Stanley L. Engerman. *Time on the Cross: The Economics of American Negro Slavery*. 2 vols. Boston: Little, Brown & Co., 1974.

Ford, Lacy K., Jr. *Origins of Southern Radicalism: The South Carolina Upcountry, 1800–1860*. New York: Oxford UP, 1988.

Frederickson, George M. *The Black Image in the White Mind: The Debate on Afro-American Character and Destiny, 1817–1914*. New York: Harper & Row, 1971.

Friedman, Lawrence M. *A History of American Law*. New York: Simon and Schuster, 1973.

Frier, Bruce W. *The Rise of the Roman Jurists: Studies in Cicero's Pro Caecino*. Princeton: Princeton UP, 1985.

Fumaroli, Marc. *L'Age de L'Eloquence: Rhetorique et "res literaria" de la Renaissance au seuil de l'epoque classique*, Hautes Etudes Medievales et Modernes, 43. Geneva: Droz, 1980.

Genovese, Eugene. *The Political Economy of Slavery*. New York: Pantheon Books, 1966.

———. *Roll, Jordan, Roll: The World the Slaves Made*. New York: Pantheon Books, 1974.

Graff, Gerald. *Professing Literature: An Institutional History*. Chicago: U of Chicago P. 1987.

Grafton, Anthony. *Defenders of the Text: The Traditions of Scholarship in an Age of Science, 1450–1800*. Cambridge, MA: Harvard UP, 1991.

Grafton, Anthony, and Lisa Jardine. *From Humanism to the Humanities*. Cambridge, MA: Harvard UP, 1986.

Grafton, Anthony, and Ann Blair, eds. *The Transmission of Culture in Early Modern Europe*. Philadelphia: U of Pennsylvania P, 1990.

Grassi, Ernesto. *Renaissance Humanism: Studies in Philosophy and Poetics*. Medieval and Renaissance Texts and Studies, 51. Binghamton, NY: Center for Medieval and Early Renaissance Studies, 1988.

———. *Rhetoric as Philosophy: The Humanist Tradition*. University Park: Pennsylvania State UP, 1980.

Gutman, Herbert G. *Slavery and the Numbers Game: A Critique of* Time on the Cross. Urbana: U of Illinois P, 1975.

Harper, Clio, comp. *Prominent Members of the Early Arkansas Bar*. Typescript bound by the Work Projects Administration, #6715-3, Oct. 1940, *AHC*.

Hart, H. L. A. *Essays in Jurisprudence and Philosophy*. Oxford: Clarendon, 1983.

Hindus, Michael S. *Prison and Plantation: Crime, Justice, and Authority in Massachusetts and South Carolina, 1767–1878*. Chapel Hill: U of North Carolina P, 1980.

Honore, Anthony M. *Tribonian*. London: Duckworth, 1978.

Hont, Istvan, and Michael Ignatieff, eds. *Wealth and Virtue: The Shaping of Political Economy in the Scottish Enlightenment*. Cambridge, England: Cambridge UP, 1983.

Horsnell, Margaret E. *Spencer Roane: Judicial Advocate of Jeffersonian Principles*. New York: Garland Publishing, 1986.

Horwitz, Morton J. *The Transformation of American Law 1780–1860*. New York: Oxford UP, 1992.

Howington, Arthur F. *What Sayeth the Law: The Treatment of Slaves and Free Blacks in the State and Local Courts of Tennessee.* New York: Garland, 1986.

Hubbell, Harry M. *The Influence of Isocrates on Cicero, Dionysius, and Aristides.* New Haven: Yale UP, 1914.

Hughes, Robert. *The Fatal Shore.* New York: Alfred A. Knopf, 1987.

Hurst, James Willard. *The Growth of American Law: The Law Makers.* Boston: Little, Brown & Co., 1950.

Isocrates. *Antidosis* (Speech of Self Defense). Trans. Gilbert Highet. Loeb Classical Library. Cambridge, MA: Harvard UP, 1929.

Jaeger, Werner R. *Paideia: The Ideals of Greek Culture.* Trans. Gilbert Highet. New York: Oxford UP, 1944.

Jenkins, W. S. *Pro-Slavery Thought in the Old South.* Chapel Hill: U of North Carolina P, 1935.

Jennings, Thelma. *The Nashville Convention: Southern Movement for Unity, 1848–1851.* Memphis: Memphis State UP, 1980.

Johnson, Nan. *Nineteenth-Century Rhetoric in North America.* Carbondale: Southern Illinois UP, 1991.

Jonsen, Alfred, and Stephen Toulmin. *The Abuse of Casistry: A History of Moral Reasoning.* Berkeley: U of California P, 1988.

Jordan, Winthrop D. *White over Black: American Attitudes toward the Negro, 1550–1812.* Chapel Hill: U of North Carolina P, 1968.

Kairys, David, ed. *The Politics of Law: A Progressive Criticism.* New York: Pantheon Books, 1982.

Kennedy, George A. *The Art of Persuasion in Greece.* Princeton: Princeton UP, 1963.

——. *The Art of Rhetoric in the Roman World 300 B.C.–A.D. 300.* Princeton: Princeton UP, 1972.

——. *Classical Rhetoric and Its Christian and Secular Tradition from Ancient to Modern Times.* Chapel Hill: U of North Carolina P, 1980.

——. *Greek Rhetoric under Christian Emperors.* Princeton: Princeton UP, 1983.

Kimball, Bruce A. *Orators and Philosophers: A History of the Idea of Liberal Education.* New York: Teachers College Press, 1986.

King, Margaret L. *Venetian Humanism in an Age of Patrician Dominance.* Princeton: Princeton UP, 1986.

Kitzhaber, Albert R. *Rhetoric in American Colleges, 1850–1900.* Dallas: Southern Methodist UP, 1990.

Klein, Rachel N. *Unification of a Slave State: The Rise of the Planter Class in the South Carolina Backcountry, 1760–1808.* Chapel Hill: U of North Carolina P, 1990.

Kristeller, Paul Oskar. *Renaissance Thought and Its Sources.* Ed. Michael Mooney. New York: Columbia UP, 1979.

Lacour-Gayet, Robert. *Everyday Life in the United States before the Civil War.* Trans. Mary Ilford. New York: Frederick Ungar Publishing Co., 1969.

Lamont, Corliss. *The Philosophy of Humanism.* New York: Philosophical Library, 1957.

Lane, Anne J., ed. *The Debate over Slavery: Stanley Elkins and His Critics.* Urbana: U of Illinois P, 1971.

Lang, Meredith. *Defender of the Faith: The High Court of Mississippi 1817–1875.* Jackson: UP of Mississippi, 1977.

LaPiana, William P. *Logic and Experience: The Origin of Modern American Legal Education.* New York: Oxford UP, 1993.

Levi, Albert W. *Humanism and Politics: Studies in the Relationship of Power and Value in the Western Tradition.* Bloomington: Indiana UP, 1969.

Lobban, Michael. *Common Law and English Jurisprudence 1760–1850.* New York: Oxford UP, 1991.

Lumpkin, Ben G., and Martha N. Lumpkin, comps. *The Lumpkin Family of Virginia, Georgia, and Mississippi.* Clarkesville, TN: privately printed, 1973.

MacDowell, Douglas M. *Athenian Homicide Law in the Age of the Orators.* Manchester: Manchester UP, 1963.

McMillan, Malcolm Cook. *Constitutional Development in Alabama, 1798–1901: A Study in Politics, the Negro, and Sectionalism.* Chapel Hill: U of North Carolina P, 1955.

Mandrou, Robert. *From Humanism to Science 1480–1700.* Trans. Brian Pearce. Atlantic Highlands, NJ: Humanities Press, 1979.

Marks, Henry S. *Who Was Who in Florida.* Huntsville, AL: Strode Publishers, 1973.

Marrou, Henri I. *A History of Education in Antiquity.* Trans. George Lamb. New York: Sheed and Ward, 1956.

Martines, Lauro. *The Social World of the Florentine Humanists 1390–1460.* Princeton: Princeton UP, 1968.

Meynard, Virginia G. *The Venturers: The Hampton, Harrison, and Earle Families of Virginia, South Carolina, and Texas.* Easley, SC: Southern Historical Press, 1981.

Miller, Perry. *The Life of the Mind in America: From the Revolution to the Civil War*. New York: Harcourt, Brace & World, 1965.

Mitchel, W. J. T., ed. *On Narrative*. Chicago: U of Chicago P, 1980.

Murphy, James J., ed. *Renaissance Eloquence: Studies in the Theory and Practice of Renaissance Rhetoric*. Berkeley: U of California P, 1983.

Nelson, John S., Allan Megill, and Donald N. McCloskey, eds. *The Rhetoric of the Human Sciences: Language and Argument in Scholarship and Public Affairs*. Madison: U of Wisconsin P, 1987.

Oakes, James. *Slavery and Freedom: An Interpretation of the Old South*. New York: Alfred A. Knopf, 1990.

Owen, Thomas McAdory. *History of Alabama and Dictionary of Alabama Biography*. 4 vols. Chicago: S. J. Clarke, 1921.

Papke, David Ray, ed. *Narrative and the Legal Discourse: A Reader in Storytelling and the Law*. Liverpool, England: Deborah Charles Publications, 1991.

Parks, Edilbert P. *The Roman Rhetorical Schools as a Preparation for the Courts under the Early Empire*. Johns Hopkins University Studies in Historical and Political Science (Series 63) 2. Baltimore: Johns Hopkins UP, 1945.

Perelman, Chaim. *Justice, Law, and Argument: Essays on Moral and Legal Reasoning*. Trans. William Kluback. Dordbrecht, Netherlands: D. Reidel Publishing Co., 1980.

Perelman, Chaim, and Lucie Olbrechts-Tyteca. *The New Rhetoric: A Treatise on Argumentation*. Trans. John Wilkinson and Purcell Weaver. Notre Dame, IN: U of Notre Dame P, 1969.

Phillips, Ulrich B. *American Negro Slavery: A Survey of the Supply, Employment and Control of Negro Labor as Determined by the Plantation Regime*. 1918. Gloucester, MA: Peter Smith, 1959.

——. *Life and Labor in the Old South*. Boston: Little, Brown & Co., 1929.

Pocock, John G. A. *The Machiavellian Moment: Florentine Political Thought and the Atlantic Republican Tradition*. Princeton: Princeton UP, 1975.

Posner, Richard. *The Economics of Justice*. Cambridge: Harvard UP, 1981.

Pound, Roscoe. *The Formative Period of American Law*. Boston: Little, Brown & Co., 1938.

Quintilian. *Institutio Oratoria* (On the Education of an Orator). Trans. H. E. Butler. Loeb Classical Library. Cambridge, MA: Harvard UP, 1921.

Rabil, Albert, Jr., ed. *Renaissance Humanism: Foundations, Forms, and Legacy*. 3 vols. Philadelphia: U of Pennsylvania P, 1988.

Randall, John Herman. *Aristotle*. New York and London: Columbia UP, 1960.

Richard, Carl J. *The Founders and the Classics: Greece, Rome, and the American Enlightenment*. Cambridge, MA: Harvard UP, 1994.

Ricoeur, Paul. *Time and Narrative*. Chicago: U of Chicago P, 1984.

Ryman, Dean E., comp. *Joseph Henry Lumpkin: An Unintentional Autobiography*. Atlanta: Atlanta Bar Association, 1913.

Schauinger, Joseph H. *William Gaston, Carolinian*. Milwaukee: Bruce Publishing Co., 1949.

Schubert, Glendon. *The Judicial Mind: The Attitudes and Ideologies of Supreme Court Justices 1946–1963*. Evanston, IL: Northwestern UP, 1965.

———. *The Judicial Mind Revisited: Psychometric Analysis of Supreme Court Ideology*. New York: Oxford UP, 1974.

Schwarz, Philip J. *Twice Condemned: Slaves and the Criminal Laws of Virginia, 1705–1865*. Baton Rouge: Louisiana State UP, 1988.

Seigel, Jerrold E. *Rhetoric and Philosophy in Renaissance Humanism*. Princeton: Princeton UP, 1968.

Smith, John David. *An Old Creed for the New South: Proslavery Ideology and Historiography, 1865–1918*. Westport, CT: Greenwood Press, 1985.

Sprague, Rosamond Kent, ed. *The Older Sophists*. Columbia: U of South Carolina P, 1972.

Stampp, Kenneth M. *The Peculiar Institution: Slavery in the Antebellum South*. New York: Alfred A. Knopf, 1956.

Stephenson, Wendell Holmes. *Alexander Porter: Whig Planter of Old Louisiana*. New York: Da Capo Press, 1969.

Tarr, G. Alan, and Mary Cornelia Aldis Porter. *State Supreme Courts in State and Nation*. New Haven: Yale UP, 1988.

Taylor, Orville W. *Negro Slavery in Arkansas*. Durham: Duke UP, 1958.

Toulmin, Stephen. *The Uses of Argument*. Cambridge, England: Cambridge UP, 1958.

Toulmin, Stephen, Richard Rieke, and Allan Janik. *An Introduction to Reasoning*. New York: Macmillan, 1979.

Tushnet, Mark V. *The American Law of Slavery, 1810–1860: Considerations of Humanity and Interest*. Princeton: Princeton UP, 1981.

Ullmann, Walter. *Medieval Foundations of Renaissance Humanism*. Ithaca: Cornell UP, 1977.

Van Deburg, William L. *Slavery and Race in American Popular Culture*. Madison: U of Wisconsin P, 1984.

Warnick, Barbara. *The Sixth Canon: Belletristic Rhetorical Theory and Its French Antecedents*. Columbia: U of South Carolina P, 1993.

Warren, Charles. *A History of the American Bar*. Cambridge: Cambridge UP, 1912.

Watson, Alan. *Slave Law in the Americas*. Athens: U of Georgia P, 1989.

Wellman, Paul I. *The House Divides: The Age of Jackson and Lincoln, from the War of 1812 to the Civil War*. Garden City, NY: Doubleday & Co., 1966.

White, James B. *Justice as Translation: An Essay in Cultural and Legal Criticism*. Chicago: U of Chicago P, 1990.

———. *When Words Lose Their Meaning: Constitutions and Reconstitutions of Language, Character, and Community*. Chicago: U of Chicago P, 1984.

Wiecek, William M. *The Sources of Antislavery Constitutionalism in America, 1760–1848*. Ithaca: Cornell UP, 1977.

ARTICLES

Achard, Guy. "Pourquoi Ciceron a-t-il-ecrit le *De Oratore?*" (Why did Cicero write the *De Oratore?*). *Latomus* 46 (1987): 318–29.

Bevilacqua, Vincent M. "Rhetoric and the Circle of Moral Studies: An Historiographic View." *Quarterly Journal of Speech* 55 (1969): 343–57.

Boyd, Joseph A., Jr. "A History of the Florida Supreme Court." *University of Miami Law Review* 35 (Sept. 1981): 1019–66.

Boyett, Gene W. "Quantitative Differences between the Arkansas Whig and Democratic Parties, 1836–1850." *Arkansas Historical Quarterly* 34 (1975): 217–21.

Braden, Waldo W. Introduction. *Oratory in the Old South 1828–1860*. Ed. Waldo W. Braden. Baton Rouge: Louisiana State UP, 1970.

Brady, Patrick S. "Slavery, Race, and the Criminal Law in Antebellum North Carolina: A Reconsideration of the Thomas Ruffin Court." *North Carolina Central Law Journal* 10 (1979): 248–60.

Braet, Antoine. "The Classical Doctrine of *Status* and the Rhetorical Theory of Argumentation." *Philosophy and Rhetoric* 20 (1987): 79–93.

Brinton, Alan. "Quintilian, Plato, and the Vir Bonus." *Philosophy and Rhetoric* 16 (1983): 167–84.

Burton, Steven J. "Law as a Practical Reason." *Southern California Law Review* 62 (1989): 747–93.

Chase, Anthony. "Toward a Legal Theory of Popular Culture." *Wisconsin Law Review* (1986): 527–69.

Clark, Gregory, and S. Michael Halloran. Introduction. *Oratorical Culture in Nineteenth-Century America: Transformations in the Theory and Practice of*

Rhetoric. Ed. Gregory Clark and S. Michael Halloran. Carbondale: Southern Illinois UP, 1993. 1–28.

Cohen, Herman. "Hugh Blair's Theory of Taste." *Quarterly Journal of Speech* 44 (1958): 265–74.

Cottrol, Robert J. "Liberalism and Paternalism: Ideology, Economic Interest and the Business Law of Slavery." *American Journal of Legal History* 31 (1987): 359–73.

Dart, Henry Plauche. "The History of the Supreme Court of Louisiana." *Louisiana Historical Quarterly* 4 (1921): 14–71.

Dart, William Kernan. "The Justices of the Supreme Court." *Louisiana Historical Quarterly* 4 (1921): 113–24.

Dieter, Otto A. L. "Stasis." *Speech Monographs* 17 (1950): 345–69.

Elkins, James R. "On the Emergence of Narrative Jurisprudence: The Humanistic Perspective Finds a New Path." *Legal Studies Forum* 9 (1985): 123–56.

Ely, James W., Jr., and Terry Calvani. "Foreword." *Vanderbilt Law Review* 32 (1979): 1–6.

Eskridge, William N., Jr., and Philip P. Frickey. "Statutory Interpretation as Practical Reasoning." *Stanford Law Review* 42 (1990): 321–84.

Farber, Daniel A. "Legal Pragmatism and the Constitution." *Minnesota Law Review* 72 (1988): 1331–78.

Farber, Daniel A., and Philip P. Frickey. "Practical Reason and the First Amendment." *UCLA Law Review* 34 (1987): 1615–56.

Fede, Andrew. "Legal Protection for Slave Buyers in the U.S. South: A Caveat Concerning *Caveat Emptor.*" *American Journal of Legal History* 31 (1987): 322–58.

——. "Legitimized Violent Slave Abuse in the American South, 1619–1865: A Case Study of Law and Social Change in Six Southern States." *American Journal of Legal History* 29 (1985): 93–150.

Ferguson, Robert A. "The Judicial Opinion as Literary Genre." *Yale Journal of Law and the Humanities* 2 (1990): 201–19.

Fernandez, Mark. "From Chaos to Continuity: Early Reforms of the Supreme Court of Louisiana, 1845–1852." *Louisiana History* 25 (1984): 19–37.

Finkelman, Paul. "Exploring Southern Legal History." *North Carolina Law Review* 64 (1985): 77–116.

——. "Slaves as Fellow Servants: Ideology, Law, and Industrialization." *American Journal of Legal History* 31 (1987): 269–305.

Fisher, Robert B., Jr. "The Louisiana Supreme Court, 1812–1846: Strangers in a Strange Land." *Tulane Civil Law Forum* 1 (1973).

Fisher, William W., III. "Ideology and Imagery in the Law of Slavery." *Chicago-Kent Law Review* 68 (1993): 1051–83.

Flanigan, Daniel L. "Criminal Procedure in Slave Trials in the Antebellum South." *Journal of Southern History* 40 (1974): 537–64.

Frickey, Philip P. "Congressional Intent, Practical Reasoning, and the Dynamic Nature of Federal Indian Law." *California Law Review* 78 (1990): 1137–1239.

Genovese, Eugene. "Materialism and Idealism in the History of Negro Slavery in the Americas." *Journal of Social History* 1 (1968): 371–94.

Genovese, Eugene, and Elizabeth Fox-Genovese. "Slavery, Economic Development, and the Law: The Dilemma of the Southern Political Economists, 1800–1860," John Randolph Tucker lecture, 23 September 1983. *Washington and Lee Law Review* 41 (1984): 1–29.

Ginzburg, Carlo. "Checking the Evidence: The Judge and the Historian." *Critical Inquiry* 18 (1991): 79–92.

Giuliani, Alessandro. "The Influence of Rhetoric on the Law of Evidence and Pleading." *Juridical Review*, new series 7 (1962): 216–51.

Gordon, Robert. "J. Willard Hurst and the Common Law Tradition in American Historiography." *Law and Society Review* 10 (1975): 9–55.

Gray, Hanna H. "Renaissance Humanism: The Pursuit of Eloquence." *Journal of the History of Ideas* 24 (1963): 497–514.

Grey, David L. "The Supreme Court as a Communicator." *Houston Law Review* 5 (1968): 405–29.

Grindle, David J. "Manumission: The Weak Link in Georgia's Law of Slavery." *Mercer Law Review* 41 (1990): 701–22.

Grube, G. M. A. "Educational, Rhetorical and Literary Theory in Cicero." *Phoenix* 16 (1962): 234–57.

Higginbotham, Leon A., Jr., and Barbara K. Kopytoff. "Property First, Humanity Second: The Recognition of the Slave's Human Nature in Virginia Civil Law." *Ohio State Law Journal* 50 (1989): 511–40.

Hohmann, Hanns. "The Dynamics of Stasis: Classical Rhetorical Theory and Modern Legal Argumentation." *American Journal of Jurisprudence* 34 (1989): 171–97.

Howington, Arthur F. "'Not in the Condition of a Horse or Ox': *Ford v. Ford*, the Law of Testamentary Manumission and the Tennessee Court's Recognition of Slave Humanity." *Tennessee Historical Quarterly* 34 (1975): 249–63.

Humphreys, S. C. "The Discourse of Law in Archaic and Classical Greece." *Law and History Review* 6 (1988): 465–93.

Hunt, Alan. "The Ideology of Law: Advances and Problems in Recent Applications of the Concept of Ideology to the Analysis of Law." *Law and Society Review* 19 (1985): 11–37.

Hunt, William. "Civic Chivalry and the English Civil War." Grafton and Blair 204–37.

Jardine, Lisa, "Humanism and Dialectic in Sixteenth-Century Cambridge: A Preliminary Investigation." Bolgar 141–54.

Karsten, Peter. "The 'Discovery' of Law by English and American Jurists of the Seventeenth, Eighteenth, and Nineteenth Centuries: Third-Party Beneficiary Contracts as a Test Case." *Law and History Review* 9 (1991): 327–81.

Kelley, Donald R. "Hermes, Clio, Themis: Historical Interpretation and Legal Hermeneutics." *Journal of Modern History* 55 (1983): 644–68.

——. "'Second Nature:' The Idea of Custom in European Law, Society, and Culture." Grafton and Blair 131–72.

Kimball, Bruce A. "Legal Education, Liberal Education, and the Trivial *Artes*." *Journal of General Education* 38 (1986): 182–210.

LeDuc, Don R. "'Free Speech' Decisions and the Legal Process: The Judicial Opinion in Context." *Quarterly Journal of Speech* 62 (1976): 279–87.

Liu, Yameng. "Aristotle and the Stasis Theory: A Reexamination." *Rhetoric Society Quarterly* 21 (1991): 53–59.

Makau, Josina M. "The Supreme Court and Reasonableness." *Quarterly Journal of Speech* 70 (1984): 379–96.

Miller, Thomas P. "John Witherspoon and Scottish Rhetoric and Moral Philosophy in America." *Rhetorica* 10 (1992): 381–403.

Morris, Thomas D. "'As if the Injury Was Effected by the Natural Elements of Air, or Fire': Slave Wrongs and the Liability of Masters." *Law and Society Review* 16 (1981–82): 569–99.

——. "Slaves and the Rules of Evidence in Criminal Trials." *Chicago-Kent Law Review* 68 (1993): 1209–40.

——. "'Villeinage . . . as it existed in England, reflects but little on our subject': The Problem of the 'Sources' of Southern Slave Law." *American Journal of Legal History* 32 (1988): 95–137.

Nadeau, Ray. "Classical Systems of Stases in Greek: Hermagoras to Hermogenes." *Greek, Roman, and Byzantine Studies* 2 (1959): 53–71.

Nash, A. E. Kier. "Fairness and Formalism in the Trials of Blacks in the State Supreme Courts of the Old South." *Virginia Law Review* 56 (Feb. 1970): 64–100.

———. "A More Equitable Past? Southern Supreme Courts and the Protection of the Antebellum Negro." *North Carolina Law Review* 48 (1970): 197–242.

———. "Negro Rights, Unionism, and Greatness on the South Carolina Court of Appeals: The Extraordinary Chief Justice John Belton O'Neall," *South Carolina Law Review* 21 (1969): 141–90.

———. "Reason of Slavery: Understanding the Judicial Role in the Peculiar Institution." *Vanderbilt Law Review* 32 (1979): 8–223.

Nelson, William. "The Impact of the Antislavery Movement upon Styles of Judicial Reasoning in Nineteenth-Century America," *Harvard Law Review* 87 (1974): 513–66.

Olsen, Stephen T. "Patrick Henry's 'Liberty or Death' Speech: A Study in Disputed Authorship." *American Rhetoric: Context and Criticism*. Ed. Thomas W. Benson. Carbondale: Southern Illinois UP, 1989. 19–65.

Paulsen, James W. "A Short History of the Supreme Court of the Republic of Texas." *Texas Law Review* 65 (Dec. 1986): 237–303.

Pocock, John G. A. "Cambridge Paradigms and Scotch Philosophers: A Study of the Relations between the Civic Humanist and the Civil Jurisprudential Interpretations of Eighteenth-Century Social Thought." Hont and Ignatieff 235–52.

Posner, Richard A. "The Jurisprudence of Skepticism." *Michigan Law Review* 86 (1988): 827–91.

Prill, Paul. "Cicero in Theory and Practice: The Securing of Good Will in the *Exordia* of Five Forensic Speeches." *Rhetorica* 4 (1986): 93–110.

Prince, William S. "St. George Tucker, Bard on the Bench." *Virginia Magazine of History and Biography* 84 (1976): 266–82.

Reder, Randall O. "The Antebellum Supreme Court of Florida." *Florida Bar Journal* 58 (Dec. 1984): 664–69.

Resnik, Judith. "Constructing the Canon." *Yale Journal of Law & the Humanities* 2 (1990): 221–30.

Riga, Peter J. "The American Crisis over Slavery: An Example of the Relationship between Legality and Morality." *American Journal of Jurisprudence* 26 (1981): 80–111.

Rosner, Mary. "Reflections on Cicero in Nineteenth-Century England and America." *Rhetorica* 4 (1986): 153–82.

Schafer, Judith K. "'Guaranteed against the Vices and Maladies Prescribed by Law': Consumer Protection, the Law of Slave Sales, and the Supreme Court in Antebellum Louisiana." *American Journal of Legal History* 31 (1987): 306–21.

——. "The Long Arm of the Law: Slave Criminals and the Supreme Court in Antebellum Louisiana." *Tulane Law Review* 60 (1986): 1247–88.

——. "Sexual Cruelty to Slaves: The Unreported Case of *Humphreys v. Utz.*" *Chicago-Kent Law Review* 68 (1993): 1313–40.

Scheppele, Kim Lane. "Facing Facts in Legal Interpretation." *representations* (Spring 1990): 42–77.

Schoeck, Richard J. "Humanism and Jurisprudence." Rabil 3:310–26.

——. "Lawyers and Rhetoric in Sixteenth-Century England." Murphy 331–55.

——. "Rhetoric and Law in Sixteenth-Century England." *Studies in Philology* 50 (1953): 110–27.

Soifer, Aviam. "Status, Contract, and Promises Unkept." *Yale Law Journal* 96 (1987): 1916–59.

Stephenson, Mason W., and D. Grier Stephenson, Jr. "'To Protect and Defend': Joseph Henry Lumpkin, the Supreme Court of Georgia, and Slavery." *Emory Law Journal* 25 (Summer 1976): 579–608.

Stevens, Linton C. "Machiavelli's *Virtù* and the Voluntarism of Montaigne." *Renaissance Papers* (1967): 120–30.

Stockbridge, Jessie Folsom. "Georgia Judge *Hanged* Twice." *Atlanta Journal* 23 Nov. 1930: 6.

Swint, Henry L. "Ezechiel Birdseye and the Free State of Frankland." *Tennessee Historical Quarterly* 3 (1944): 226–36.

Tinker, Edward Larocque. "Jurist and Japer—François Xavier Martin and Jean Leclerc." *Bulletin of the New York Public Library* 39 (1935): 675–97.

Tushnet, Mark V. "The American Law of Slavery, 1810–1860: A Study in the Persistence of Legal Autonomy." *Law and Society Review* 10 (Fall 1975): 119–86.

——. "Critical Legal Studies: A Political History." *Yale Law Journal* 100 (1991): 1515–44.

Waltz, Robert. "Arkansas Slaveholdings and Slaveholders in 1850." *Arkansas Historical Quarterly* 12 (1953): 38–74.

Warnick, Barbara. "Charles Rollin's *Traite* and the Rhetorical Theories of Smith, Campbell, and Blair." *Rhetorica* 3 (1985): 45–66.

Watson, Alan. "Seventeenth-Century Jurists, Roman Law, and the Law of Slavery." *Chicago-Kent Law Review* 68 (1993): 1343–54.

Wedgewood, Ruth. "The South Condemning Itself: Humanity and Property in American Slavery—A Review of Andrew Fede, *People without Rights* (Garland Press 1992)." *Chicago-Kent Law Review* 68 (1993): 1391–98.

Wetlaufer, Gerald B. "Rhetoric and Its Denial in Legal Discourse." *Virginia Law Review* 76 (1990): 1545–97.

White, James B. "Rhetoric and Law: The Arts of Cultural and Communal Life." Nelson, Megill, and McCloskey 298–318.

Wiethoff, William E. "Common Law Reflections of a Forensic 'Urge' in the Art of Letter Writing." *Southern Communication Journal* 56 (1991): 268–78.

——. "Critical Perspectives on Perelman's Philosophy of Legal Argument." *Journal of the American Forensic Association* 22 (1985): 88–95.

——. "The Logic and Rhetoric of Slavery in Early Louisiana Civil Law Reports." *Legal Studies Forum* 12 (1988): 441–58.

——. "Machiavelli's 'Heroic' Political Oratory." *Southern Speech Communication Journal* 47 (1981): 10–22.

Wright, Warren E. "Judicial Rhetoric: A Field for Research." *Speech Monographs* 31 (1964): 64–72.

INDEX

Abolition, judicial perceptions of,
70, 80, 82, 86, 91, 92–93, 107–8,
114, 120

Adams, John Quincy, 18

Alabama: high court judges of, 2;
organization of appellate courts
of, 142

Allen, John J., 80, 128; lifespan and
judicial tenure of, 4; *Martin v.
Martin*, 80; *Wynn v. Carrell*, 80

Aristotle, 16–18, 23, 26, 30–31

Arkansas: high court judges of, 2;
organization of appellate courts
of, 136

Baldwin, Briscoe G., 77–78, 128, 155;
lifespan and judicial tenure of, 4;
Peter v. Hargrave, 38–40, 160

Baltzell, Thomas, 69, 119–20; lifespan
and judicial tenure of, 2; *McRaeny
v. Johnson and Moore*, 120

Bay, Elihu H., 58, 103; lifespan and
judicial tenure of, 3; *Gist v. Cole*,
103–4; *Kinloch v. Harvey*, 104

Belles lettres. *See* Blair, Hugh

Blair, Hugh, 19–20, 25, 28

Brockenbrough, William, 128; lifespan
and judicial tenure of, 4; *Davenport
v. Commonwealth*, 36–37;
Commonwealth v. Carver, 78;

Commonwealth v. Turner,
78–79

Brooke, Francis T., 26, 38; lifespan
and judicial tenure of, 4; *Anderson's
Ex'ors v. Anderson*, 78; *Allen v.
Freeland*, 78, 156

Butler, Andrew P., 9–10, 22–23, 59,
107–8, 138, 139; lifespan and
judicial tenure of, 3; *Felder v.
Louisville, Cincinnati and
Charleston Railroad Co.*, 59–60

Cabell, William H., 28–30, 36, 127, 129,
154; lifespan and judicial tenure of,
4; *Randolph v. Randolph*, 30–31, 77;
Paup's Adm. v. Mingo, 31, 127

Carr, Dabney, 26–28, 129; lifespan and
judicial tenure of, 4; and *Old
Bachelor*, 26, 31, 79, 160; *Jones v.
Mason*, 37; *Randolph v. Randolph*,
37–38; *Allen v. Freeland*, 79;
Dabney v. Taliaferro, 79; *Manns v.
Givens*, 79, 81; *Paup's Adm. v.
Mingo*, 127

Catron, John, 46, 47, 96–97, 98,
135–36; lifespan and judicial tenure
of, 4; *Fisher's Negroes v. Dabbs*, 46,
95–96, 136; *Loftin v. Espy*, 95; *Dred
Scott*, 96, 97, 135

Channing, Edward T., 18, 159